BOTANICAL BLOCK PRINTING

Pavilion
An imprint of HarperCollins*Publishers* Ltd
1 London Bridge Street
London SE1 9GF

www.harpercollins.co.uk

HarperCollins*Publishers*
Macken House,
39/40 Mayor Street Upper
Dublin 1, D01 C9W8,
Ireland

10 9 8 7 6 5 4

First published in Great Britain by
Pavilion, an imprint of HarperCollins*Publishers* Ltd 2024

 A catalogue record for this book is available from the British Library.

ISBN 978-0-00-860773-9

Printed and bound in RR Donnelly in China

Publishing Director: Stephanie Milner
Editor: Ellen Simmons
Copyeditor: Katie Hardwicke
Senior Designer: Alice Kennedy-Owen
Photography: Eva Nemeth
Artworking: maru studio G.K.
Proofreader: Sarah Epton
Indexer: Hilary Bird
Production Controller: Grace O'Byrne

The information provided in book is for educational purposes only. Foraging for wild plants or mushrooms carries inherent risks, and some plants and mushrooms are poisonous and/or deadly. HarperCollins and the Author are not responsible for any consequences arising result of consuming or using wild plants and mushrooms and you eat them at your on risk. It is illegal to forage on private land in the UK without the permission of the landowner. HarperCollins and the Author do not encourage readers to forage on private, protected or cultivated land. Please consult with an expert before engaging in foraging activities or consuming any wild food.

BOTANICAL BLOCK PRINTING

A creative step-by-step handbook to make art inspired by nature

PAVILION

ROSANNA MORRIS

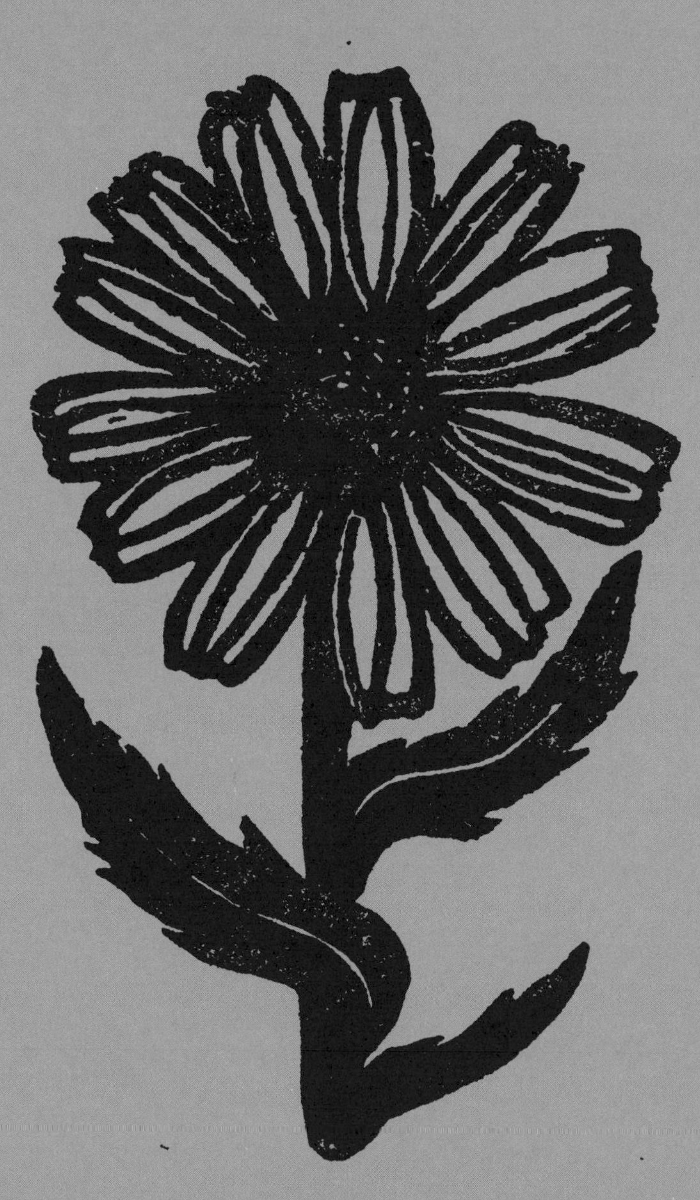

Introduction

My Printmaking Journey

I first got excited about the world of print at the age of 18, during my foundation diploma at the Bristol School of Art. We took a trip to Paris, where I encountered huge relief wheat pastes of plants and people displayed around the city. Once home, I felt so inspired and wanted to make my drawings 'big', to take the ink scribbles in my sketchbook out into the world. I began carving huge, life-sized woodcuts from ply I found in skips, following botanical and agricultural themes, and pasting them up on abandoned walls around the city.

I found the process of relief printmaking so liberating – making my small ink drawings huge, bold, and imposing. I fell in love with how the process of making a relief print turned the lightest lines into something so unquestionably solid and bold. I also succumbed to the sculptural process of carving the block, the physical action of going against the grain, and the satisfying process of removing matter, refining your image, and inking up the remains.

I went on to study illustration at Camberwell School of Art, drawn to the school by rumours of its beautiful printmaking studios and its historical association with the Arts and Crafts Movement. I spent most of my time in the grand and well-equipped print rooms, exploring all the different processes of printmaking from etching to lithography, whilst all the while continuing carving and printing relief blocks at home.

After graduating, my interest in printmaking took me to Mexico. It was while learning from printmakers in San Cristobal that I realized the potential of print as a medium for connection with the land. Collectives there were making their own papers and inks, creating prints that were rooted in the very land they were depicting. In Oaxaca, I saw first-hand how printmaking collectives were embedded in their community, with studios that opened onto the street, making posters and prints about local political themes and working to facilitate real change.

Once back in the UK, I joined a group of other practising printmakers and set about building the printmaking studio and collective, Cato Press. For many years we ran courses, events, and a members' facility with the aim of bringing printmaking into our community. To this day I still work from the same studio that we built on the top floor of a large, red brick factory, with windows looking out onto the urban landscape.

Growing up in an urban environment, first on a council estate and later in the dense concrete jungle that is east Bristol, my first memories are of picking dandelions from the cracks in the paving slabs, hunting for snails and woodlice, yearning for nature. For most of us, our first drawings are of flowers, trees, and plants. In my own work, I continually come back to making images that follow botanical themes and our human connection with the land. My creative process these days usually starts in the fields and woodlands on the outskirts of the city, collecting plants to be studied and then developed into prints back at my studio. In my mind, the natural world is not something other than us; it is part of us and in exploring and depicting it we are simply sharing part of what it means to be human.

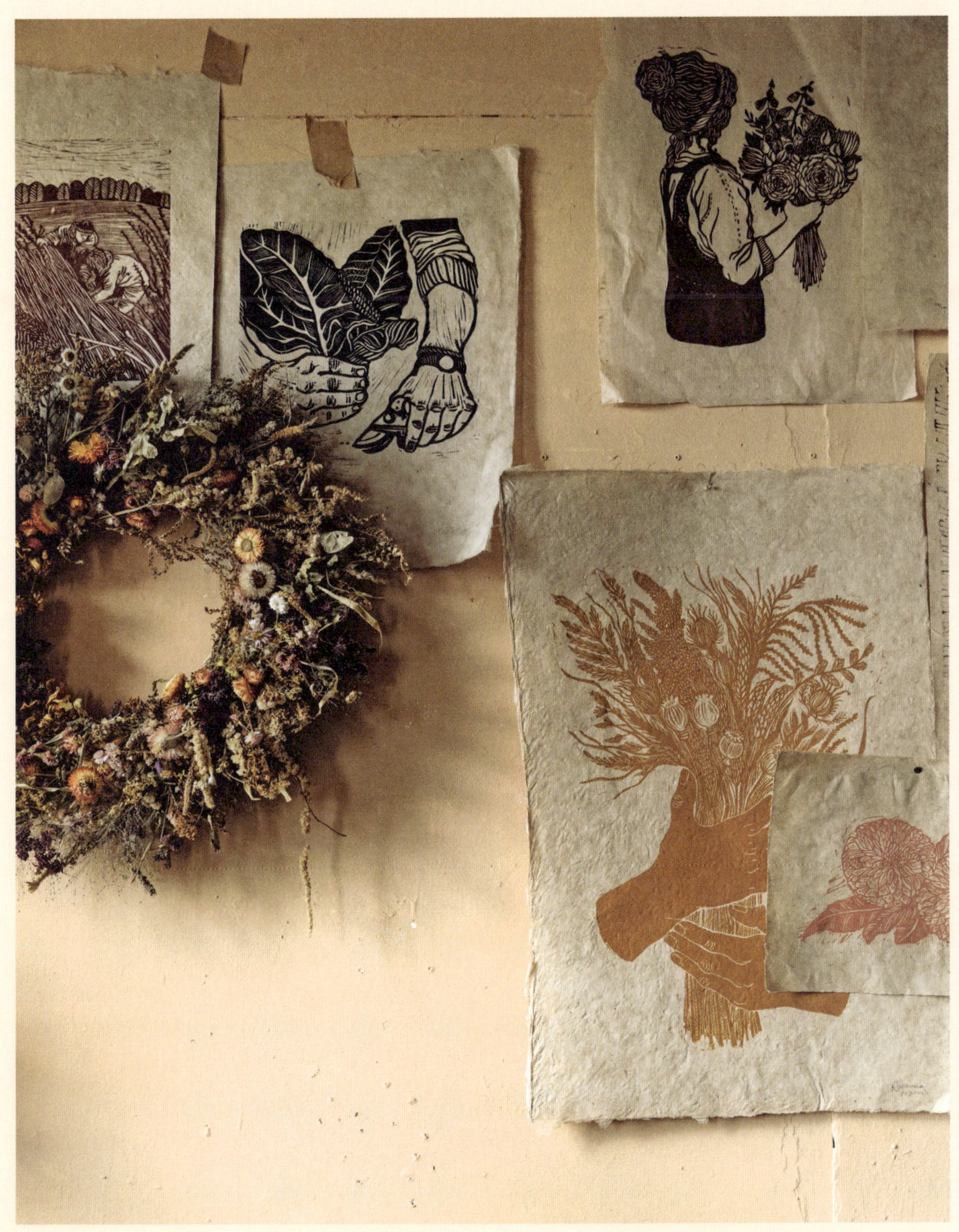

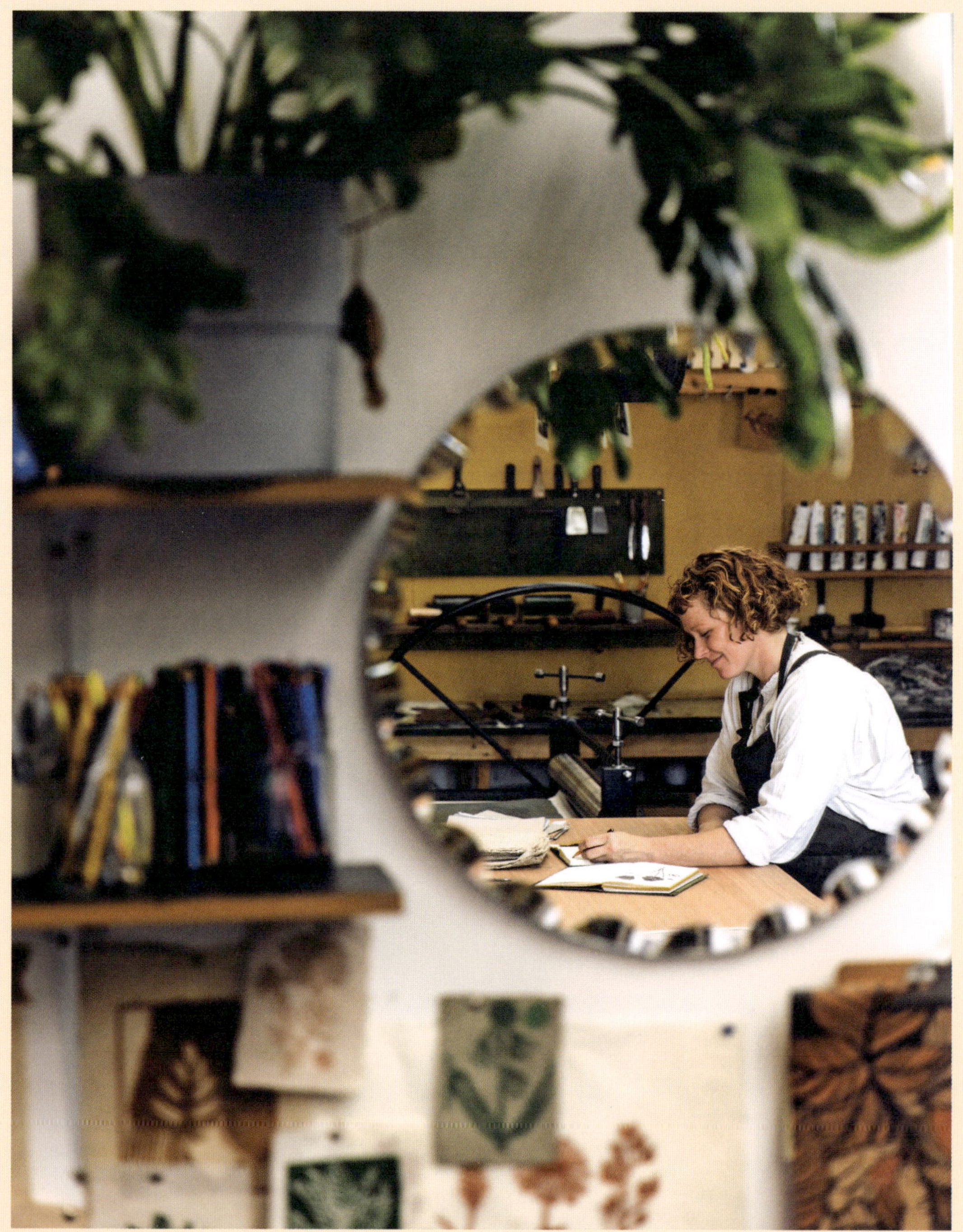

How to Use This Book

Bringing together and consolidating all the experience I have gained from the last decade of fulltime printmaking, I have written this book for those new to the art and for those who already have some experience. The book is intended to work as a straightforward, concise, and practical guide to exploring different printmaking processes, and then later as a companion that you can reference either from home at the kitchen table or a dedicated printmaking studio.

The book is best read from front to back, with each chapter outlining important techniques and steps involved in a complete printmaking practice. The first chapter introduces the specialist tools and materials you may need as you explore different printmaking techniques. Chapter two outlines setting up your work space, either at home or in a dedicated studio, and finishes with a practical project to get you started making prints. If you are new to printmaking, don't miss this exercise as it really helps to get you used to your tools and what is possible with relief print.

In the third chapter, I explore the foundations of all good image making in drawing, design, and practical techniques for developing your skills. In the fourth chapter we get down to the nitty gritty of making prints, transferring techniques, registration, and editioning. The final chapters explore techniques for taking your practice further: onto fabric, through multiple colours and, finally, how to make your own inks from the land.

The world of creative art can sometimes feel a little intimidating when you're starting out. However, I believe printmaking doesn't have to be complicated and in *Botanical Block Printing*, my aim is to keep it simple, practical, and accessible, giving you the tools to take printmaking into your own hands so that you can concentrate on the fun bit – making beautiful botanical prints.

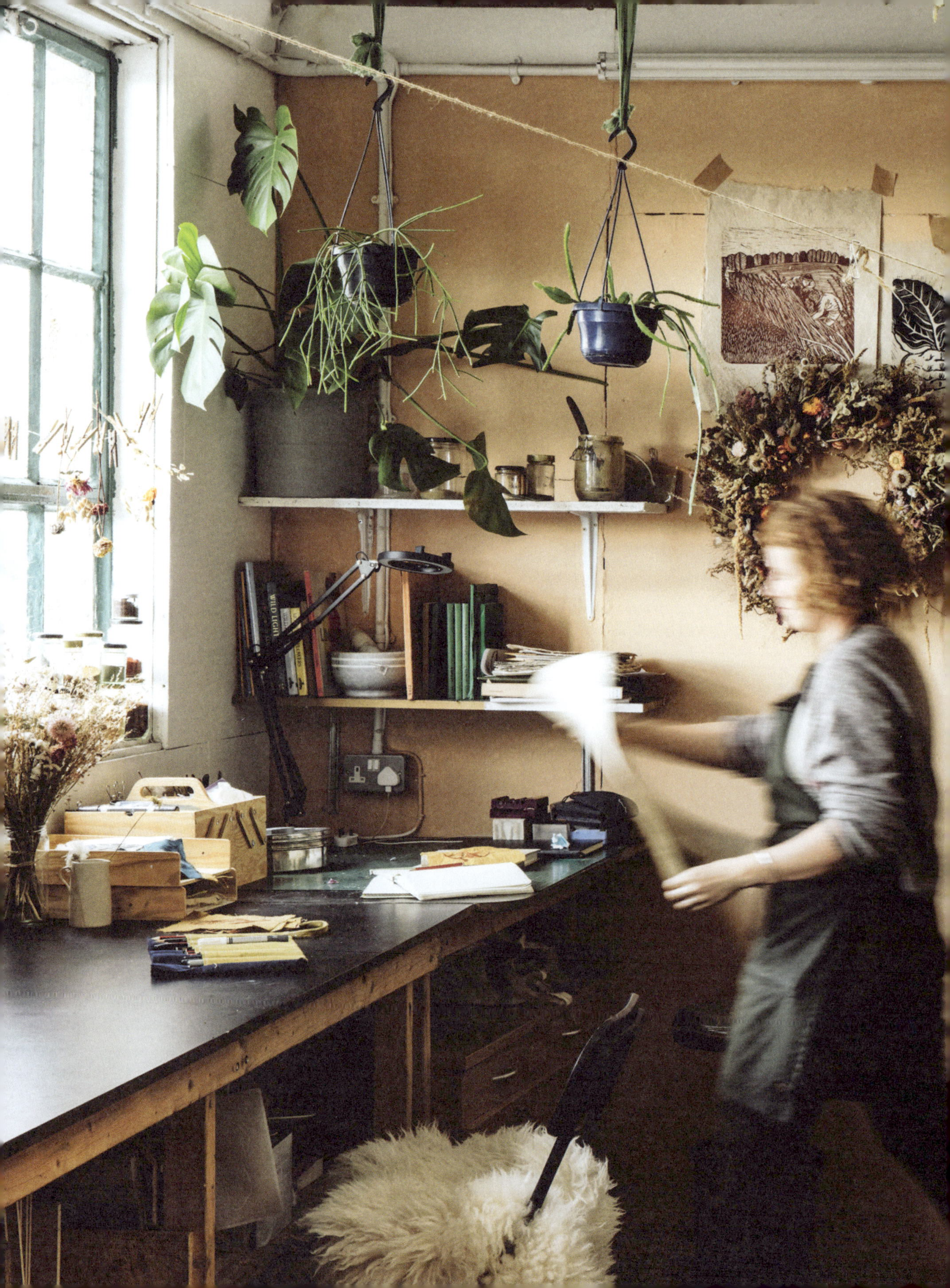

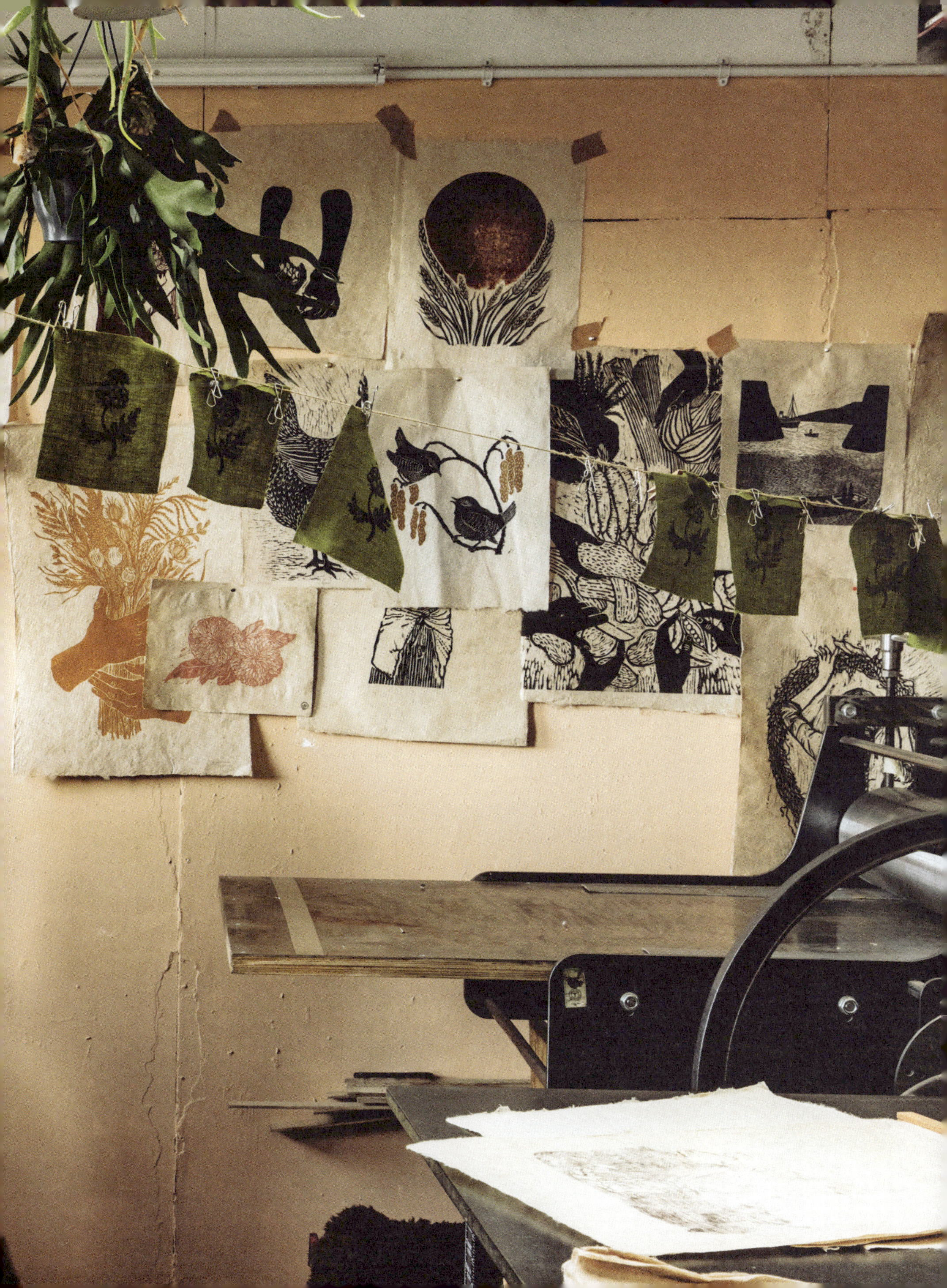

TOOLS & MATERIALS

In this chapter, I will outline all the basic tools needed for relief printmaking. It's not a comprehensive list; it would be almost impossible to cover every single tool to do with print out there in the world. Instead, I've focused on the tools I use and why.

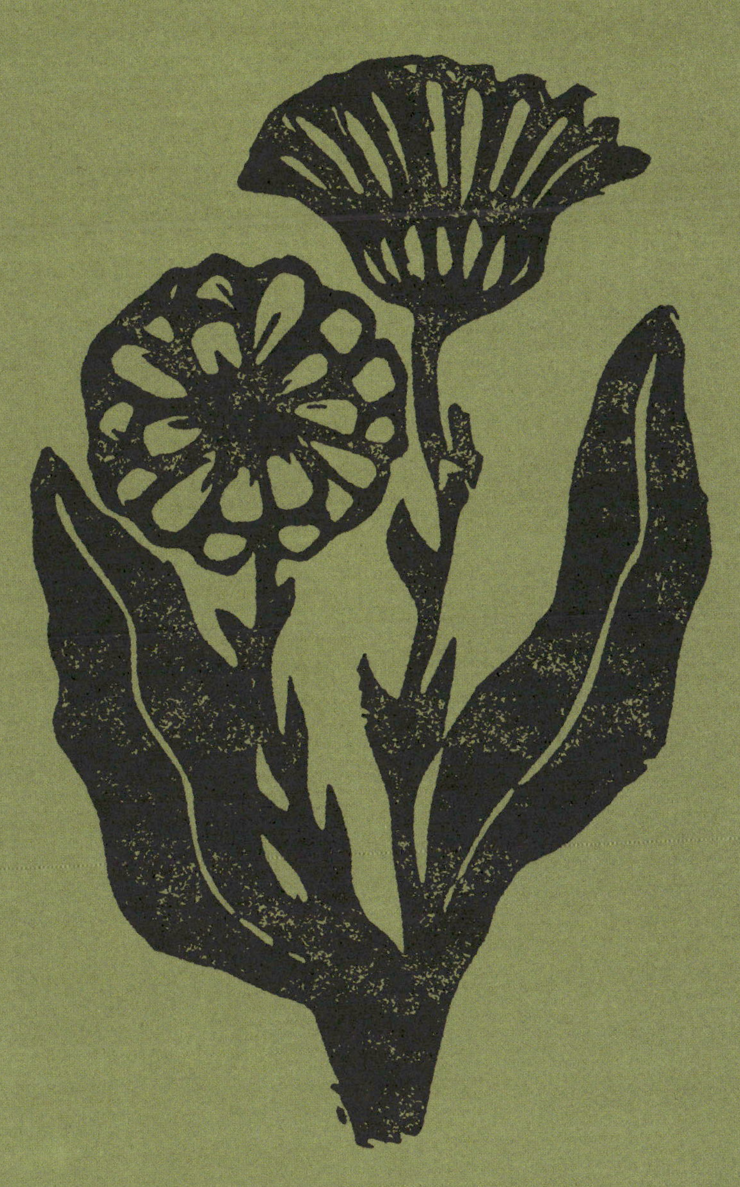

Surfaces

You can make relief prints in several ways, from the simplest form of direct printing from found materials, such as dried leaves and flowers, to carved blocks of lino or wood. There are several options to choose from and it's worth trying them out to see which suits your style.

Linoleum

A great starting point for relief printmaking, linoleum, or lino, was first used for flooring and soon adopted by artists for its ease of carving. It is available in multiple sizes, from single sheets to packs. Small sizes are ideally suited to experimenting when you first start out.

GREY 'BATTLESHIP' LINO

This readily available lino gets its name from its use on battleships up until the 1950s. It is made from linseed oil, cork dust, and pine resin with a backing of hessian or jute, which means it can break down and be easily composted once cleaned, although this does take time.

I really love working with grey lino. It's technically 'half baked' so is much softer than flooring lino, with a super-smooth surface that cuts like butter. It also has a very satisfying way of peeling away when carved, which makes it very popular with printmakers.

Grey lino is available cut to size in a variety of packs or by the roll, which is great for making very large prints. You can also buy it backed onto wood at 'type height', which means it's at the correct height to be printed on traditional letterpress printing machines.

TIP *Lino backed onto a wood surface helps with longevity, as it keeps your blocks in better condition while in storage. It's easy enough to back your blocks onto wood yourself with a bit of patience, wood glue, and some clamps to keep the surfaces together as they dry.*

MARMOLEUM

Much frowned upon by the general artist community, Marmoleum, or old flooring lino, is in my opinion a much under-used resource. It usually has a hessian backing and comes away in satisfying cut pieces when carved. If you do decide to go down this route, sharp tools and a bit of elbow grease are a must, as it can be a lot tougher to cut than traditional art store lino, and may crumble slightly. I've been collecting Marmoleum for years from skips, flooring shops, bins, and scrap stores. By re-using it you save it from landfill and it can give you truly beautiful results. Don't confuse it with flooring vinyl, which is rubbery and rips when you try to carve it.

I've made a lot of my larger prints from discarded Marmoleum and this allowed me to be more experimental and fluid in my making than the pressure that is felt when using expensive materials. I'd highly recommend it to anyone who wants to push their practice and be more experimental.

TIP *Old, hard lino can be slightly softened by brushing on a layer or two of linseed oil and leaving to soak for a couple of days before use. You can also use an iron, radiator, or hairdryer to soften the surface with a little heat before you begin carving.*

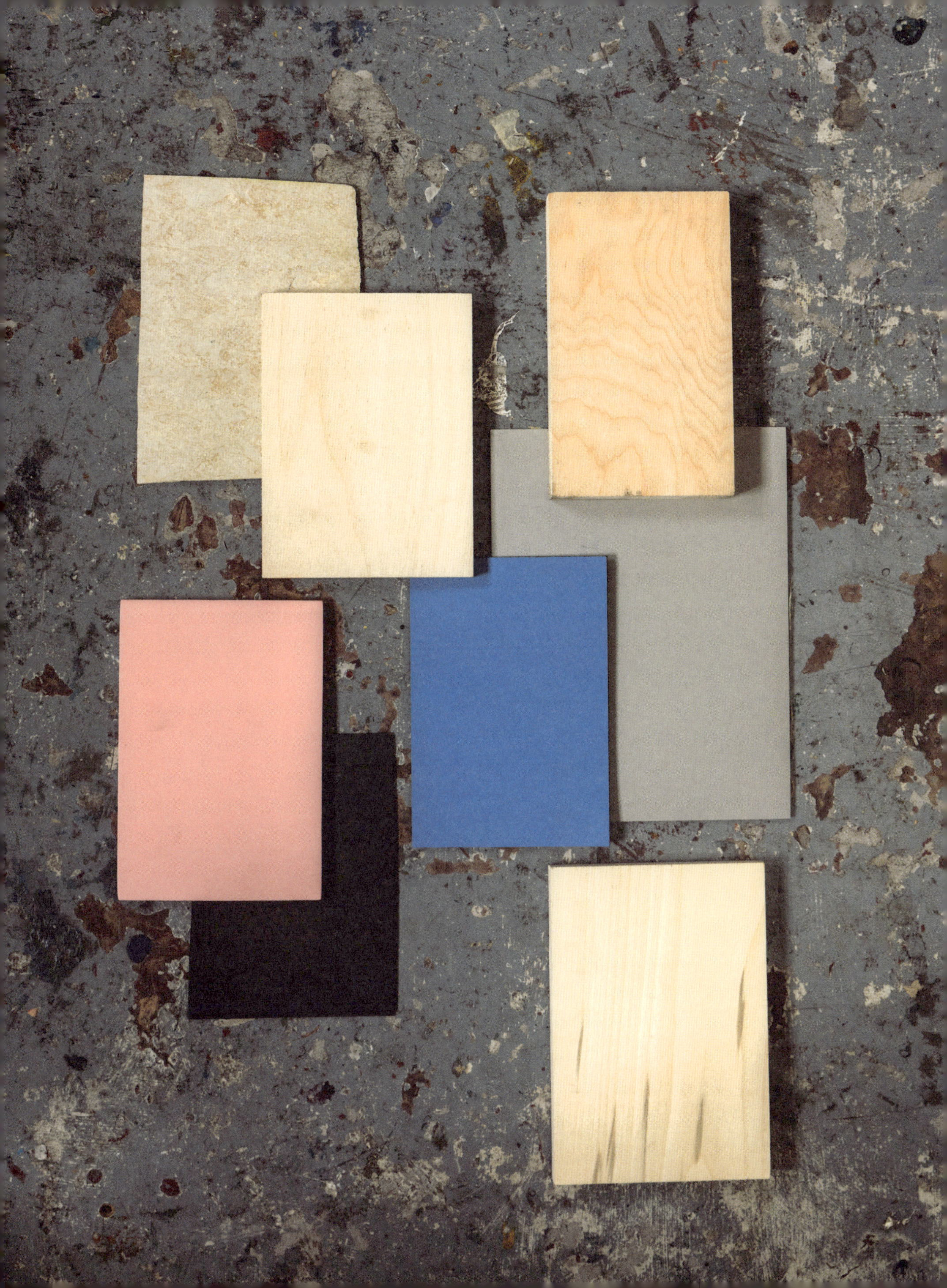

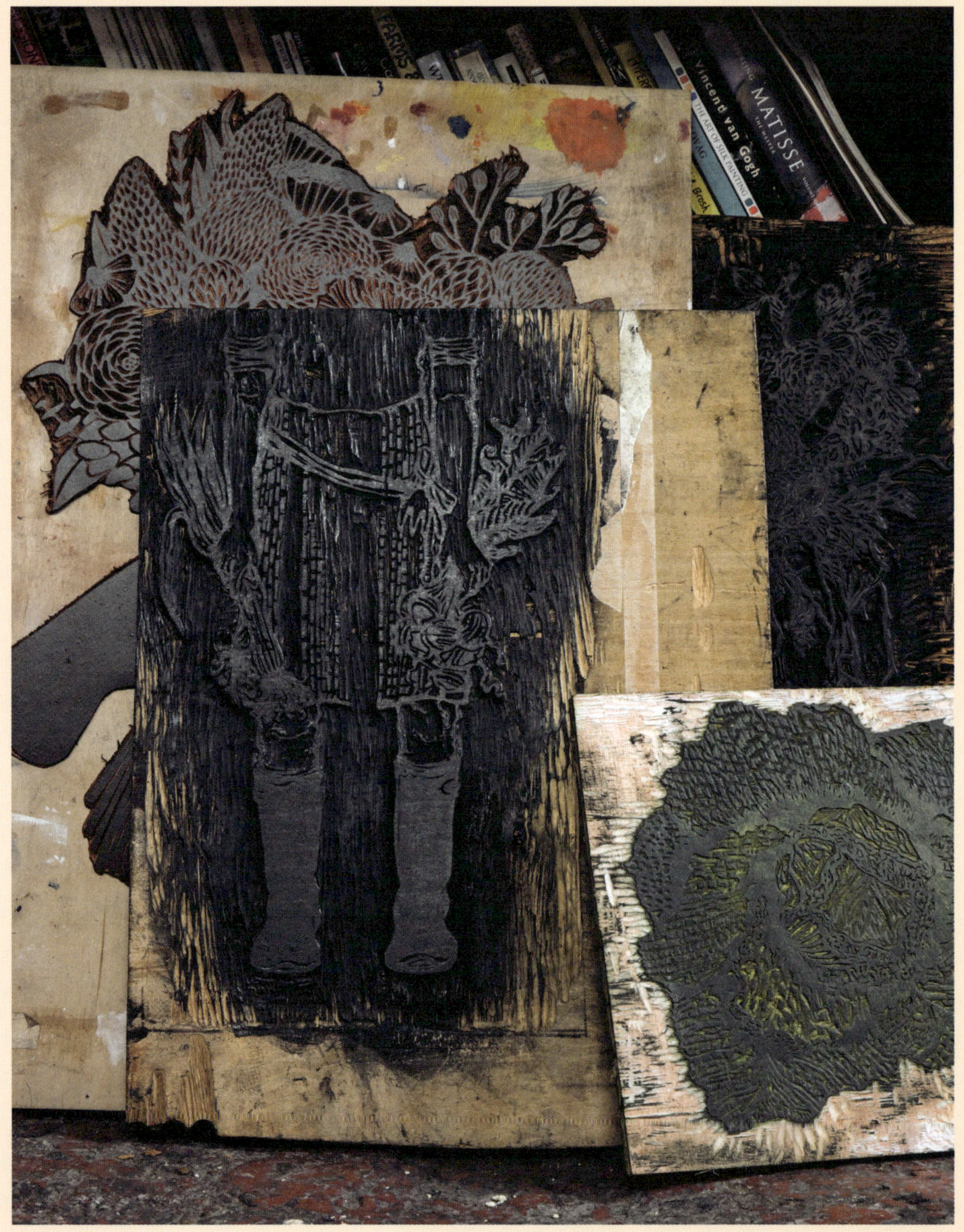
MATISSE
Vincent van Gogh

OTHER CARVING SURFACES

Softcut block – Usually cream or grey and made from a rubbery plastic surface, this is super-easy to carve, and is good for people with mobility issues. It's very supple but can be frustratingly soft when carving, and fine detail can get lost from high pressure at the printing stage, so it's best to keep things bold when using this material.

Speedy carve lino – Popular in the US, this pink lino is great if you want to re-use your block time and again and get it wet. Its longevity is better than hessian-backed lino for fabric printing but it is comparatively expensive.

Japanese vinyl – Softer and more flexible than battleship lino and very satisfying to carve. It is however limited in its size, so not recommended if you want to make larger prints. Double-sided with a black core so that you can see your cut lines clearly.

Vinyl flooring – There are lots of different types that often have an artificial wood grain or stone effect on one side and are smooth on the other. It cuts easily but can wrinkle and tear depending on how good the quality is, and it is rubbery and thinner than traditional lino. It often comes in massive rolls and is difficult to dispose of, so I wouldn't recommend buying it new; however, if you can save it from the tip it's definitely worth using.

Wood

You can purchase different woods for carving from art supply shops but I prefer to salvage wood from skips or tips. I like how the shape of the wood I find often inspires the final print and I enjoy the grain and the roughness that wood gives my images. Many of my favourite prints that I've made were influenced by the wood I used to carve them.

My 'Boots' print was carved from a large block of ply I found in East London. Its narrow form and a few knots in the grain, made me stop my design just above the knee, and now, on reflection, it's this that I feel makes the print feel rooted and weighted, rather than overworked. It's nice to be open to the happy accidents that come from using found materials.

BIRCH PLY

This is the traditional wood used for relief printmaking. If purchased from an art shop the grade will usually be slightly higher, along with the price tag. You can also buy ply from builders' merchants at a much cheaper rate. Carving ply is not for the faint-hearted and takes considerably more effort than lino. Be prepared to sharpen your tools regularly and to potentially lose pieces that chip away when you go against the grain.

JAPANESE PLY

Tomo-shin from Japan is made specifically for printmaking and usually used for Japanese woodblock printing with water-based inks. It's a much softer and gentler experience for carving than birch ply, and can, of course, also be used for general relief print. It's very silky to use, cuts like butter, and generally you're not so limited by the direction of the grain, as it holds its carved edges satisfyingly well.

MDF

Use with caution – the supple and soft buttery surface of MDF is very tempting, but the glue used to bind it all together is highly toxic and shouldn't be used without a face mask. I recommend only cutting in a well-ventilated space and being mindful of dust extraction as you go. It will also need to be sealed before use as it is very porous and will absorb ink and moisture like a sponge.

Carving Tools

People's tools and preferences are as varied as the artists themselves and no one tool can be categorically ruled as the best. Below are a variety of the most popular on the market, but which of them you come to love will be down to you and the way you work.

Cutting Blade Shapes

Essentially, with carving tools each type is just a variation on the handle shape, while the shapes of the cutting blades themselves remain relatively standard. There are two basic blade shapes: V-shaped and U-shaped.

V-shaped gouges – The V-shaped tool can make a fine and continuous line; it has the ability to vary in depth and is great for the finest of detailed work. You can utilize the tip of the blade to create a tapered end to your cut, which has a nice effect when repeated.

U-shaped gouges – This tool is great for clearing large areas of the block and defining edges. It has a rounded tip, which allows you to make rounded dots and smooth out bold edges on your design.

Flat scoop gouges – The perfect tool for clearing large flat spaces in your design, smoothing down ripples in the lino that could later pick up ink, and creating clear, flat areas in your prints.

Knives and scalpels – Great for defining the edges of very intricate designs. Many printmakers choose to define all the edges of their designs with a scalpel first and then cut up to the line with a U tool. In Japanese tool sets this knife tool is called a 'hangito', and is used to remove areas of the block by making two opposing cuts that form a kind of ravine.

Choosing Your First Tools

Include both a V-shaped and U-shaped tool in your basic set, and choose tools that sit comfortably in your hand. Linocutting tools are available with interchangeable blades, or look for Japanese woodcarving sets. Beginners' sets are an inexpensive way to explore the options before you commit to more expensive tools that can last a lifetime.

RED-HANDLED ALL-IN-ONE LINOCUT TOOLS

These are readily available in most art shops. They are a great start for a beginner and have the convenience of being able to switch out blades as you dull them, saving lots of sharpening time. However, as they develop and spend more time cutting, most printmakers find the need to change blades regularly can become time-consuming and choose to upgrade.

JAPANESE STRAIGHT-HANDLED TOOLS

These come in a range of shapes and gouges and have been developed for carving wood. I find the strong, straight shape of the handles lend themselves to working on a larger scale. They are very practical for vigorous work as you can put a lot of strength behind them, and I love using them for clearing away larger areas of the block.

If you enjoy the shape of these tools and get really into carving wood, you can buy traditional Japanese tools with long blades, which move up the inside of the handle as you sharpen and wear away the blade. Found at specialist printmaker suppliers, they are designed to last a whole lifetime of carving.

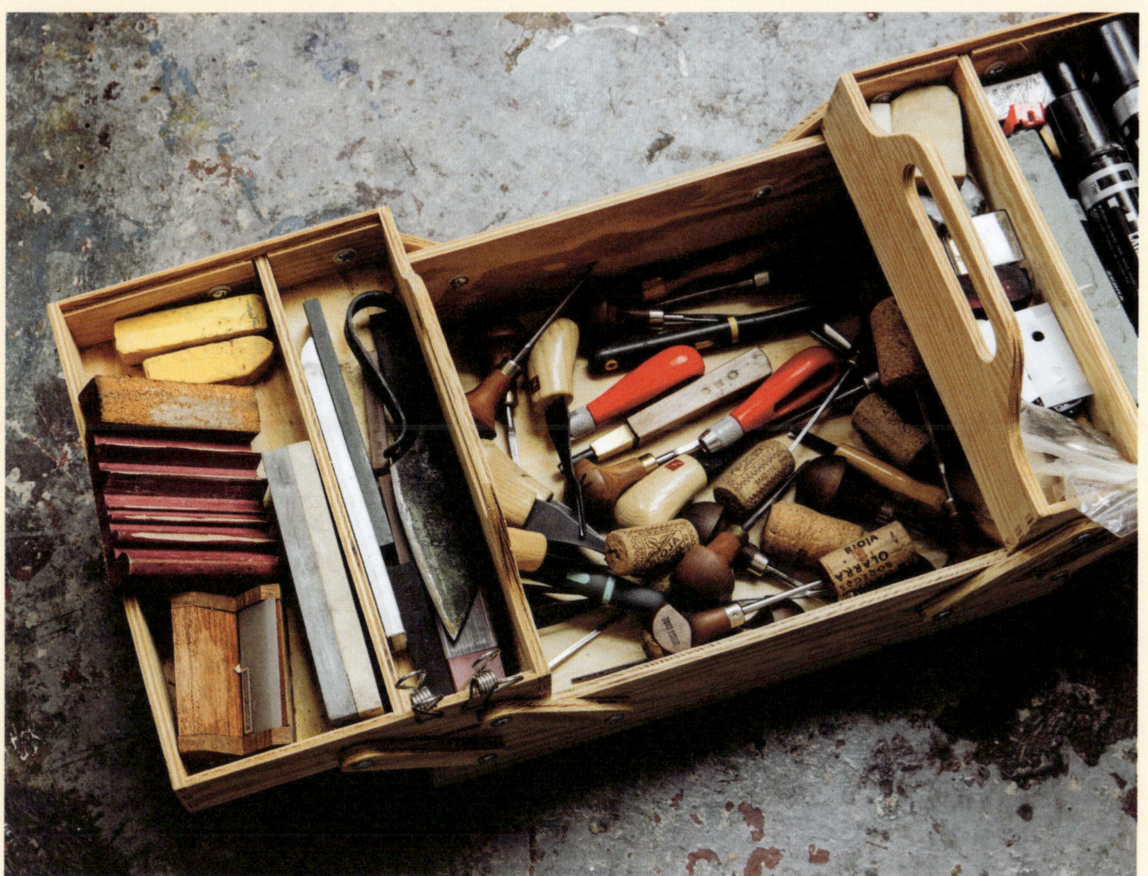

PFEIL TOOLS

These mushroom-handled tools were originally designed for carving end-grain woodblocks for wood engraving. However, they are also excellent for ply and lino, are ergonomic and comfortably designed to sit in the palm of your hand, and are great for getting fine detail into your blocks.

Pfeil tools come in a huge variety of gouge sizes, which you can buy in packs of six. If you are ready to invest, I suggest starting with the smallest V and a large U. Although expensive they are very strong and designed to last. If you take care of them and keep on top of burnishing and sharpening (see page 57), they could last a lifetime.

FLEX-CUT TOOLS

The newest handle shape on the market, these tools are ergonomic and nimble to use. Again, for me the small V and the large U are the most useful gouges, but it's worth experimenting and, like the Pfeil tools, you can buy them in multi packs with a range of V- and U-gouge sizes.

Rollers

Rollers, or brayers, are used to apply ink to the relief image on the plate. Good-quality rollers make all the difference to the quality of your final print, but they can be prohibitively expensive when you are starting out. A hard roller is best for relief printmaking; if your roller is too soft, it will lay too much ink into the grooves in your carving and pick up unwanted marks in your final print.

Choosing Rollers

Choose a roller that is slightly larger than your block, to allow you to ink up the whole block in one go. This limits the lines that can appear at the ink's edge and leave streaks through your image. If you only have a small roller and a big block to ink, those lines are still avoidable; you just need to take a little more care in your application. Sometimes having a small roller is handy for touch ups or inking specific areas in a reduction (see page 158).

Check the hardness of the roller, or 'shore' number; this indicates the hardness of the material the roller is made from. The lower the number, the softer the roller, so a 30-shore roller is soft and a 60-shore roller is hard.

The thickness of the roller determines how much ink it can put down in a single run. This isn't important for tiny blocks but if you are inking up big stuff it helps, and the added weight makes the job of spreading out the ink and applying it easier.

BUDGET ROLLERS

Red-, blue-, or black-handled Essdee and metal-handled rollers are readily available, relatively hard and inexpensive. They are sturdy and long-lasting if taken care of, and with a bit of elbow grease you can get good coverage on your block and produce lovely prints. Blues are softer and sold as 'fabric' rollers; blacks are typically harder.

MID-RANGE ROLLERS

My favourite in this price range are the Japanese, red-handled rollers, specifically, the hard red rubber ones. I still use mine daily and often favour them over the bigger, heavier, and more expensive rollers. They are lighter on the wrists and great for smaller prints, and are also simple to take apart, making clean-up much easier.

TOP-RANGE ROLLERS

These rollers are big, beautiful, and expensive. The weight of them allows the ink to gently glide onto your block with much less effort. Available from most specialist printmaking supply shops, their price tag makes them prohibitively expensive when you are just starting out. However, once you are ready to invest, they are a joy to use; they have been created to last a lifetime and, with care and good housekeeping, they will.

In this range you have a choice between rollers made from nitrile rubber, a long-lasting and hard black roller, and durathene, a green and slightly softer material but equally long-lasting when well cared for. Note that the green durathene rollers do not like white spirit and can degrade over time, so clean with natural substances or get a rubber one if you use solvents.

FABRIC ROLLERS

Although you can use any of the rollers listed above for rolling fabric ink onto your blocks, I've found that tight foam rollers are great for this task. They make the, often slippery, fabric ink adhere to your block more easily and with less 'smearing'. Look for rollers with a foam coating that's relatively tight and will apply the ink evenly.

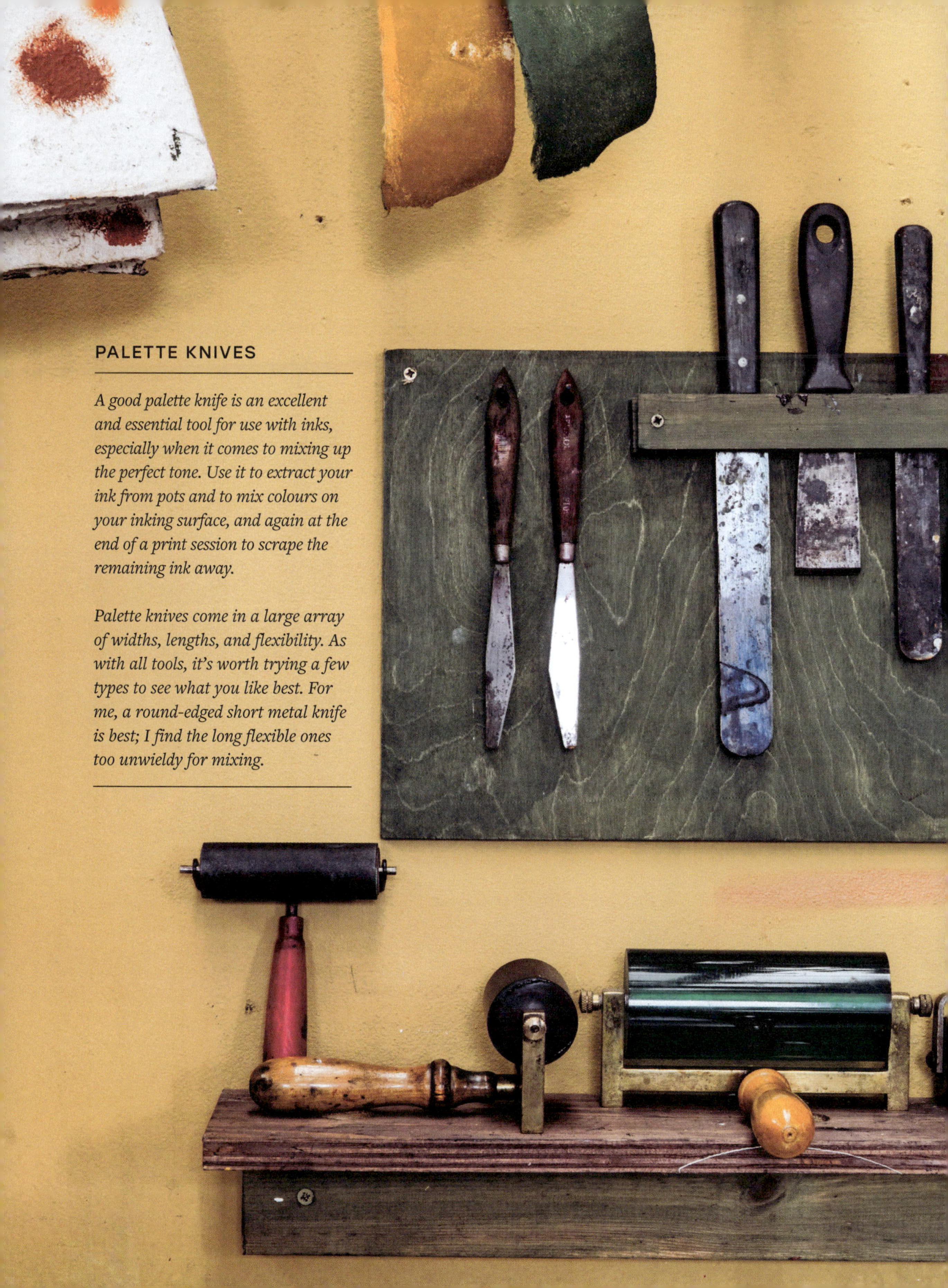

PALETTE KNIVES

A good palette knife is an excellent and essential tool for use with inks, especially when it comes to mixing up the perfect tone. Use it to extract your ink from pots and to mix colours on your inking surface, and again at the end of a print session to scrape the remaining ink away.

Palette knives come in a large array of widths, lengths, and flexibility. As with all tools, it's worth trying a few types to see what you like best. For me, a round-edged short metal knife is best; I find the long flexible ones too unwieldy for mixing.

Printmaking Inks

Ink is an essential part of the process that is too often overlooked, as the ink you choose will affect your final image just as much as the design, carving, and paper choice. There is a huge variety of ink types and brands to choose from. Which you go for comes down to the main choice: water or oil-based inks?

Inks and Other Materials

There's nothing more disheartening than a smudgy print when you've put hours into the carving process, so having a good-quality printmaking ink on hand, whether you're printing in a studio or at home, is essential. Before you decide which type of ink you'll use, take into account factors such as drying time, pigmentation, fastness, and viscosity.

Oil-based inks are the traditional standard for printmaking; however, they need a lot more elbow grease to clean up. As a result, schools and students generally begin printing with water-based inks.

I often use good-quality, oil-based inks in my work that have been processed to wash down, or clean up, using soap and water rather than harsh chemicals. They are also much more practical to use at home, on the kitchen table, and even to include children in the activity without worrying about using solvents.

As there are so many inks to try, I have listed below the ones that I most like to use.

WATER-BASED PRINTMAKING INKS

Adigraf Inks – A professional water-based option, these inks are water-soluble and highly pigmented. They are available in 24 colours and can be cleaned down with warm soapy water. These are a great option for home printing and an easy, chemical-free clean-up. These inks are quick to dry and in the right conditions could be dry within a few hours of printing, which is ideal for layering up colour, but also important to be mindful of if you're planning a long lunch break in the middle of an edition!

OIL-BASED PRINTMAKING INKS

Cranfield Caligo Safe Wash – These linseed-based inks come in a great range of colours and tube sizes. They are easy to find in most art shops and I especially recommend their 'Safe Wash' range, which has allowed me to move away from using solvents in the studio. The pigment and consistency for printing is high and almost indistinguishable from other premium oil-based inks. You can also use the Caligo Safe Wash inks on fabric with very little fading when washed.

Cranfield inks come in tubes, cartridges, and tins. I recommend starting out with tubes as they will keep your ink in good condition for longer. I tend to go for the cartridges in the studio, as I get through a lot and the tins, although more economical, dry out quickly in between uses.

These inks can dry fast, sometimes overnight in warm weather. If you want them to dry more slowly, see opposite for details on extending drying times.

Hawthorn Stay Open – A small printmaking business with a gorgeous array of ink colours, their inks are wonderful to work with and highly pigmented, suitable for all types of printmaking. When printing in relief, some transparent ink should be added to reduce their strength, which has the added benefit of making them go further, so you get more prints for your money. They come in pots and will not skin up for two years or more.

These take a little longer to dry than Cranfield inks and that should be factored in when printing an edition, especially if you want to print multiple colours.

Speedball® inks – Speedball® professional printmaking inks are perfect for most of your projects. Their fabric inks are also brilliant and worth investing in as they are colour-fast after repeated washing and a nice consistency to work with. I've found they roll on better with a tight foam roller rather than a usual rubber roller.

Drying time is really quick with these inks; in warm weather prints will be ready to sign an edition by the next day.

INK DRYING

All the inks I've mentioned will dry on printmaking papers quite quickly. What determines the speed of drying is the absorbency of the paper and the temperature in the room; prints on more porous papers will dry quicker than others. If the paper is glossy, non-absorbent, or you are using fabric, then a few drops of drier (see below) can really help move the process along.

If you want to really speed up drying time, air circulation is key, so a slightly open window can help. Just be sure your prints are secured wherever they are drying and not likely to knock into each other and smudge in a breeze.

INK ADDITIVES

Drier – Used to speed up the drying times of inks, this is great in winter when the air is cold and drying times increase massively, or when you have a quick turnaround on a project. Cranfield produce wax driers, which are non-toxic, but take care if you are using traditional cobalt driers as they are very poisonous. A little goes a long way.

Extender – Used to extend the pigment of the ink, it naturally also makes the inks more translucent and can create some nice effects when layering colours. Be careful not to dilute too much, or at least to do a few test prints with your ink before you commit to a full run. It also increases drying times, so is worth considering if you're on a tight turnaround.

Retarder – Used to extend the drying times of your inks, great for when you're planning a long day of printmaking in the heat of the summer to keep your inks fresh.

Copper-plate oil – Available in Thin, Medium, and Thick, boiled linseed plate oil can change the viscosity of your ink without diluting it or thinning it. I also use this when creating printmaking oil from my own pigments. If using premade inks, just a few drops at a time will loosen them up.

Transparent ink – A brilliant ink specifically made to help get the level of transparency you need for your prints. This really helps to aid with multicolour prints, as you overlay layers of ink that would otherwise bleed into each other.

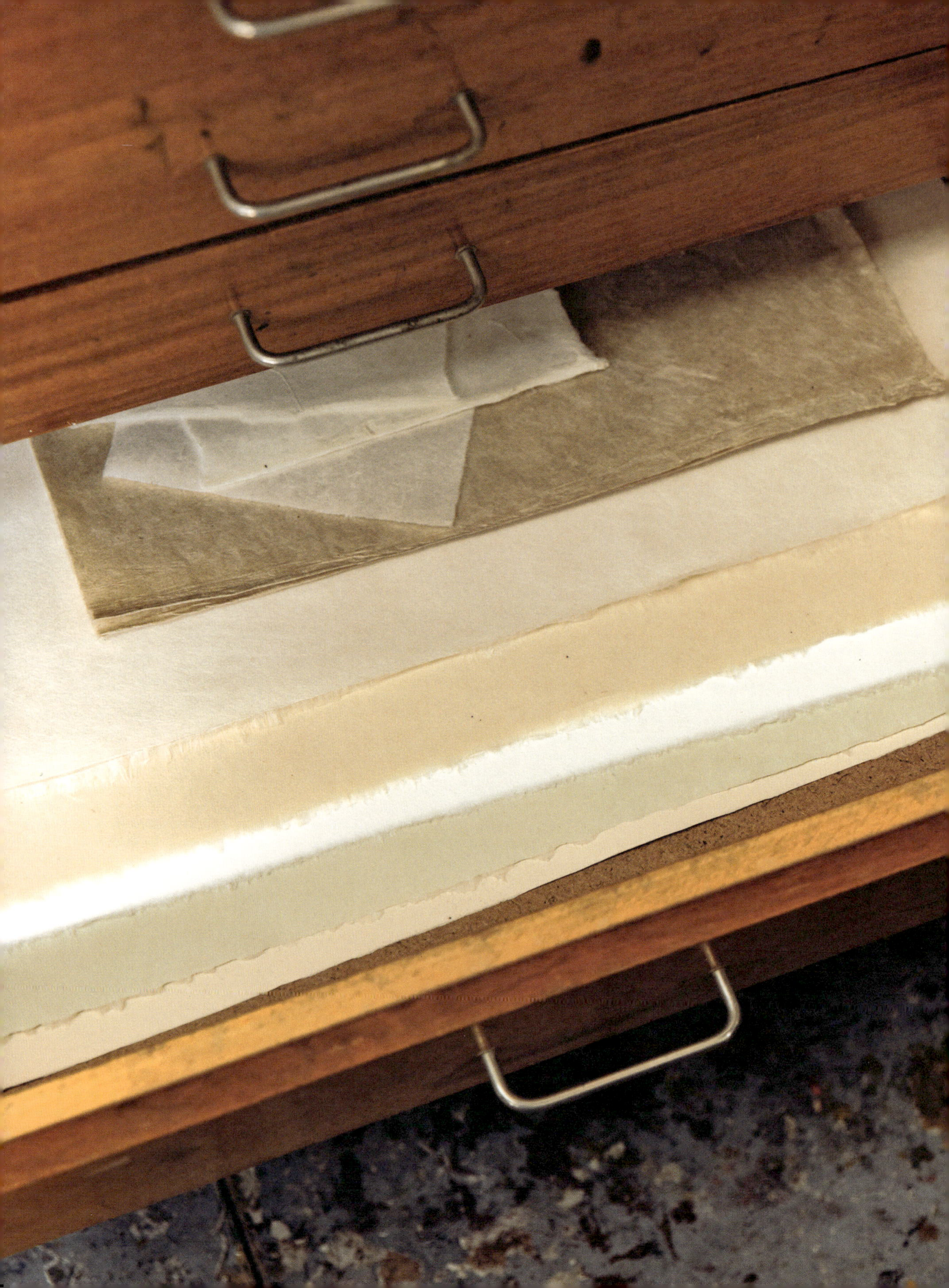

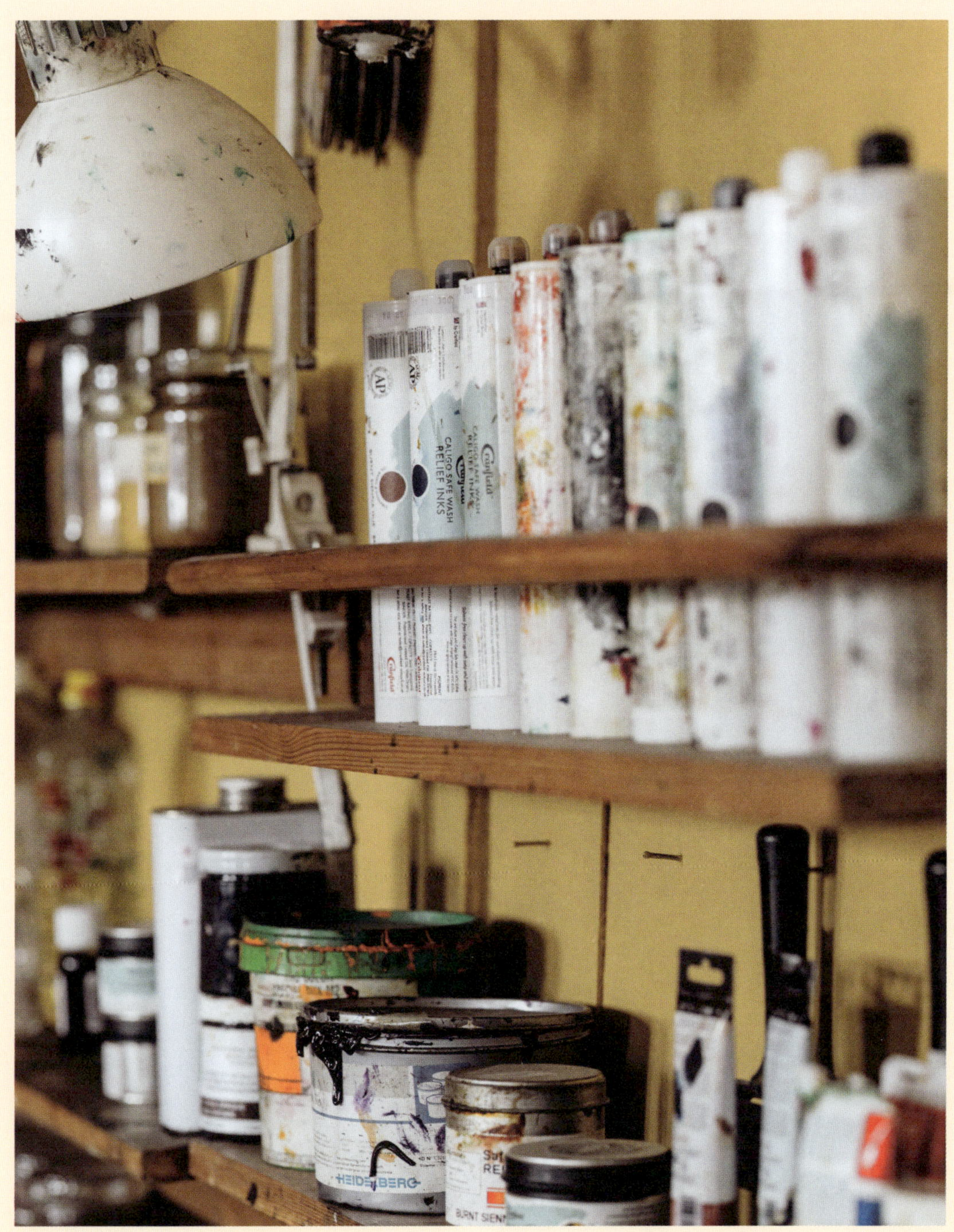
CALIGO SAFE WASH
RELIEF INKS
HEIDELBERG
BURNT SIENN

Printing Papers

The printmaking paper you choose is as much about your final design as the print itself, it can lend warmth, texture, and feel to your final image, so it's not a decision to be made lightly.

Paper for Printing

The most important thing to consider when coming to choose your paper is that it is acid-free, known as archival paper. This means that it will last many years without discolouring, whereas papers that contain acid will yellow and degrade over time.

Texture is another important quality to consider. Although beautiful, a more textured paper can interfere with your block and the quality of your final print. It's worth experimenting before deciding to print an entire edition.

Paper weight is measured in 'grams per square meter' (GSM). The higher the GSM, the heavier the weight, and generally the higher the cost and quality of the paper. When hand-printing, it's important to be aware of the GSM, as thicker papers are much harder to burnish by hand, but can create lovely, embossed effects when used with a press.

Printmaking papers usually come in large A1 sheets that must be cut down for smaller prints. You can use a large metal ruler for this or a deckled edge ruler with a ridged edge, much like a bread knife, which is particularly useful when working with handmade papers to produce a natural, wavy, irregular edge.

HOW TO CUT PAPER

With a metal ruler and water
Lay your paper out on a cutting mat and measure out where you want to cut. Line the metal ruler up and use a paintbrush and some water to dampen the edge of the paper – you may have to go over this a couple of times depending on the thickness of your paper. Once fully damp, apply pressure on the ruler with one hand and you should be able to rip the paper towards yourself cleanly.

With a deckled-edge ruler
Lay your paper flat on a cutting mat and measure out where you want to cut. Hold the ruler down with as much pressure as you can and rip the paper upwards, away from the ruler. Some strength and speed are needed to get a clean edge. It's worth practising with test prints or scrap paper until you master the technique.

With a knife
Perhaps you want a hard edge for tight registration in a jig? A good sharp Stanley or craft knife combined with a cutting mat and metal ruler will do a good job of this.

EUROPEAN PAPERS

Fabriano – Smooth, Italian paper with a whole range of colours and choices available. You can also buy these in packs of A4 sheets, which are great for printing editions of small prints.

Somerset – Beautiful cotton rag papers, Somerset papers have been made in the same place in southwest England since the 1700s. They come in a huge range of weights and colours and are expensive for a reason: they make beautiful prints. Once you have a print that you're happy with and ready to edition, buy yourself some Somerset.

Zerkall – A great German paper that is cost effective and smooth to print with. I particularly like the Rough 'Antique' sheets.

JAPANESE PAPERS

Paper-making is an ancient craft in Japan and people spend entire lifetimes mastering it. The intricate techniques used to construct the papers make them incredibly versatile, often stronger than fabric. There are a number of different papers to explore; here are some of my favourites.

Kozo – The general name for Japanese papers made with long-fibred mulberry bark. Incredibly strong yet malleable and great for printmaking.

Kitakata – The general name for papers made from the Gampi bush. Considered to be a very luxurious paper material, the papers are almost translucent, shiny, and strong, and come in a variety of subtle shades. Easy to find in sheets or as a roll, making it great for larger prints.

OTHER ASIAN PAPERS

My favourites are the rough handmade Nepalese and Asian papers. Many moons ago, I was lucky enough to spend a month in Bhaktapur, a beautiful Nepalese town, where I witnessed the process of harvesting and making these beautiful papers. I love the raw warmth and textural quality they bring to my prints.

Lokta – Made from the pulp of the Lokta tree, a small Himalayan bush. The papers are rough to the touch, undyed and come in a variety of weights. Because of the raw untreated nature of the fibre, it's not uncommon to find lumps of bark, grit, or even stone wrapped up in the paper fibres. It's always worth checking each sheet over before you send it through the press, as rogue stones can damage your blocks and press.

Cotton rag – Made in India from cotton rag pulp, these papers are very thick, and are great for embossing but will need a press to get an even and good print.

Bhutanese papers – Made from a Bhutanese variety of the Lokta bush, these papers are also made in the Himalayas. They have a smoother and more consistent finish than the Lokta papers and are slightly easier to work with and edition.

OTHER PAPER SUPPLIES

Below are two pretty essential sundries that you will need to keep in good supply in the studio.

Newsprint – A cheap paper option that's very useful for sandwiching between prints to keep your blankets and rollers clean. Also useful for creating a registration matrix (see page 110) or for wiping and removing excess ink. I often use newsprint for the first proof of a new block. You can buy newsprint in large bags from packaging suppliers online, or from art shops.

Tissue paper – Another studio essential, available to bulk buy cheaply from packaging suppliers, use it for layering up prints for storage or for wrapping around prints when sending. Make sure it's described as undyed and acid-free.

Fabric for Printing

The main consideration when printing on fabric is the thread count: too few and you will lose a lot of detail in your print. You want to choose something absorbent that will allow you to make a neat and uniform print.

Generally, natural fibres are best for absorption, such as cottons, hemps, or linens. Try to avoid anything synthetic with a plastic feel as the ink will have a hard time sticking to the surface. When starting out and experimenting, raid your cupboards or charity shops for old pillowcases, tablecloths, or T-shirts.

Barens & Presses

Once the plate is inked, you need to apply pressure to transfer the image to the paper. This can be done in two ways: by hand using a baren, or using a printing press. When starting out, a baren, which can be as basic as a humble wooden spoon, is the simplest method best suited to small prints at the kitchen table. After you've spent some time printing by hand, you may want to invest in something a little less back-breaking for printing your editions. I'll give you some ideas of the types of presses that you can choose from.

Types of Barens

A baren is a flat surface, often disc-shaped, that can be held face down on the back of your paper when laid on an inked block, rotating in circular rubbing motions to transfer the ink to the paper.

Handmade papers naturally have lots of lumps and irregular areas on their surface. When working with handmade papers, I've found it's important to layer a piece of tracing paper or similar between your baren and your print. This protects the delicate paper by creating a barrier that reduces rips or tears under high pressure.

WOODEN SPOON

It takes strength and determination but there's nothing to stop you creating beautiful artworks with the humblest of objects: the wooden spoon. I spent years using my trusty wooden spoon to pull prints at home, and it now has a lovely soft and polished sheen to it. When hunting for the perfect wooden spoon, you want something that is strong and has a good flat scoop to cover as much surface area as possible.

METAL SPOON

Metal spoons can be great for applying high pressure to specific parts of your block, but watch out if using for your whole design, as they can heat up very quickly from friction; with the repeated movement needed to pull a print, you can easily burn your fingers!

JAPANESE BARENS

Traditional barens are used in Japanese printmaking for hand-burnishing woodcuts. They are made from a coil of bamboo rope with a bamboo leaf wrapped around them. They are beautiful objects and work well for both wood and linocuts, making them great for pulling prints at home. However, over time and with a lot of printing, they do wear down and will need recovering or replacing.

SPEEDBALL® BARENS

These barens are designed to be used in two ways: either hand-burnishing paper onto the block or the other way around, with the block face down onto your surface and applying pressure from above. They have a large handle which can be held with two hands, making it possible to use your full strength when pushing on the back of the block to help the ink transfer. Being able to print your blocks face down also helps with the arrangement and placement of your design.

GLASS BARENS

Available from specialist glass blowers in lots of beautiful designs, these usually have a good weight to them, which helps with applying less pressure than lighter barens. They also have the added benefit of looking beautiful in the studio. Expensive but long-lasting.

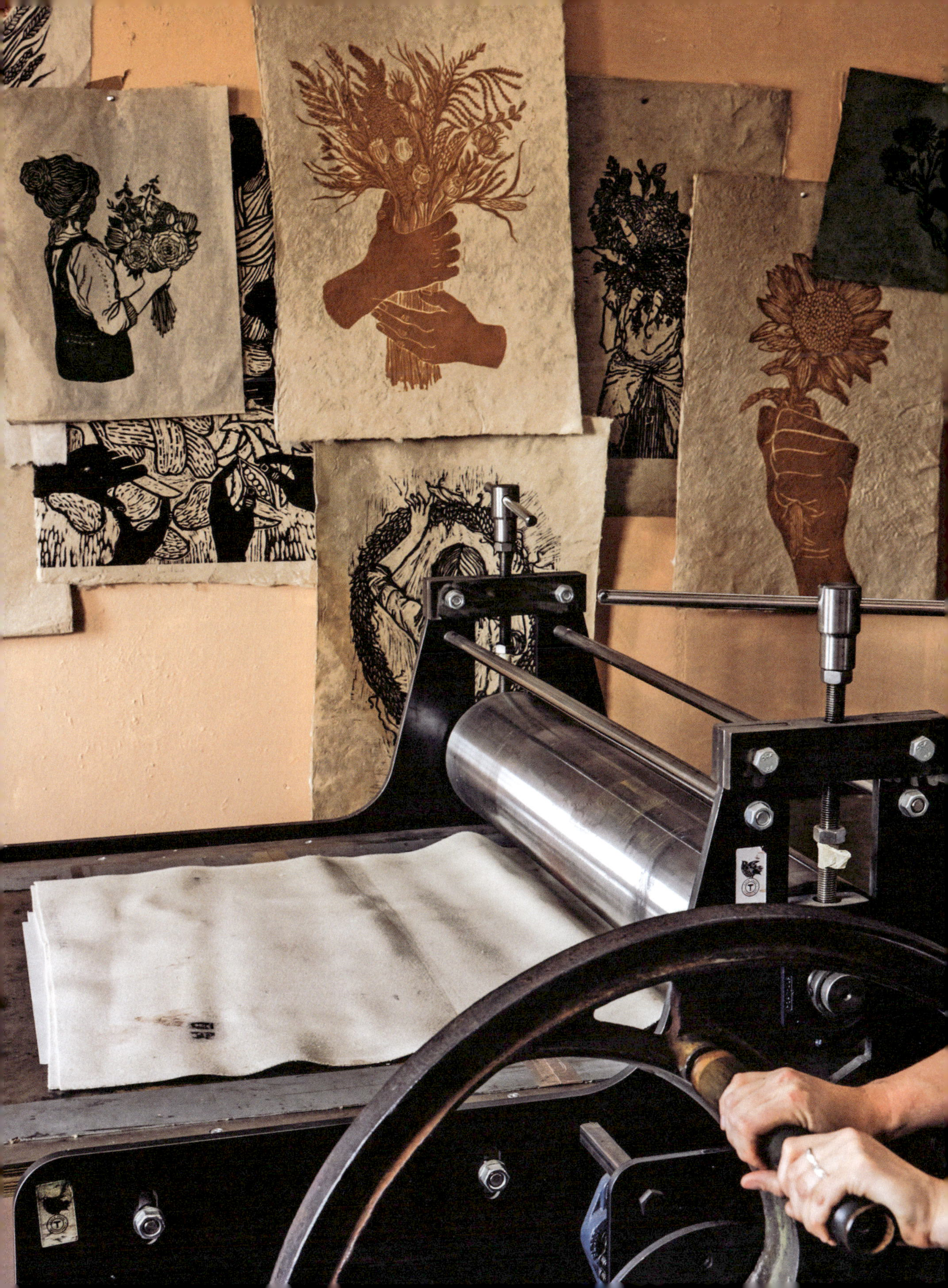

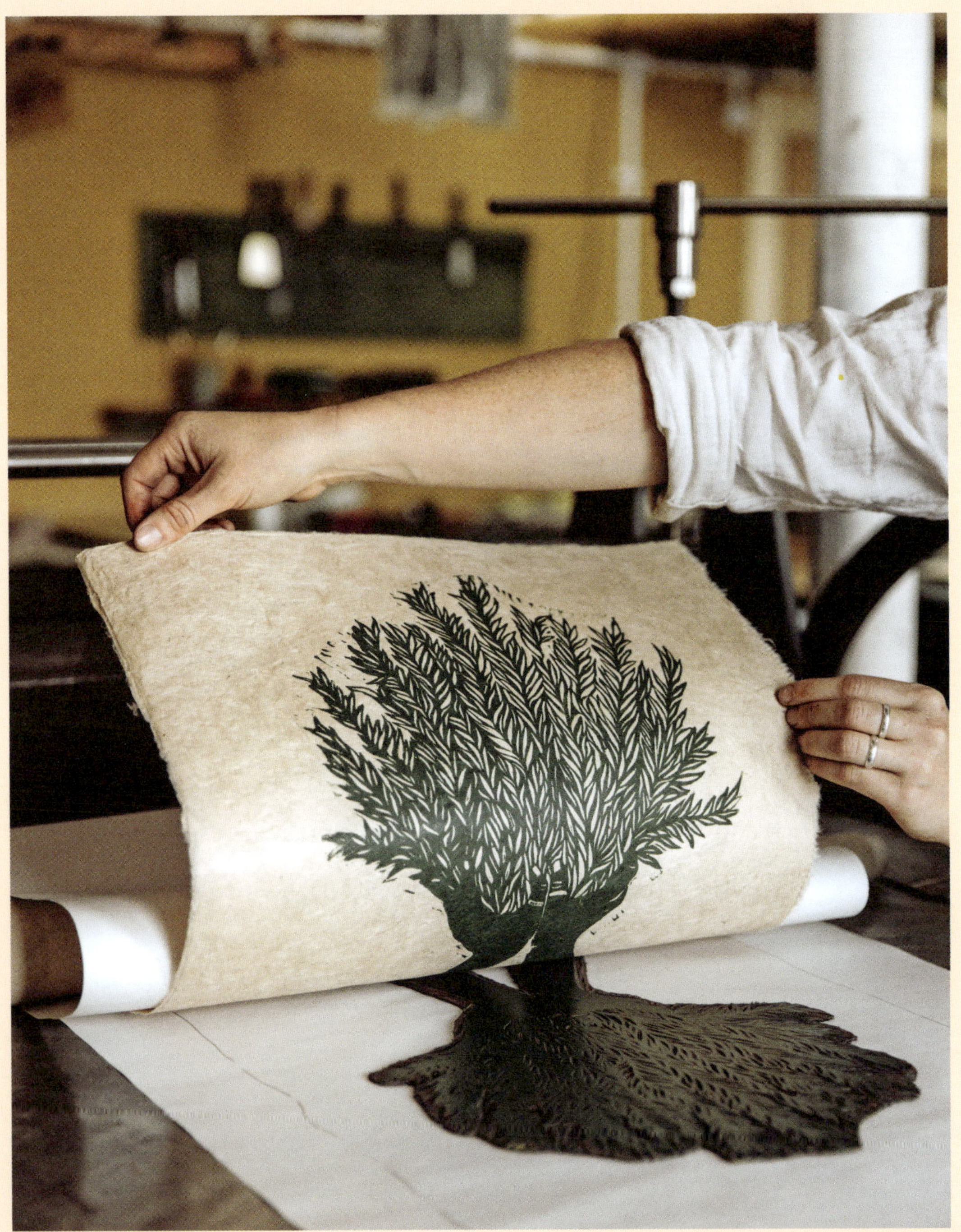

BALL-BEARING BARENS

Although expensive, these barens do wield beautiful results. They are formed of little metal balls sitting in a plastic casing that roll independently across the print, allowing it to pick up details and apply pressure along the way. A great alternative to a press if you need to be able to pack your studio away in between print runs.

Types of Presses

There are a huge range of printmaking presses out there for you to choose from, and which press you go for will be determined by your budget and the space you have to house it. Below is a list of the most popular presses I've used and enjoyed.

ADANA PRESSES

Adana presses are small, tabletop letterpress machines. They are great for printing letterpress projects at home and can be used for your carved blocks if you take the time to make them 'type height'. You can do this by gluing the correct thickness of wood to your block or woodblock with wood glue. Once dried they will be ready for inserting into the press and printing.

BOOK PRESSES

You can often pick these traditional book presses up in reclamation yards and charity shops. Originally made for pressing books together while gluing their spines, book presses can be effective for making relief prints. You essentially make a sandwich of two wooden boards and layer your prints, paper, and newsprint in the middle; they then work by applying pressure from above by turning the screw.

TABLETOP ETCHING PRESS

There are a range of small, economical tabletop etching presses on the market. I'd recommend going for the biggest and heaviest you can afford. The only exception to this is if you plan on running workshops or printing on the move, in which case light and foldable will be preferred.

TIP *When printing an edition, a lot of pressure is needed, and this can cause a small press to move all over the place if it hasn't got enough weight – use a strong clamp to hold your press down to your table.*

TABLETOP VERTICAL PRESSURE PRESSES

There are great tabletop relief presses out there; a popular example is the 'Woodzilla press', that is relatively economical. It works by applying pressure from above with a mechanical handle. Start with an A4 press bed as, generally, the bigger you go the more pressure is needed, and it can turn into quite the workout.

FREESTANDING ETCHING PRESSES

Etching presses work by applying a high amount of pressure onto thin metal sheets, which in turn pull the ink from the plates. Using them for relief printing requires a slightly different set-up: you need to make runners for your press bed that allow the central rollers to sit at an even height as you roll the block through the press. These runners also allow you to set the pressure before your block is inked and in place, which can be handy. I use etching presses to work on a large scale as they don't limit the size of my blocks.

ALBION & OTHER VERTICAL MOTION PRESSES

These sought after presses are a huge investment and take specialists to move and set them up. Originally designed to print letterpress posters, newsletters, and pamphlets, these presses were the workhorses of print shops all over the world. However, with the invention of digital print they became obsolete and are now wholly in the domain of artists. To print on these presses, you need to layer up packing and boards to achieve 'type height'. You are also limited to the size of the bed; the biggest I've come across is A1. They work by applying pressure from above by pulling a huge arm across the body of the press. Printing an edition with them is a physical task, but a very rewarding one (see page 116).

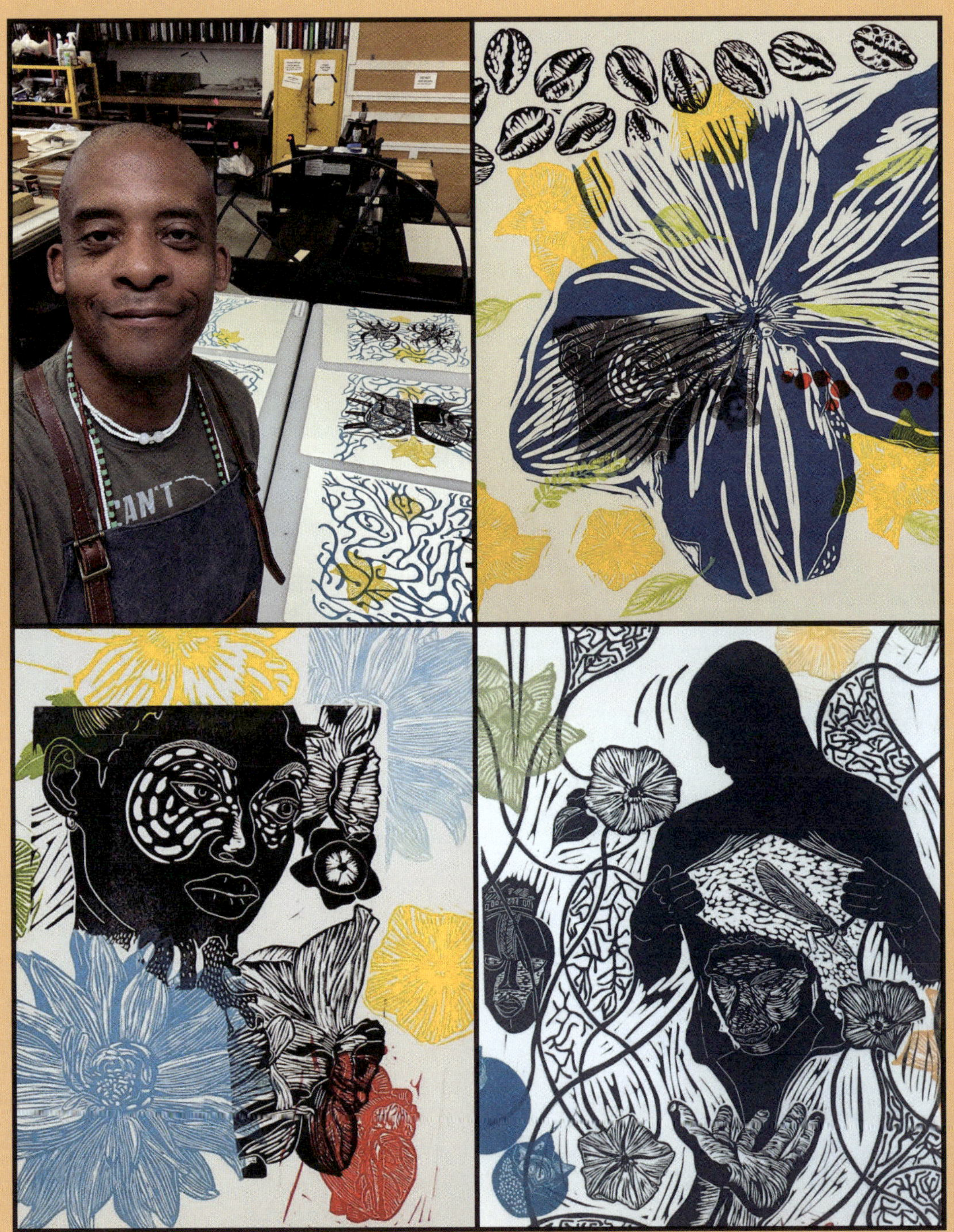

Tenjin Ikeda

Where do you work and what materials do you work with?
I primarily work out of my home on the dining room table. Even though I have a designated space in my home, the lighting is better in the dining room. When it is time to print my work, I visit Guttenberg Arts in New Jersey where they have presses and I pay for time in the studio space. I work with linoleum mostly, but have done some woodcuts in the past. I take images from photos – tracing them and transferring onto the linoleum – as well as drawing directly on the surface of the lino. There are no pre-planned ideas, it all comes together intuitively.

How did you start making prints?
I started printing 23 years ago. I had been painting for several years, then stopped due to frustration with the art world. I started dancing professionally for about two years but was drawn back to visual arts and working with paper, which led me to printmaking. I went to the Arts Student's League in Manhattan, New York and signed up for a class and have been printing ever since. It was and still is something that feels very natural, almost second-nature, to me.

Where do you go for inspiration for your work?
My inspiration comes from my culture, spiritual beliefs, dreams, conversations, music, and looking at the way other artists express themselves in unique ways. Living life in all of its simplicities and complexities is inspiration enough.

Can you explain a little about how drawing is part of your practice?
Drawing is key to my practice. In order to take a contoured flat drawing and give it dimension, I have to understand the technical basics of drawing; where the light is coming from, how to push something forward and move something in the background to give shape and form. I'm not very good at filling up sketchbooks and usually lose interest. I mainly draw directly onto the linoleum surface. There are times that I trace an image from a photograph before transferring it to the linoleum.

What's your favourite botanical piece that you've made?
I don't necessarily have a favourite. I love nature – especially flowers and leaves for their simultaneous beauty, strength, and fragility. They are a microcosm of life itself.

What does a typical day in the studio look like for you?
The motivation to work can come out of nowhere – often when I need to channel energy because the world is too overwhelming. If an idea comes to me and I am in the space to explore, I usually put on music. When I print I'm usually listening to the genre of house – which is a type of upbeat dance music.

What's the best advice you'd give to a new printmaker?
Your limitations in this medium are up to you. There are some incredible artistic expressions that are out there to see in printmaking. Also, keep your hands behind the cutting tools. If you do slip and cut yourself, I say: Congratulations! You have officially entered the world of printmaking – at least the relief side of it.

GETTING STARTED

What I love about relief printmaking is how relatively simple and accessible it is. You need so little to get started and a lot of the things you do need you'll likely have at home already: a wooden spoon for a baren, or glass from a picture frame for an inking slab. You can even repurpose old, discarded wood or floor linoleum for your design blocks.

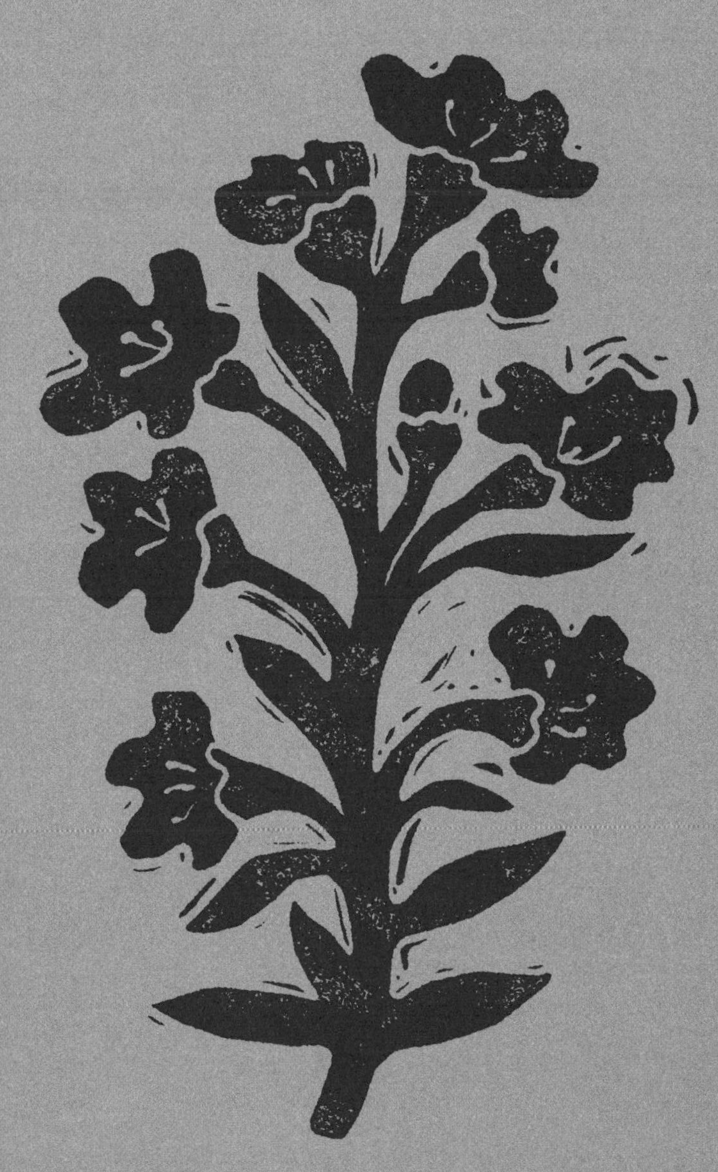

Kitchen Table Studio

When I first came back to printmaking after university, I spent many years printing on my kitchen table. With my newborn son in a Moses basket next to me, I spent days carving and hand-burnishing my designs. It was creatively liberating to realize I didn't need the extensive equipment used in my university print studio, and that I could take things into my own hands, literally, and start making prints at home.

Basic Set-up

Over the years, I've worked in big professional and specialist print studios as well as garden sheds and old stone barns (with no running water!). I believe it's possible to set up a functioning workshop space almost anywhere; you just need a few basic things.

- A desk or kitchen table: somewhere to draw, carve, and print your blocks.
- Access to a water source to clean up: this is essential but can be engineered and brought in via a big bottle or bucket if needs must.
- A couple of nails in the wall: to hang a piece of string and pegs to clip your prints up for drying.
- A wooden spoon or baren for burnishing.
- A piece of strong glass or smooth sturdy plastic for inking.
- Basic carving tools, a roller, decent ink, and paper.
- Rags, newsprint, and washing-up liquid for the clean-down.
- A relatively large box with a lid to keep all your bits in when you pack down at the end of the day and to keep everything together, especially if you live with children.

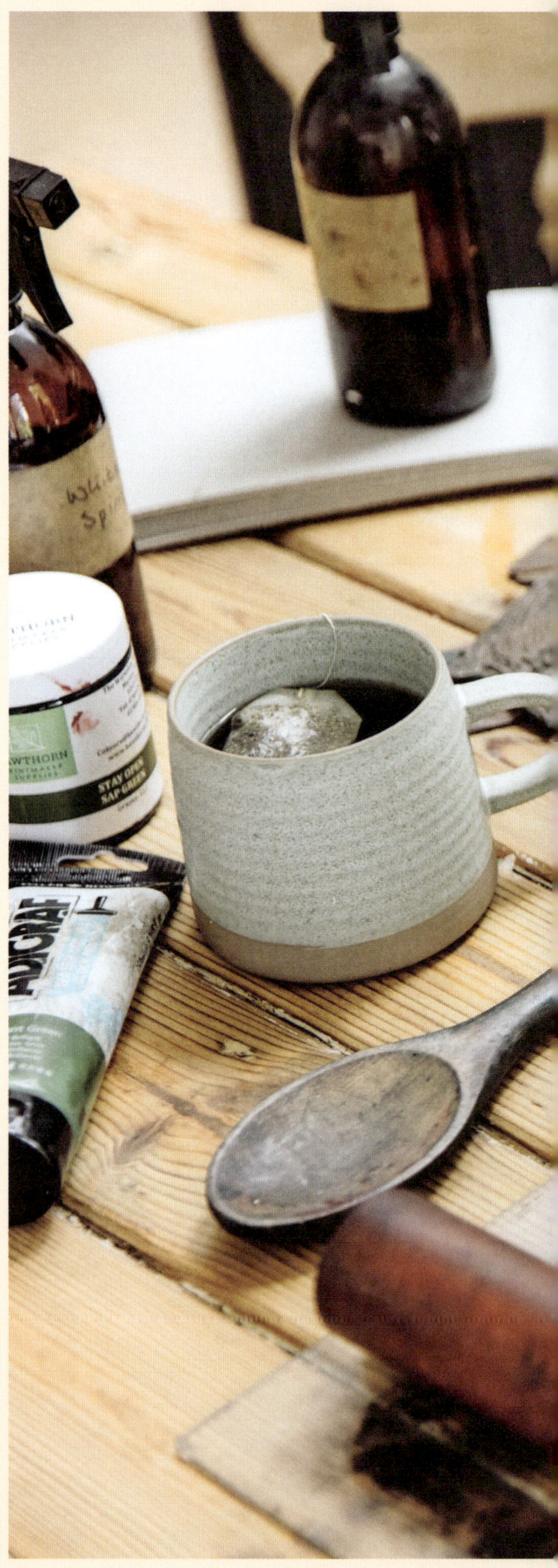

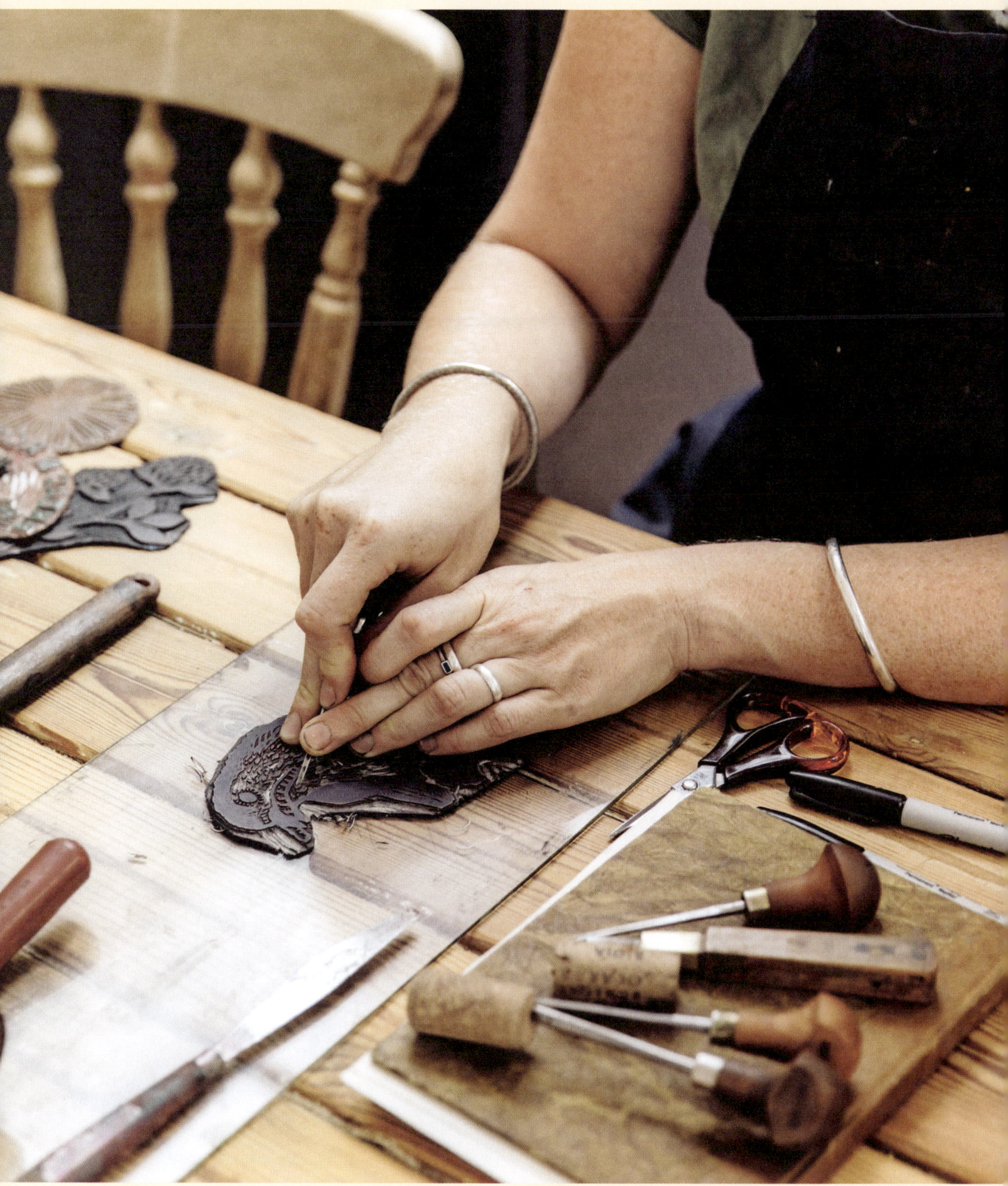

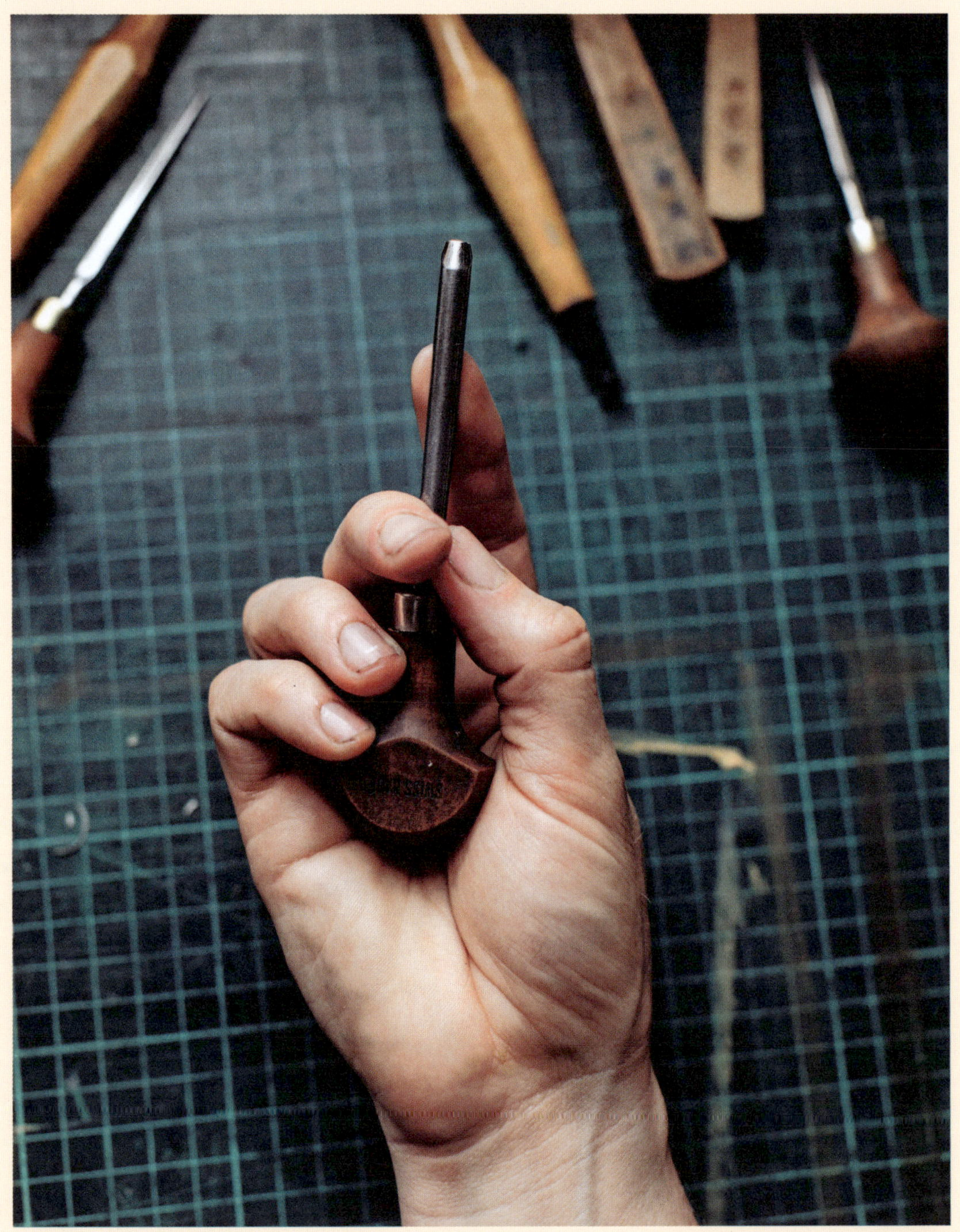

Basic Carving Techniques

How to Hold Your Tools

Grip the tool in your hand, as shown opposite. It's important that you feel comfortable and have enough clear space around you to apply good pressure through from your elbow to make the cut. Whether you are right-handed or left-handed, your non-dominant hand will be used to steady the tool-holding hand as you apply pressure.

HOW DEEP TO CUT?

You want to aim for about a 35-degree angle; however, this will vary from cut to cut. With practice you will find an angle that works for you. You don't need to cut away very much to create a mark for relief prints. However, if your angle is too high, and you cut too deep, you will likely tear your cut and create a fuzzy muffled edge on your print.

Another thing to consider when working with lino is not cutting so deep that you cut through to the hessian backing, as this can make your lino weaker and vulnerable to parts of your design breaking off and getting lost.

There's no science to the order in which you should carve your blocks and everyone has their own methodology for this. Some like to start with the fine detail and get the tricky bits out of the way first, leaving the 'easier' clearing of larger areas until last. Others may prefer to warm up with the clearing and then get down to the nitty gritty of fine detail last. It all comes down to personal preference and how we tackle a challenge. In my own work, I like to postpone the harder tasks until last, much to my own detriment.

CLEANING & NEATENING THE BLOCK

Once you've finished carving out the majority of your design, you can neaten any large areas of cleared surface by using a flat U gouge to bring the carved surface down to a uniform level. Any deep ridges left in these open areas are likely to pick up ink and create 'noise' in your final print. Once you've finished all your carving, give the block a good wipe down with a brush or dry cloth to remove any carved debris or dust.

Checking Your Carving

Use a pencil and scrap paper to make a rubbing and check what you've carved, and make any adjustments. You can also use a flat marker to check the carved areas. However, if you plan to print on the same day, marker pen can come off with the ink and muddy the look of your print. Either wipe it down with a solvent before printing or use a dark printing ink to hide this for the first run.

Before you commit to printing an edition, make a proof print on scrap paper. Check for any inconsistencies or areas you might want to change before you begin the final run.

HEALTH & SAFETY

Always cut away from you and take care not to put your free hand in front of the carving blade, as it's very easy to slip and stab yourself when applying pressure. Even the most seasoned printmakers cut themselves every now and then, so get into the habit of moving your block rather than your body as you carve. You can also use bench clamps, specially designed wooden boards with a shelf, or anti-slip mats to hold the block in place.

Making a Texture Block

Creating a texture block is a great opportunity to explore your carving tools and see what they are capable of. I like to make a couple of back-up copies of my texture blocks to reference back to when creating new designs. They are a great reminder of what's possible with your tools if you are stuck in the design stage.

YOU WILL NEED
Prepared A4 lino block
Pencil
Paper for design and printing
Permanent marker pen
Ruler
Carving tools
Printing ink and rollers
Baren or printing press

TEXTURE IDEAS

Here are a few things to consider as you carve each section – be experimental and test what your tools can achieve. Try moving the block as you carve, especially for circles and S-shapes, and experiment with getting a consistency of line size, length, and depth.

Play with straight, overlapping and curved lines, jagged edges and cross-hatching. You could even try letters – but keep in mind that everything prints in reverse!

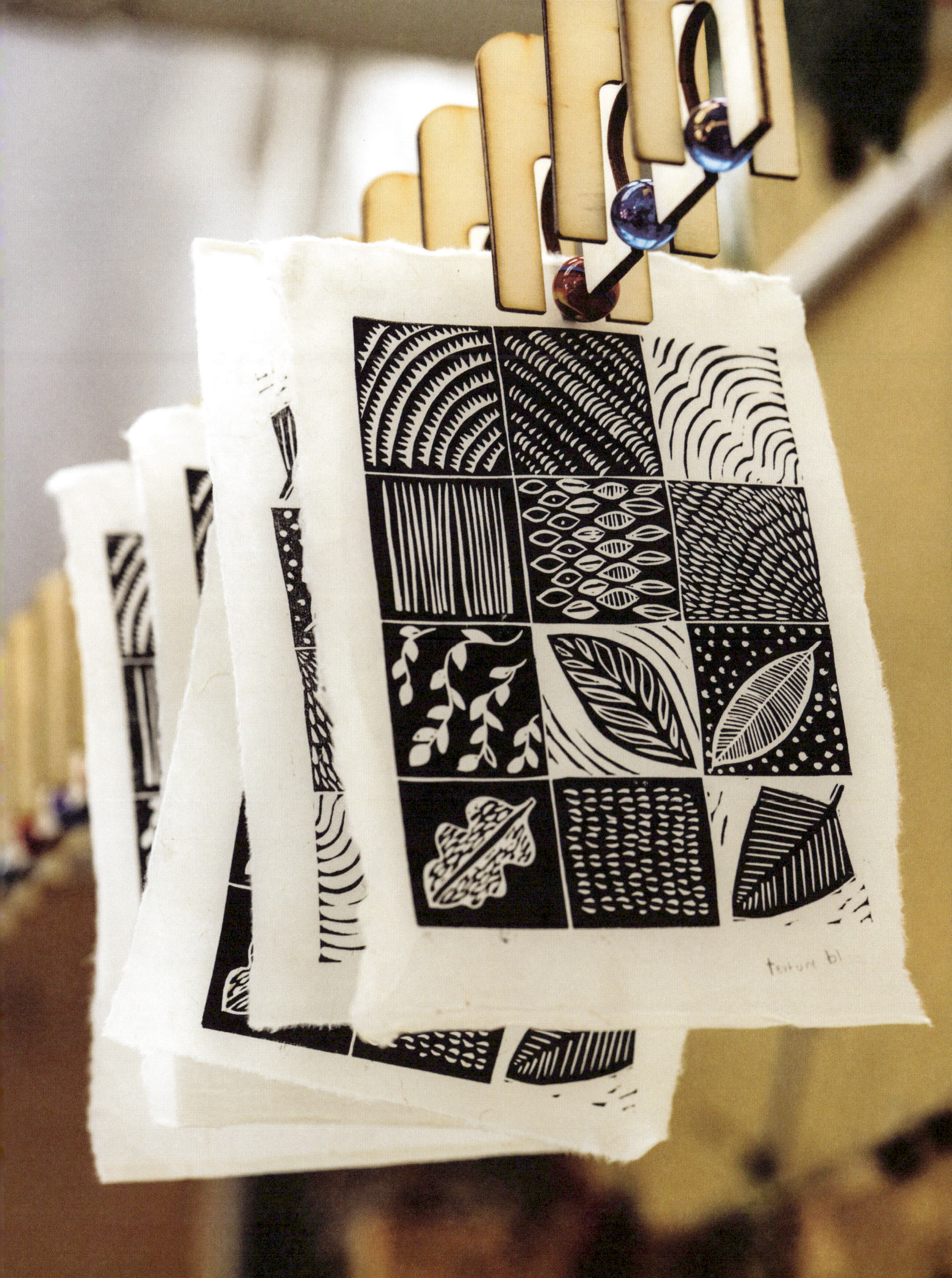

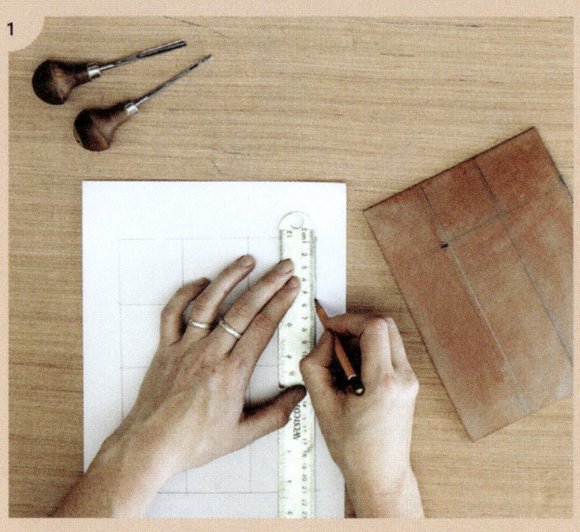

1. Using a pencil and ruler, divide the block into 5-cm (2-in) grid squares. Create an identical paper version of this grid alongside it to be used as a reference map.

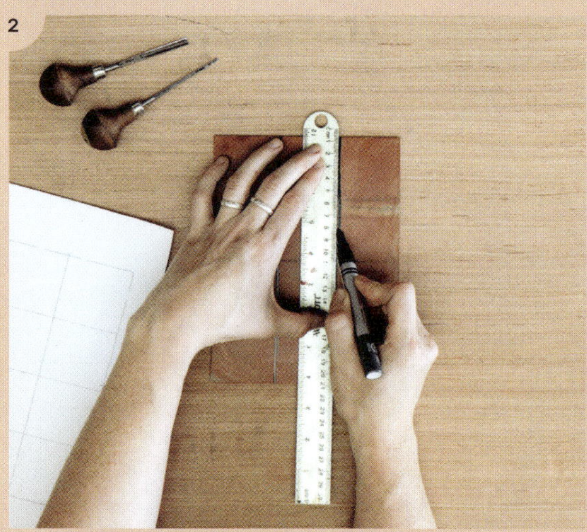

2. Use a permanent marker to go over these outlines so they don't get smudged when carving. Use a V-shaped tool to carve out each of the grid lines.

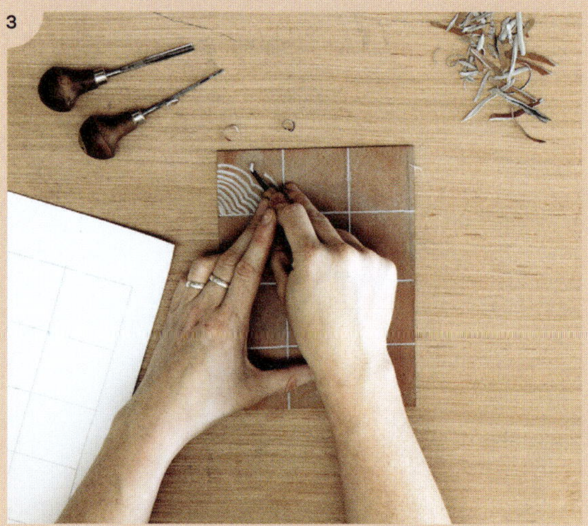

3. Now you're ready, work methodically across the lino, experimenting with different carving tools and textures for each square.

4. On the paper reference map, list each tool used as you complete each square on the grid to help you quickly identify them when you reference back later.

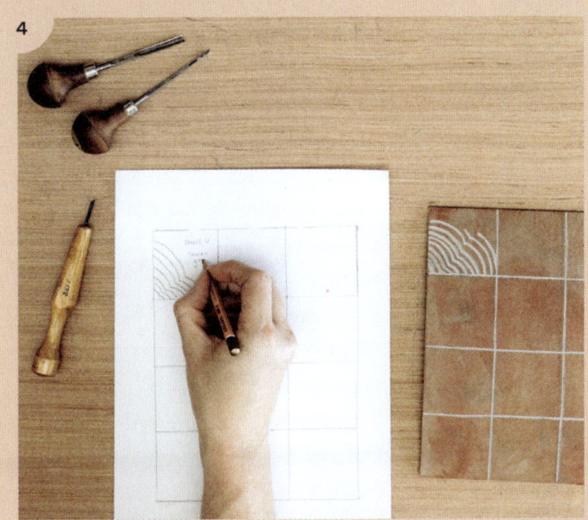

5. Once complete, use a rag to clean off any dust or cut pieces, and make a couple of proof prints.

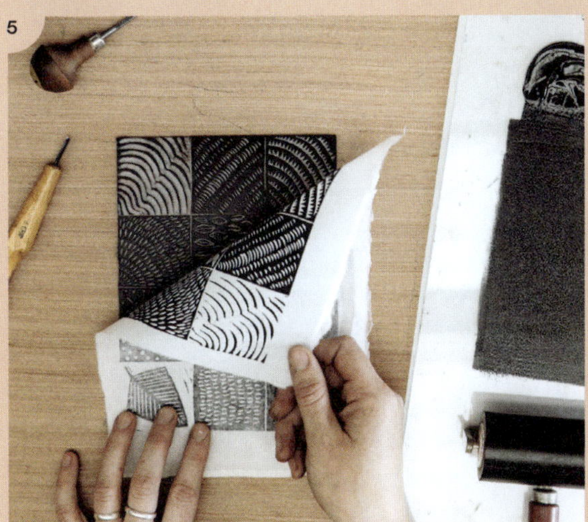

6. Reflect on what worked and what didn't and keep the texture block print in your scrapbook or pinned to your studio wall for reference in the future.

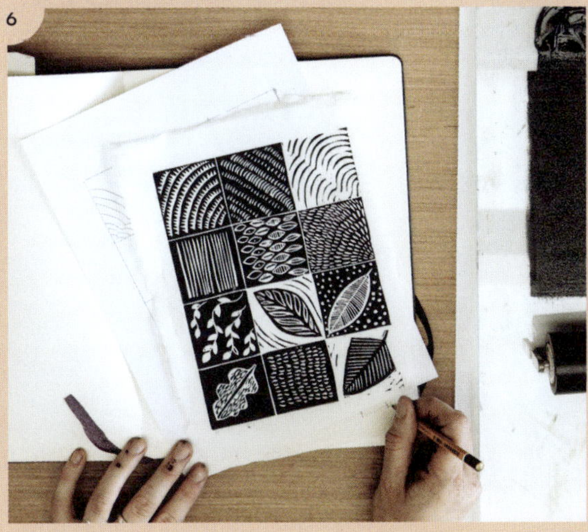

Inking Up

With time and practice every printmaker will naturally develop their own approach to inking up. How thickly you lay on the ink, the angle and corners you take as you travel across the surface, and how many times you go back over your block are all part of your own individual tastes and practice. It is these fine details that career printmakers obsess over. After all, we are not machines, and how you ink up your print has as much to do with the outcome as the design process.

TIP *Keep your fingers clean! It's very easy to get very mucky in the midst of printing. I like to keep a damp cloth with me and wipe down as I go.*

Inking Up

When you are first starting out, your main concern is with making sure to ink the whole block. Below is a basic step-by-step guide to my process of getting good prints.

YOU WILL NEED
Cleaning cloths
Roller
Printing ink
Palette knife
Inking plate
Anglepoise lamp

TROUBLESHOOTING INK PROBLEMS

- ***Too much ink*** *– loses detail and ink bulges over the edges of the design.*
- ***Not enough ink*** *– uneven ink distribution leaves some areas unprinted and patchy.*
- ***Dust/debris in the ink*** *– leaves white halos where the dust/debris blocks the ink.*
- ***Messy inking/soft roller*** *– picks up carved areas that should be clear.*

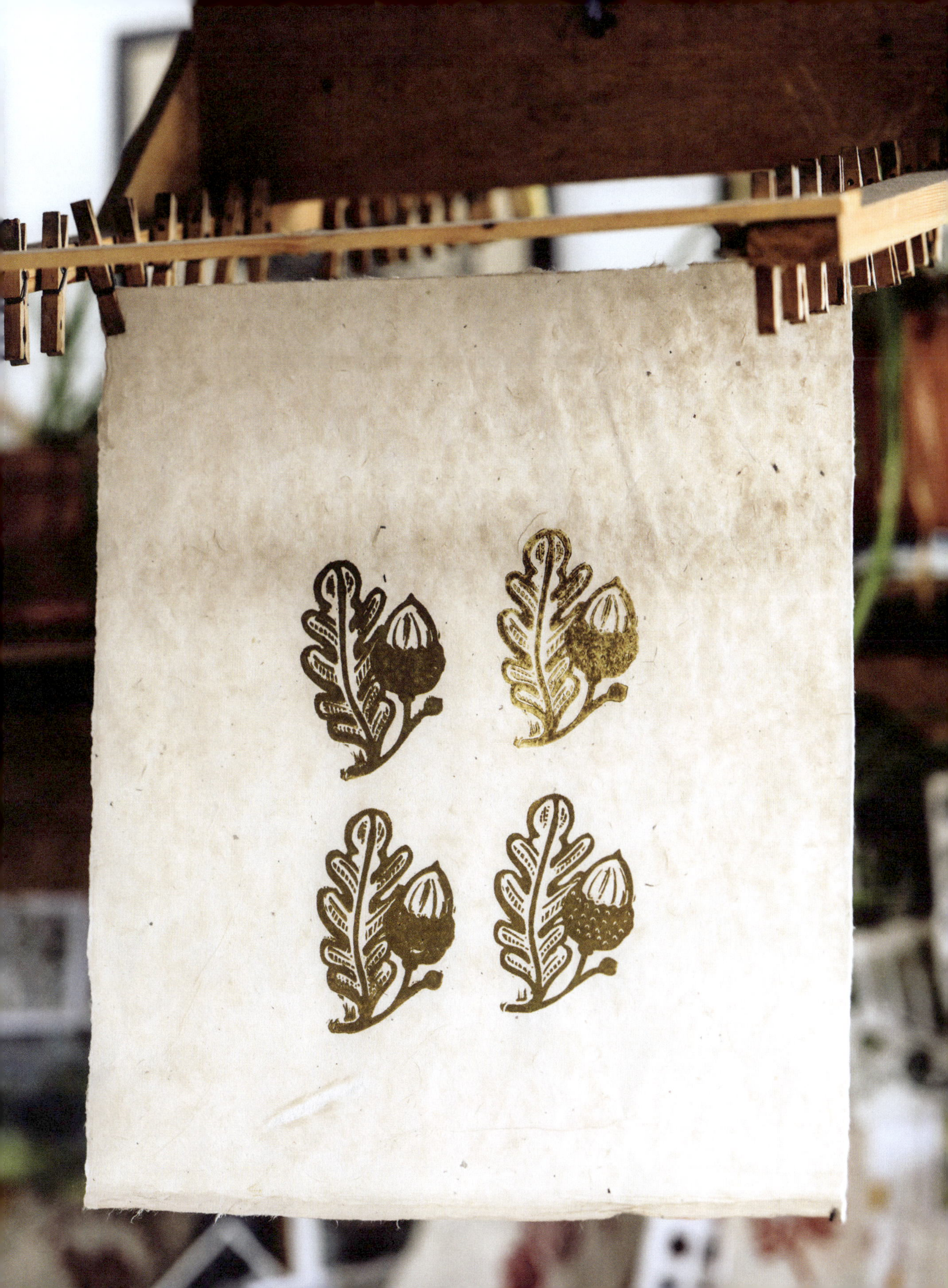

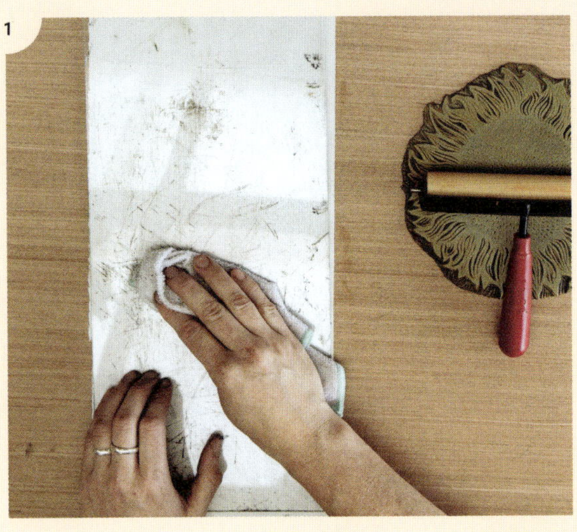

1. Before you start printing, make sure your inking area is clean. Wipe down the surface with a damp cloth and remove any fluff, dust, or debris.

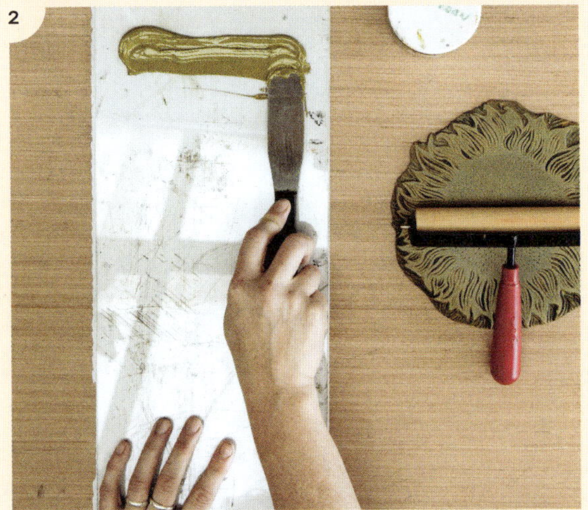

2. Choose a roller roughly the same size as your lino block to help avoid lines in your print and make inking up easier.

3. If using a tin of ink, grab a palette knife and cream off a good dollop of ink from the surface, then spread it onto your inking plate. If using a cartridge or tube, just squeeze some out and remember to pop the lid back on. Ink goes a long way, and you likely need less than you think. You can always add more but getting ink back into a tube is impossible.

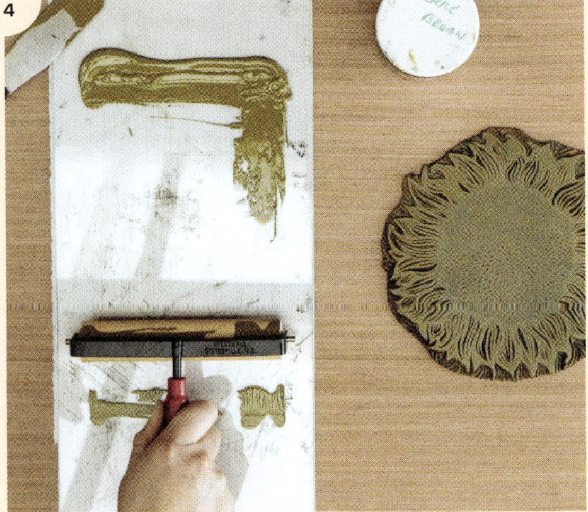

4. Warm the ink up by mixing it back and forth with the palette knife to create an even reservoir roughly the size of your roller.

5. Use your roller to pick up a little ink and, starting lower down the glass, roll back up towards your ink reservoir, stopping just before you get to the top.

6. Lift the roller and roll again from the bottom up. It's tempting to roll back and forth at this stage but you're aiming for an even distribution of ink and lifting the roller each time helps spread the ink out.

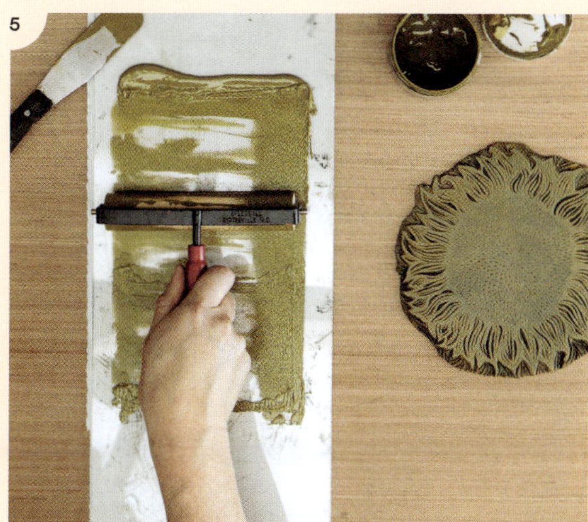

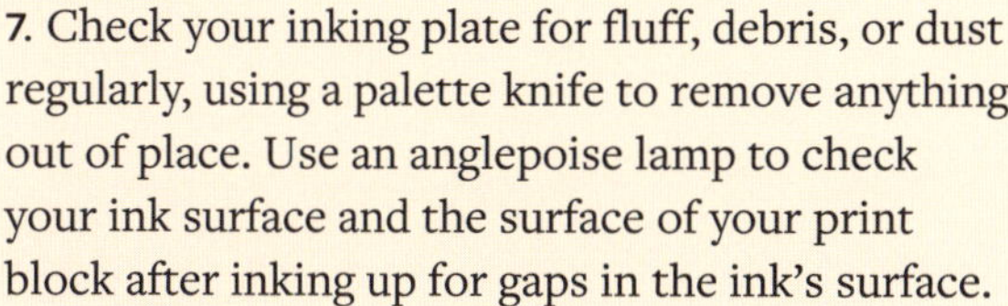

7. Check your inking plate for fluff, debris, or dust regularly, using a palette knife to remove anything out of place. Use an anglepoise lamp to check your ink surface and the surface of your print block after inking up for gaps in the ink's surface.

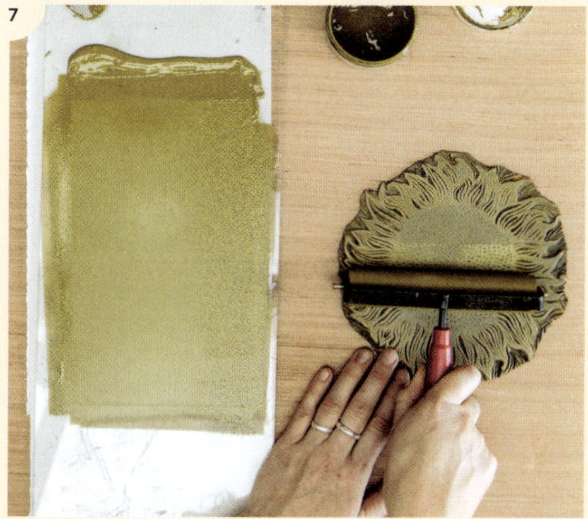

8. You're aiming for a kind of velvet consistency. Once you have an even layer of ink on your surface and the roller, you're ready to print.

9. In between printing, always leave your roller rubber-side up to protect the inked surface. Most good-quality rollers have a little stand you can sit them on just for this purpose.

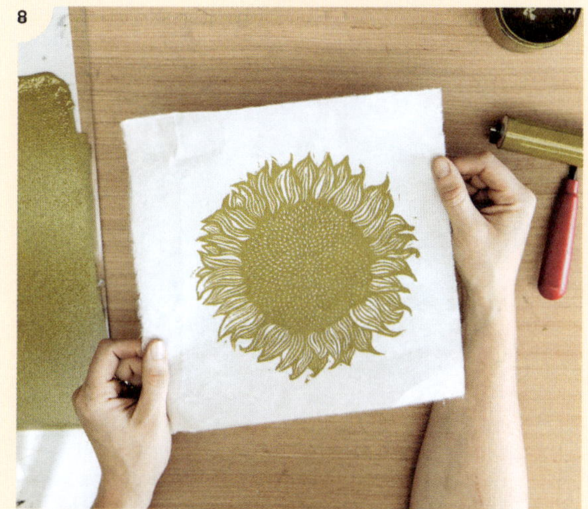

Printing with a Wooden Spoon

After inking, lay your paper onto your block and follow the steps below for printing with a wooden spoon.

YOU WILL NEED

Inked carved block
Paper
Newsprint or tracing paper
Wooden spoon

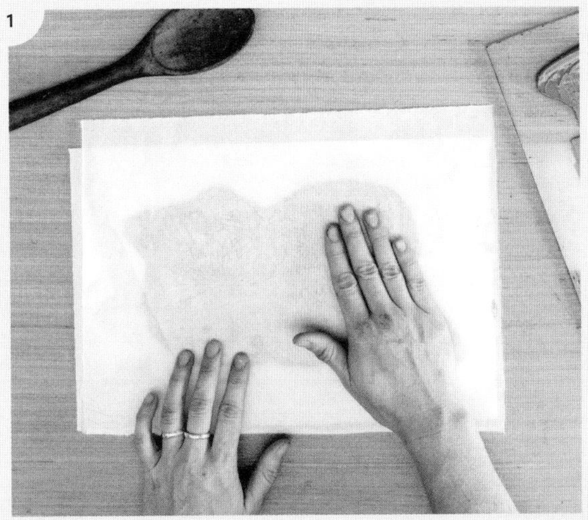

1. Gently rub the paper onto the block allowing the ink to adhere and stick it in place.

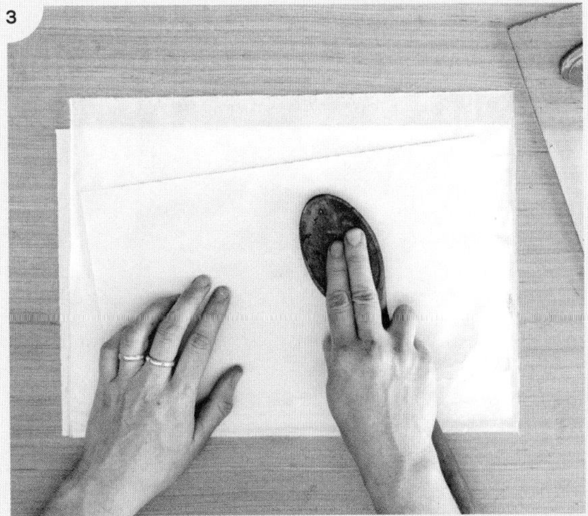

2. If you are using handmade or fine papers, it's worth layering a piece of newsprint or tracing paper between your spoon and the paper to protect it from tearing.

3. Hold the wooden spoon comfortably along its edges and begin to work methodically across your block, rubbing the wooden spoon in circular motions.

4. You can check your progress by picking up a corner of the paper while holding the rest of the print down with your other hand, to see how much you have left to go.

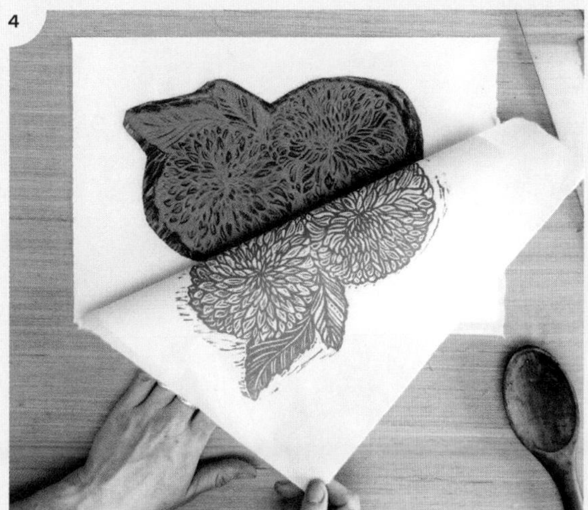
4

5. Place the paper back down carefully and continue burnishing if needed. Be careful not to move the paper at this point or you may get a double image.

6. Once you've been over the whole print, do another little rub down for luck and pull a corner to reveal.

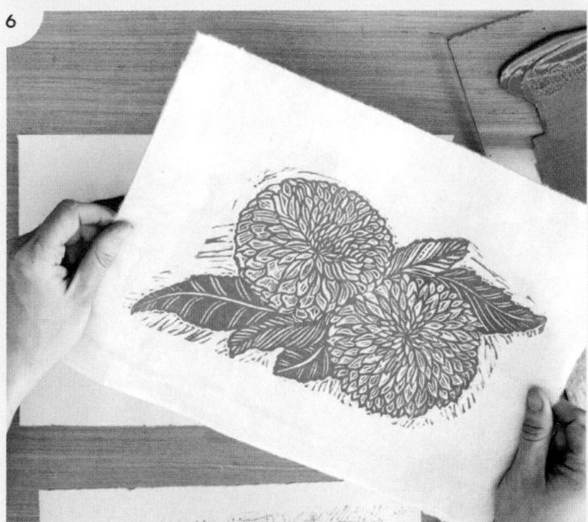
6

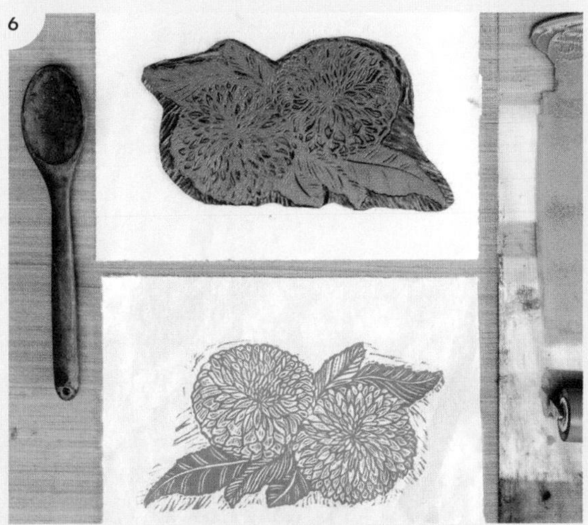
6

Leaf Inverted

Relief printing, when it's boiled down, is all about light and dark and how we choose to represent these two opposing elements. This project is a great chance to play with this concept and really get your head around the differences your choices can achieve in print. The marks we make in these two opposing images can have a huge range of effects on how an image is preserved.

YOU WILL NEED

Prepared A4 lino block
Pencil
Foraged leaves (see pages 86, 95)
Permanent marker pen
Ruler
Carving tools
Printing ink and roller
Baren or press

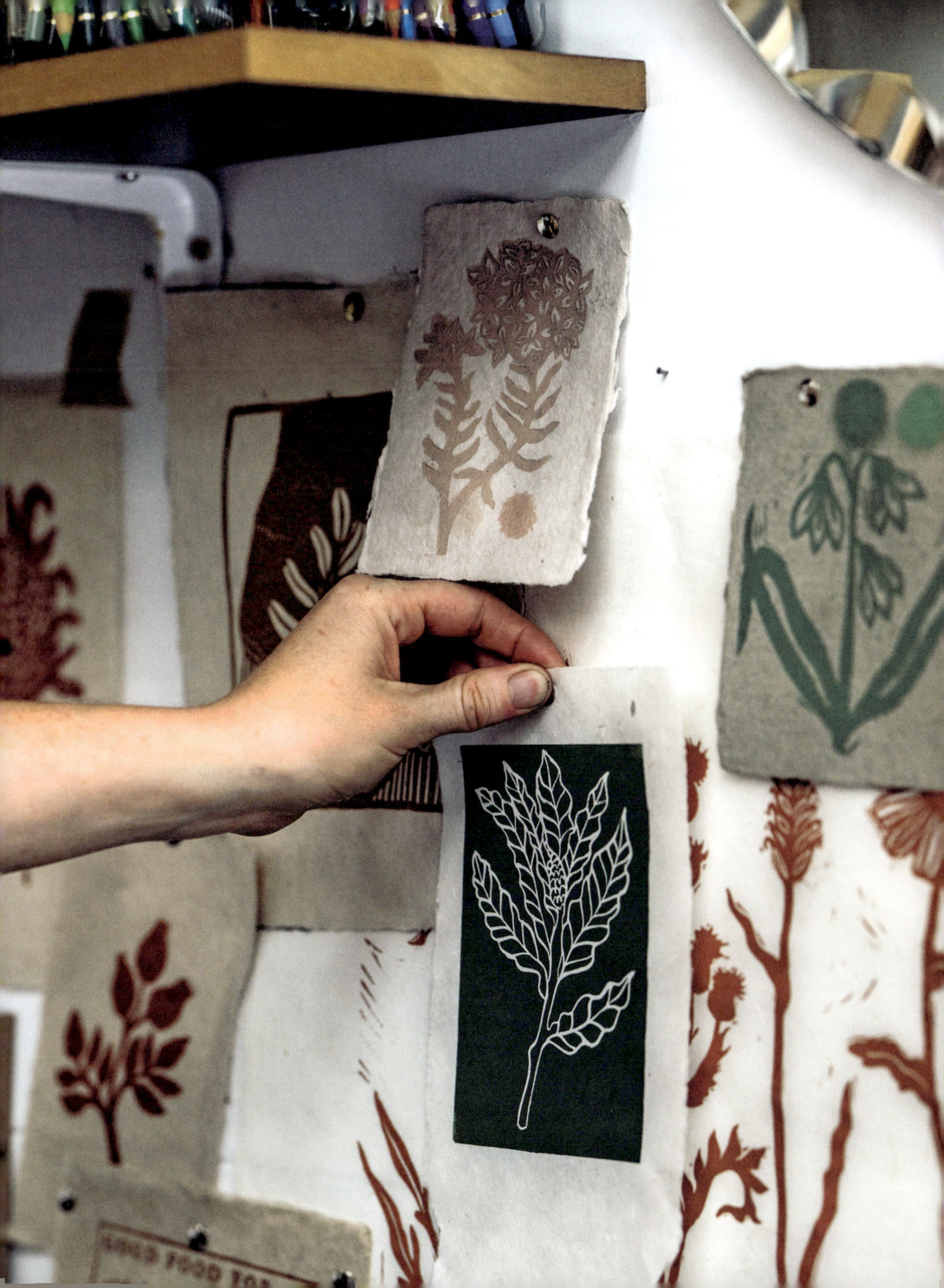

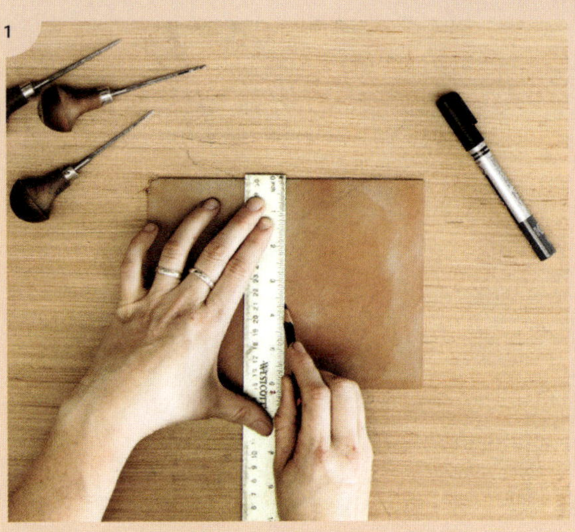

1. Divide the block in half so you have two A5 sections.

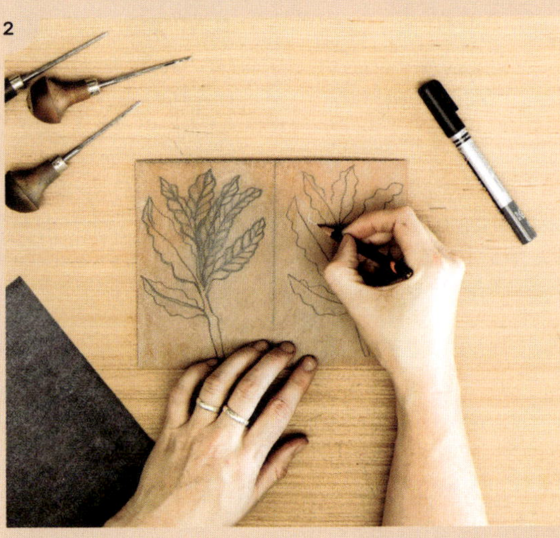

2. Draw out your leaf in pencil on both sections of the lino, taking care to keep the shape and design as similar as possible. You can also use tracing or carbon paper to make this step easier (see pages 104–105).

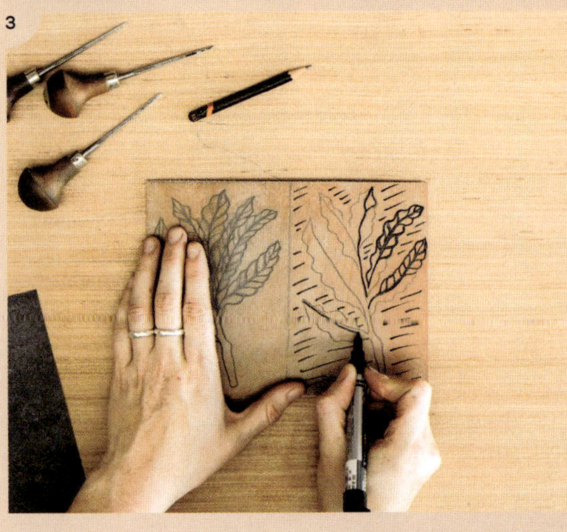

3. Go over your design with a marker, this time choosing one to be in the positive and one to be in the negative. I find being as clear as possible during this stage really helps me when I come to carve later; I mark out everything I intend to pick up ink once carved.

4. Use your texture block (see page 40) to make choices about tools and markings as you create these two opposing images.

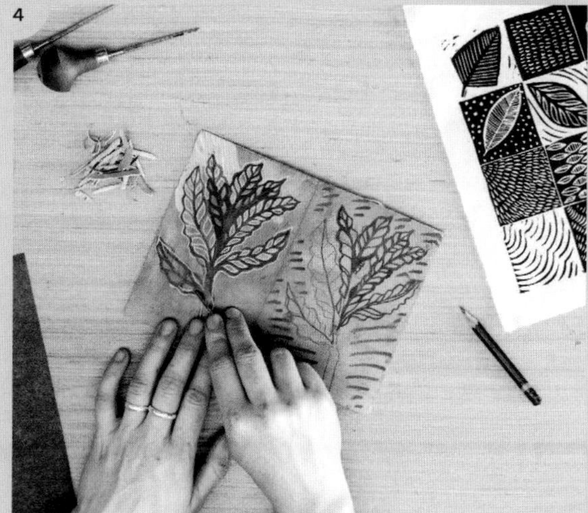

5. Clean down the block with a rag and proof print a couple of images.

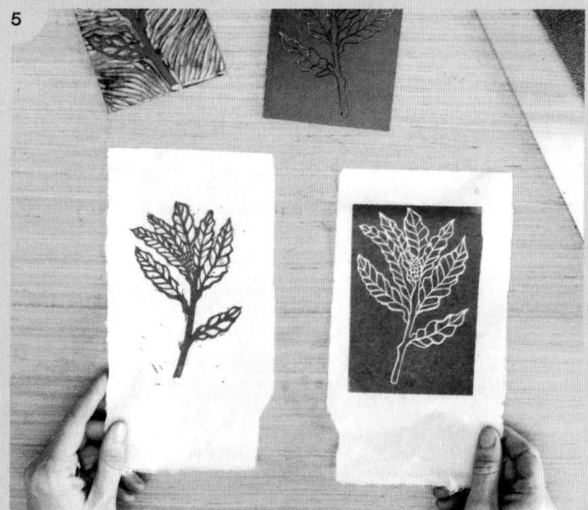

6. Reflect on what worked and what didn't and keep it in your scrapbook or pinned to your studio wall for reference in the future.

Cleaning Down

When I used to teach in my studio, we would joke that half of the printmaking process was the cleaning up! Although it's not necessarily true, many a printmaker has been caught out by the mammoth task of cleaning down at the end of the day. Always leave at least half an hour to make sure you've cleaned up properly and put everything back in its place and you'll thank yourself the next time you come back to print.

Cleaning Inks

Always wear gloves while printing and cleaning down. Even though water-based inks are generally considered harmless, it's still a good idea to wear gloves, unless you like the blue-stained hand look when you pop to the shops later!

Use newsprint to blot any remaining ink on the block after you've finished printing. For water-based inks, spray the block liberally with a mixture of 1 part washing-up liquid to 9 parts water. Use an old rag or cloth to wipe in circular motions and remove ink. Generally, with water-based inks they should lift easily without too much work.

For oil-based inks, repeat the stages above, but instead of a water-based spray use a little vegetable oil to lift the oil from the block and tools. Once most of the ink has been removed, a light cleaning liquid like Zest It, might be needed to remove the last streaks, or a stronger solvent like pure alcohol or white spirit.

For detailed prints, use an old toothbrush or scrubbing brush to remove ink from finer cuts. For the inking area or glass, use a palette knife to scrape up ink onto scrap paper. Spray the block down and rub clean.

Cleaning Rollers

Cleaning your roller after every print session is essential. Dried-on ink can completely ruin a good roller's surface, making it impossible to get a clear print, and takes hours of your time to remove and restore later. As with most tools, a few minutes spent maintaining them regularly saves you money and time later on.

Remove most of the ink first by rolling out on scrap paper. For water-based or processed inks, spray generously with a cleaning solution and use a rag to wipe clean. For oil-based inks, use rags with vegetable oil to thin and remove as much of the ink as possible.

Give the inside of the frame a clean with a strip of cloth rag, as clots can build up and hide in there, especially on budget rollers.

To finish, it's sometimes necessary to give the roller a quick wipe to remove any last streaks of ink with something alcohol, or a solvent such as Zest It. A fresh piece of paper or cloth passed through the roller at the end of cleaning should come out spotless. For best practice, use a little oil on a clean rag to seal and preserve the roller in between uses.

HEALTH & SAFETY

Always read the label and be aware of health and safety recommendations when using solvents. Good ventilation in your workspace is essential and if you're planning on using stronger solvents, invest in an industrial eye-wash station. Store your solvents and cleaning products in clearly labelled bottles away and out of reach of children.

Taking Care of Your Tools

Your prints are only as good as your tools are sharp. Regular honing, which is essentially polishing and sharpening of your blades, is a vital part of the printmaking process.

Storage

Store your tools in a sealable box or bag to keep them safe from moisture. You can also use a little vegetable oil on the blade to reduce any chance of rusting in between uses; this is especially important if you regularly work in a damp studio space or outside. I once spent a summer carving on a beach and the salty sea air put an end to the carving tools I had at the time.

A lot of printmakers use wine corks on the ends of their blades to stop the ends knocking into each other and getting blunt. Another option is sliced down pieces of traditional erasers. You might want to create a tool roll to store your tools side by side and make them easier to travel with. Use a strong and thick material like denim, and allow space for corks or rubber stops, as fabric is very easily pierced even with the bluntest of carving tools.

If storing all your print kit together in a box, wrap cloth around your rollers too, to protect the rubber.

Honing

Honing is essentially polishing, and it's generally recommended that you do this little and often throughout the carving process. I tend to aim for a break to hone every 20–30 minutes, but some printmakers do it as often as every 10 minutes. Well-honed tools reduce the need for more serious sharpening later and will help your tools last longer and your prints look crisper.

A simple honing strop can be made from any old piece of leather with a suede side; I've used an old belt, cut it down, and superglued it to a piece of wood. Essentially, it's just a soft and durable surface for you to apply your sharpening compound to. Sharpening compound is available at hardware shops and specialist art shops. It's made from chromium and aluminium oxide and comes in a few different colours and types; most printmakers use the softer yellow or pink one.

You can also purchase specialist honing kits, ready-made for carving tools, with the leather already glued to a sturdy base. Some have specially designed edges and ridges to make your job easier and for removing the bur (a thin layer of steel build-up).

WHEN TO HONE?

- *Always hone immediately after a carving session so that your tools go back into their box ready to use next time.*
- *I also hone every half an hour while I'm carving lino and maybe every 15 or 20 minutes when carving wood.*

Honing with a Honing Tool or Belt

Over time your strop will grey and blacken as small amounts of metal are removed in the honing process. This is normal and the sign of a well-seasoned and practised printmaker. When you're finished, your blade should shine brightly like a mirror.

YOU WILL NEED
Sharpening compound
Honing tool or belt

FOR V-SHAPED TOOLS

1. Apply your sharpening compound to the block liberally by rubbing back and forth.

2. Take your tool and try to align the cutting edge on one side with the strop – the angle is important here and you want to replicate the angle on the blade.

3. Stroke back across the leather, applying a small amount of pressure. With each stroke, pick the tool up and place at the beginning again, repeating the process (don't go back and forth).

4. Count your strokes and repeat evenly for the other side of the blade.

5. Find the closest matching ridged edge on the other side, apply compound, and stroke the inside of the tool to clear the bur. If using a belt, utilize the belt's edge in a similar way with compound applied and gently stroke back the bur.

FOR U-SHAPED TOOLS

Repeat the steps above, but instead of evenly stroking the tool across the honing block, use your wrist to curve the blade across the surface, making sure the angle remains the same and each part of the blade touches the honing compound evenly. This sounds tricky and at first it is, but with practice you will master it.

1
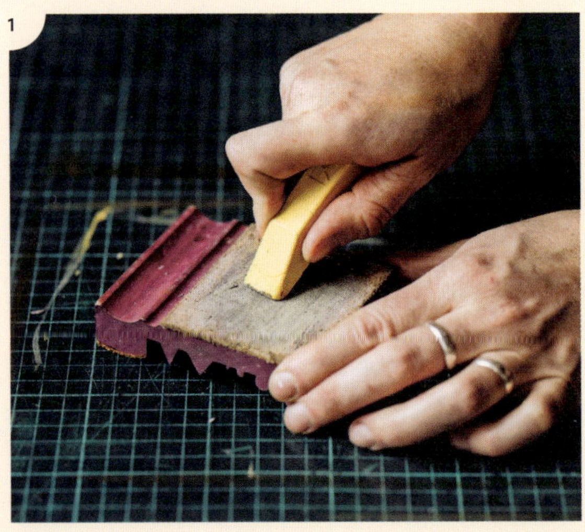

2
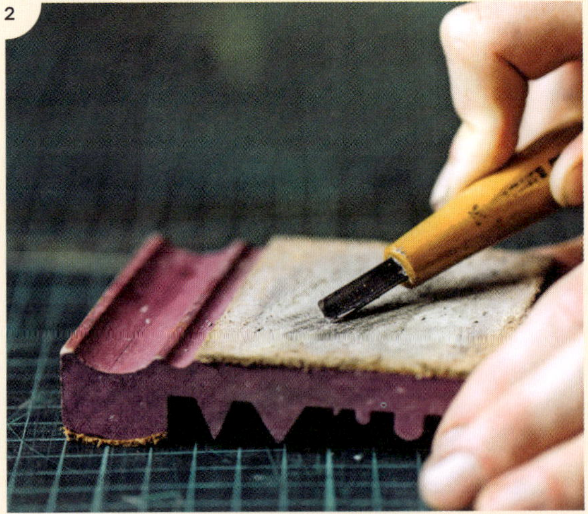

Sharpening

Eventually there comes a time in every tool's life when it will need a proper sharpening. Either it's been honed to the point of no return, or you've chipped or damaged the cutting edge. Either way, it's pretty essential as a printmaker that you get a handle on sharpening your own tools to make them last, and your prints will be all the better for it.

You should always sharpen when, even after honing, your tool feels dull to cut with and tears the lino or wood rather than slicing it, and if you notice a nick in the tool's edge, head straight to reshaping.

USING WHETSTONES

The stones for tool sharpening are usually divided into two categories: naturally mined Arkansas stones and synthetic ones. These are then available in two types: aluminate oxide, which is generally faster and cheaper; and ceramic, which is more expensive but harder wearing over time.

As you grind the tools on the rough stone you will create a bur – a thin layer of steel build-up created through grinding. You should remove this with a slipstone or leather strop before using. Slipstones are sharpening stones with one edge of their surface shaped to fit in the gouge of the tool (see step 5 below). They are intended specifically to remove the bur on carving tools after sharpening.

When sharpening your tools, it's important to utilize the entirety of your stone's surface and wear the stone evenly. Inevitably you will create grooves across the surface that will need regular flattening with a flattening block, available in hardware stores. Another simple option is to sand the surface back: use an 800-grit to rub it back and progress up to 1200-grit to create a nice smooth surface to begin sharpening again.

TIP *To help see the effect your sharpening is having on the edge of the blade, use a permanent marker to mark the edge before you begin sharpening. This will make it much easier to see if you are wearing away the blade correctly and to adjust your angle to save yourself going too far in the wrong direction.*

3

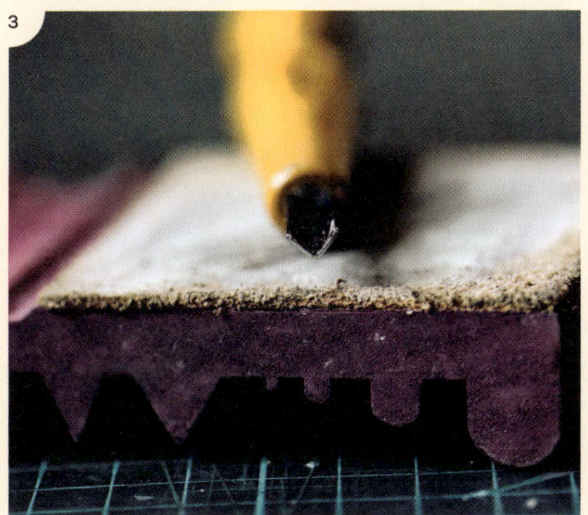

5

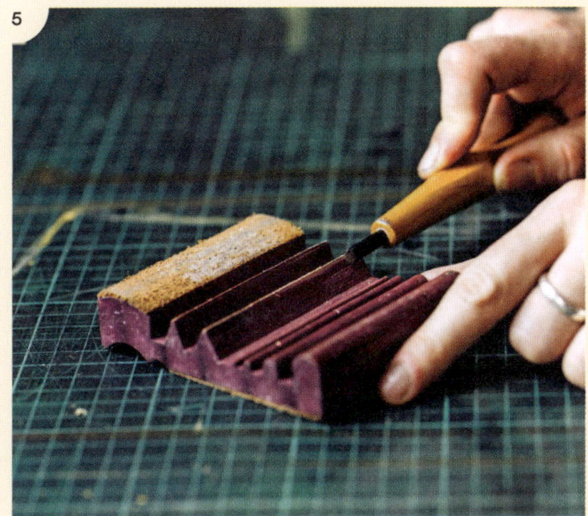

Sharpening a Chisel or Flat Gouge

Sharpening a chisel or flat gouge is arguably the simplest tool in your box to sharpen. If you can hold a consistent angle, you'll be fine.

1. Using both hands, find the blade's edge and angle so that it lies flat against the stone. You want to aim for a 25–30-degree angle.

2. Move up and down the stone gently, keeping your pressure and movements consistent with each stroke.

3. Start with ten strokes back and forth and see how your blade looks.

4. Remove the bur by turning the tool over and gently stroking the other side on the stone.

Sharpening a V-shaped Gouge

Sharpening a V-gouge is much the same as a chisel or flat gouge, but because of the meeting point in the centre it's especially important to remain consistent in the angle and the pressure you apply.

1. Using both hands, find the blade's edge and angle on one side, laying it flat against the stone. You want to aim for a 25–30-degree angle.

2. Start with ten strokes on one side and then repeat with ten on the other. Move up and down the stone gently, keeping your pressure and movements consistent with each stroke.

3. Stop and check regularly to make sure you are applying consistent pressure. Check the permanent marker on the edge to see that you have sharpened the whole of the tool.

4. Remove the bur build-up with a slipstone or similar. If you don't have the correct-sized stone, a leather belt could do.

5. After sharpening, always hone before use.

Sharpening a U-shaped Gouge

One of the hardest tools to sharpen, a U-gouge requires developing a specific twist of the wrist while maintaining consistent pressure. No mean feat, but achievable with patience and practice.

1. Start with the U-gouge in the centre of your stone; you want to get the angle of the blade edge flat to the stone's surface: aim for 25–30 degrees.

2. Using your wrists to move the tool, rotate across the tool's edge, while also rotating back and forth in circular motions across the stone. Keep your pressure and angle as consistent as possible here to maintain a steady connection between your blade's edge and the stone.

3. Check the permanent marker on the edge to see that you have sharpened the whole of the tool.

4. Use a round-edged slipstone to remove the bur that forms inside the gouge.

5. After sharpening, always hone before use.

Reshaping a Damaged Tool

Unless you are incredibly conscientious with your tools and how you keep them, at some point you're going to need to do some more serious sharpening. If your tool has come into contact with something hard, like a rogue nail in your woodblock, or been dropped from a height, it may have developed a nick in the end. When this happens it's necessary to grind it right back to basics and begin again.

1. Take a low grit stone and place your blade flat on it at a 90-degree angle on the surface.

2. Keep a consistent pressure and move the tool up and down the block until you've ground past the damage.

3. Once the blade is flat to the stone, you are ready to start to rebuild its edge.

TIP *Reshaping a tool is not for everyone and takes some confidence in your abilities to rebuild a new cutting edge. There are plenty of professionals who will do this for a fee; search online for tool sharpening services in your area. You may need to send your tools further afield, so plan ahead and make sure you have some spare tools on hand. Receiving your tools back from a professional sharpening is one of the biggest treats a printmaker can give themselves.*

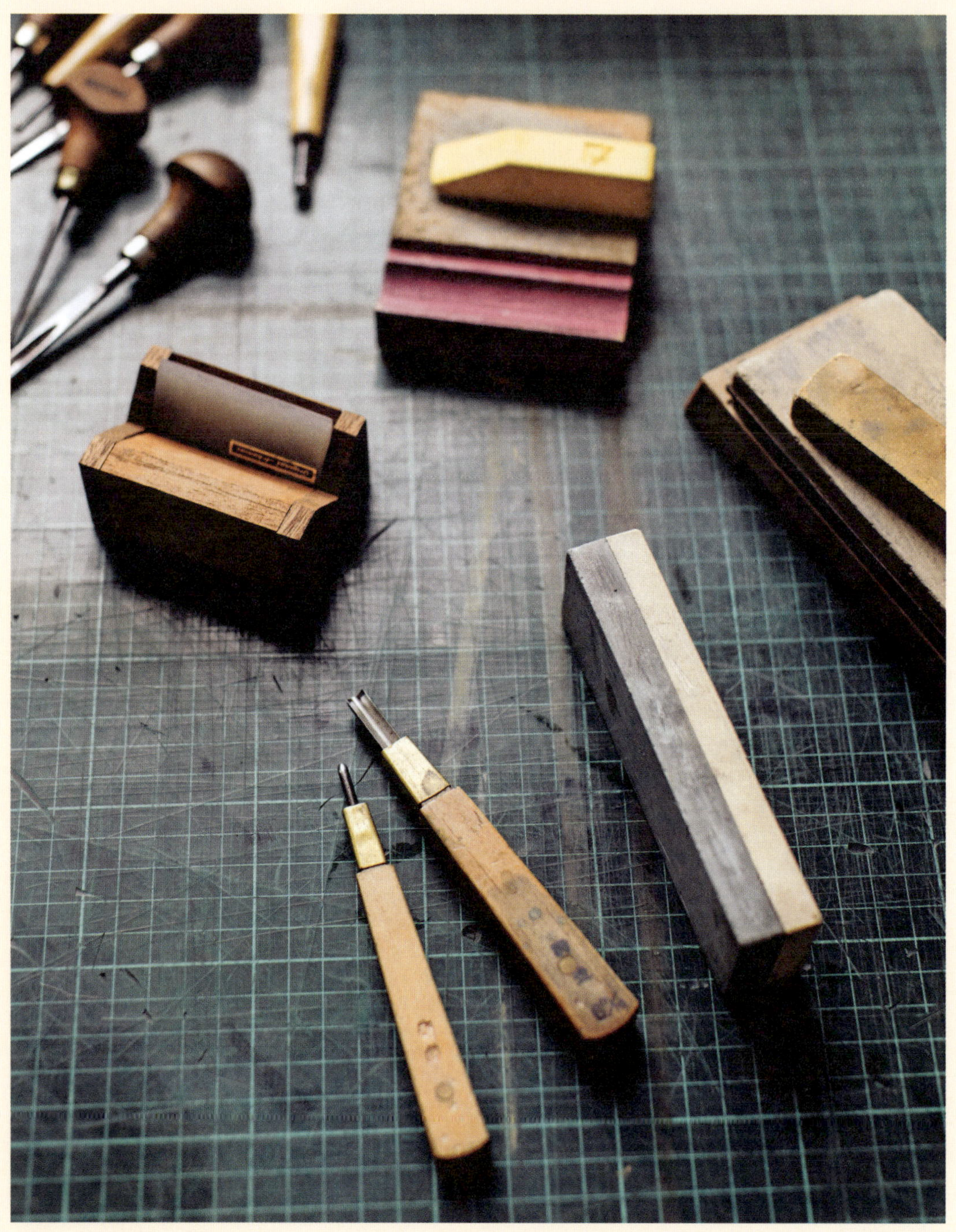

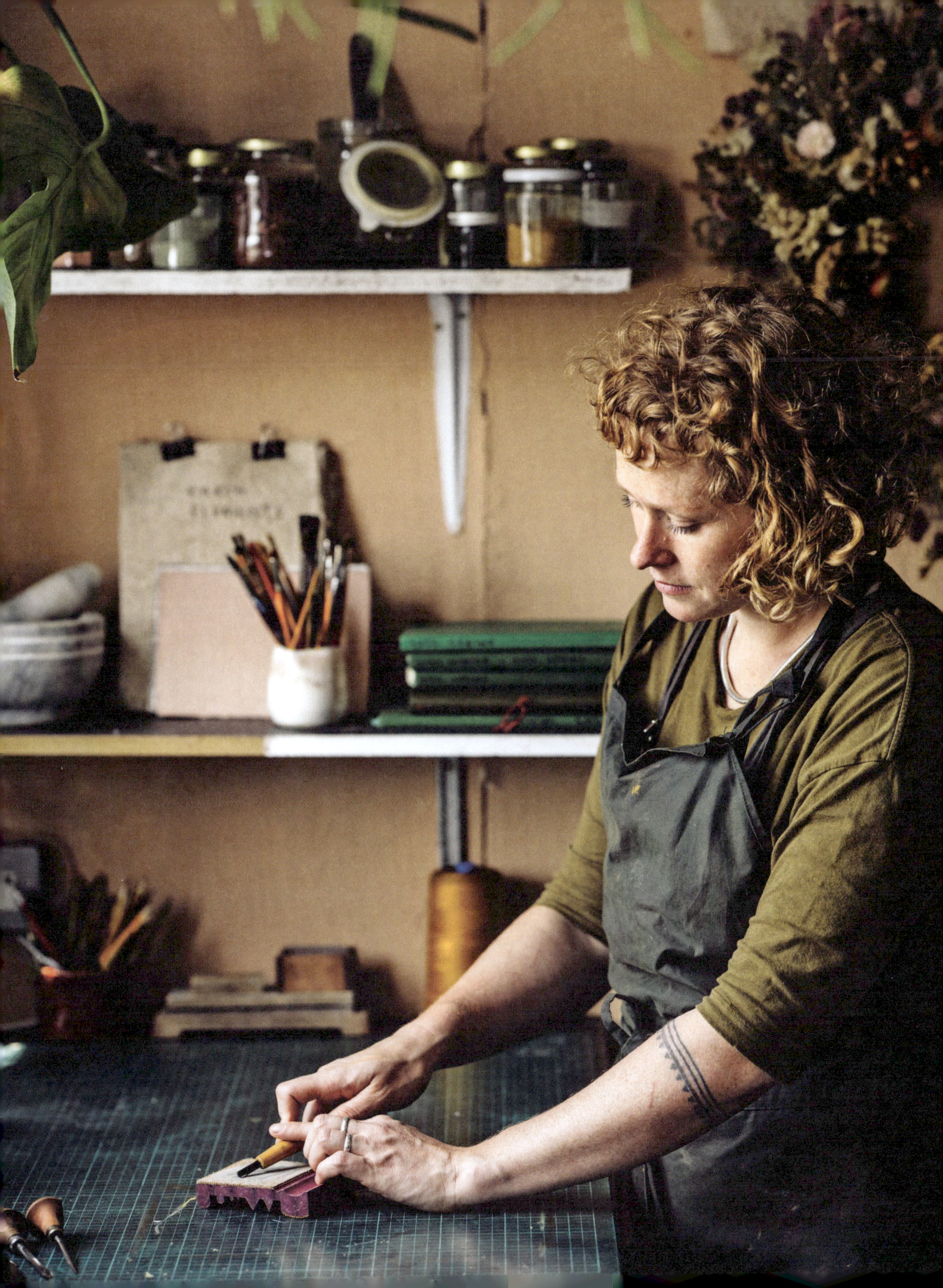

Studio Set-up

After a good long while of printing at your kitchen table, you may have outgrown this room's capacity and feel ready to set up a professional print studio, or at least a dedicated space in your home in which you can develop your practice and not have to pack down at the end of each day.

Setting Up a Professional Space

When setting up a permanent printmaking space you will need to take the following into consideration:

- The height of your workspaces: I'm 6 ft and my back has been ruined over the years by working on low tables. Make sure your desks are high enough for you to work standing up with good posture as you apply pressure.
- Access to a water source: this is essential in a proper printmaking space. In an ideal world you'd have two sinks, one for cleaning down your rollers and blocks and one for the all-essential cups of coffee that keep you going on a print run. Mixing ink and coffee is not recommended.
- Light: natural light is so important for me when drawing out my designs. I have my desk right in front of the window in my studio. If you don't have the luxury of a big window, investing in a couple of decent anglepoise lamps is a must.

THE STORY OF CATO PRESS & BOUBOULINA

When the day came that I couldn't move in my dining room without ducking or banging into multiple prints on a drying line, I knew I had to start looking for a space to work in. I was lucky enough to meet some other local printmakers who were also in need of a space. We teamed up and found a beautiful studio on the top floor of a big warehouse full of different artists. We didn't have much money, but we did have a lot of energy, enthusiasm, and vision for the kind of community print shop we wanted to create. We began hunting around for all the furniture we would need, contacting established print studios to see if they had any equipment they were getting rid of. We collected old plan chests from schools and a huge abandoned and rusty drying rack from a shed. Piece by piece, we managed to salvage a full print workshop together.

We had the studio, but we didn't have the funds or means to buy a proper etching press. My partner, a metal worker and now bladesmith by trade, optimistically volunteered himself to make us one. Somehow, he worked it out and pulled it off, creating our beautiful and massive Bouboulina from scratch, ready to sit proudly in the centre of our studio.

Our press is named after the brilliant and famous heroine from Greek history, Laskarina Bouboulina, who was a single mother of seven children and a formidable revolutionary in the Greek War of Independence in 1821. She led an armada of ships against the Ottoman Empire and became the first woman to posthumously receive the title of Admiral. We felt hers was a fitting name to christen our formidable press.

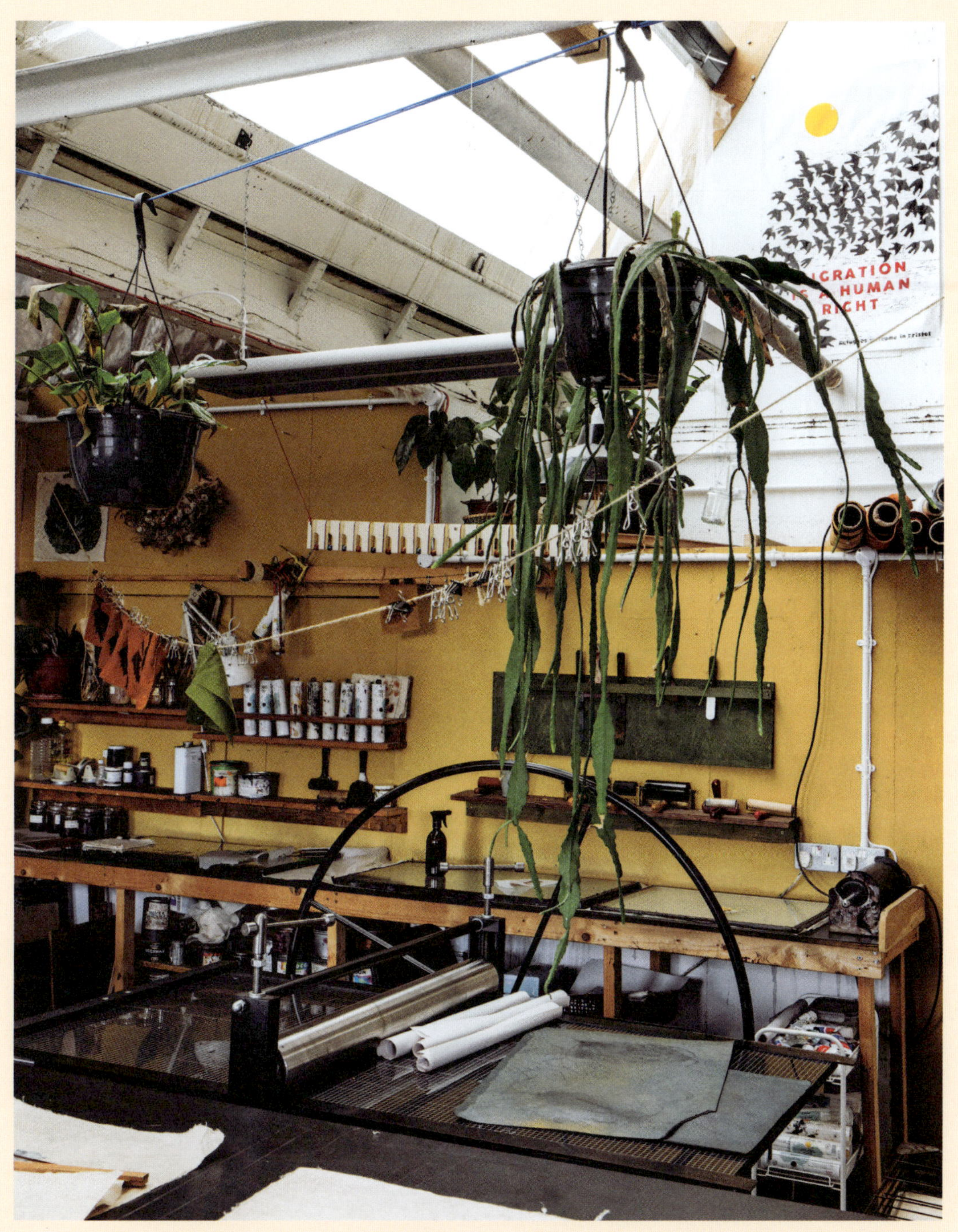
IGRATION
HUMAN
RIGHT

A CLEAN AREA & A DIRTY AREA

Most professional printmaking studios are organized into a dirty area – for inking, printing, and so on, and a clean area – for drawing, paper cutting, signing your edition, packing, etc. It's useful when designing your space to keep these things in mind and to make the process of printing an edition as simple as possible.

Inking or dirty area – For the inking area you need some strong, flat surfaces to roll out your inks. Traditionally, reinforced glass is used as it's hardwearing and quick to clean down. In our studio we have used old glass windows we found in skips. They are all different shapes and sizes and I've found this particularly useful when needing to move around my space. Having inking areas that are portable allow me flexibility, especially when working on larger prints where I can even get down on my hands and knees to ink up with my inking slab on the floor.

Another inking material is plexiglass. However, because this doesn't have the weight that an old glass window has, it can make inking up trickier. Ink can be tacky and stick to the roller or glass, which can cause a lot of movement. If you use plexiglass, screw it to the work table to stop it moving.

In ad hoc situations I've also used plain A3 sheets of lino to ink up; the smooth surface lends itself to inking and you can use a bench clamp or similar to secure it to your desk.

Keep everything in reach – Keep your rollers, palette knives, and inks near your inking area. Screw hooks into a shelf for hanging your rollers, or cut holes out of wood to slot the roller handles into.

Dirty sink – Use this sink for all cleaning down activities. Keep it separate from food and drink preparation. Drying racks or hooks on a shelf above are a great option for drying rags and blocks after cleaning.

Print drying area – A trusty string and pegs are the cheapest option for drying your prints.

Metal drying racks – Check for these old gems on second-hand websites and local buying and selling pages. They are efficient and you can fit a huge number of prints into a small space. Failing that, you can buy new from an art supply shop.

Marble print driers – Most printmakers dream of owning one of these beautifully designed objects. It took me years to be able to justify the investment, but once I finally did, it was so worth it, and it takes pride of place in my workshop. These drying racks work by sliding your paper between the wood and marble; the marble then slots into place, holding your prints tight for drying above your head.

Design or clean area – For drawing, cutting, paper prep, and so on; you want lots of light here, so I'd recommend organizing this area in front of a window. A good-sized, strong cutting mat is a must here, and shelves for books, tools, pencils, etc.

This is where you are going to be doing the majority of your designing and cutting so fill this space with things that inspire you: photos, pictures, scraps of paper collected on a pin board, jars of found objects and plants, and odds and ends you've collected.

HEALTH & SAFETY

If you do repurpose old windows and glass, be sure to regularly tape up the edges of the glass with strong electrical tape to keep it safe.

STORING ROLLERS

Rollers should never be stored with the rubber sitting on a surface or touching other rollers as this could lead to indents in the surface and uneven prints in the future. The best way to store them is either to hang them from a little hook screwed into the end or lay them upside down on their stand. If you only have the budget blue or red-handled rollers, you can create a roller shelf by cutting out holes for the handles to sit in.

PAPER & PRINT STORAGE

Somewhere clean, dark, and dry to store your prints is essential. Over time, exposure to light can degrade printmaking inks and papers and really damage your prints. At a push a sealable A1 portfolio with plastic pockets will do, but eventually you'll find that you run out of space.

A traditional architect's plan chest is ideal; they are an investment, but are the best place to store your prints long-term. I recommend getting the biggest one you can afford as they really are something you only want to buy oncc. I use an A0 plan chest with ten drawers and utilize plastic portfolio sleeves inside to separate editions and for extra protection from dust or damp.

Another cheaper and easier option, particularly if you're not working on a very large scale, is a classic domestic chest of drawers. It works in much the same way, and you can pick them up second-hand with a much smaller price tag.

PRINT BLOCK STORAGE

Your blocks, especially lino, are best stored out of sunlight in a place that doesn't get too hot or too cold. A few vertically installed shelves are a good option for woodblocks, allowing them to rest upright without all leaning on each other. For lino, which is prone to curling, a flat open drawer where they can lie on top of each other works well.

When I'm finished with an edition or retiring it for a while, I like to wrap the block up in newsprint or cloth. Label your blocks clearly to save yourself time later; I like to wrap mine in newsprint, stick a proof print to the outside of the package, and write the name and edition on the outside.

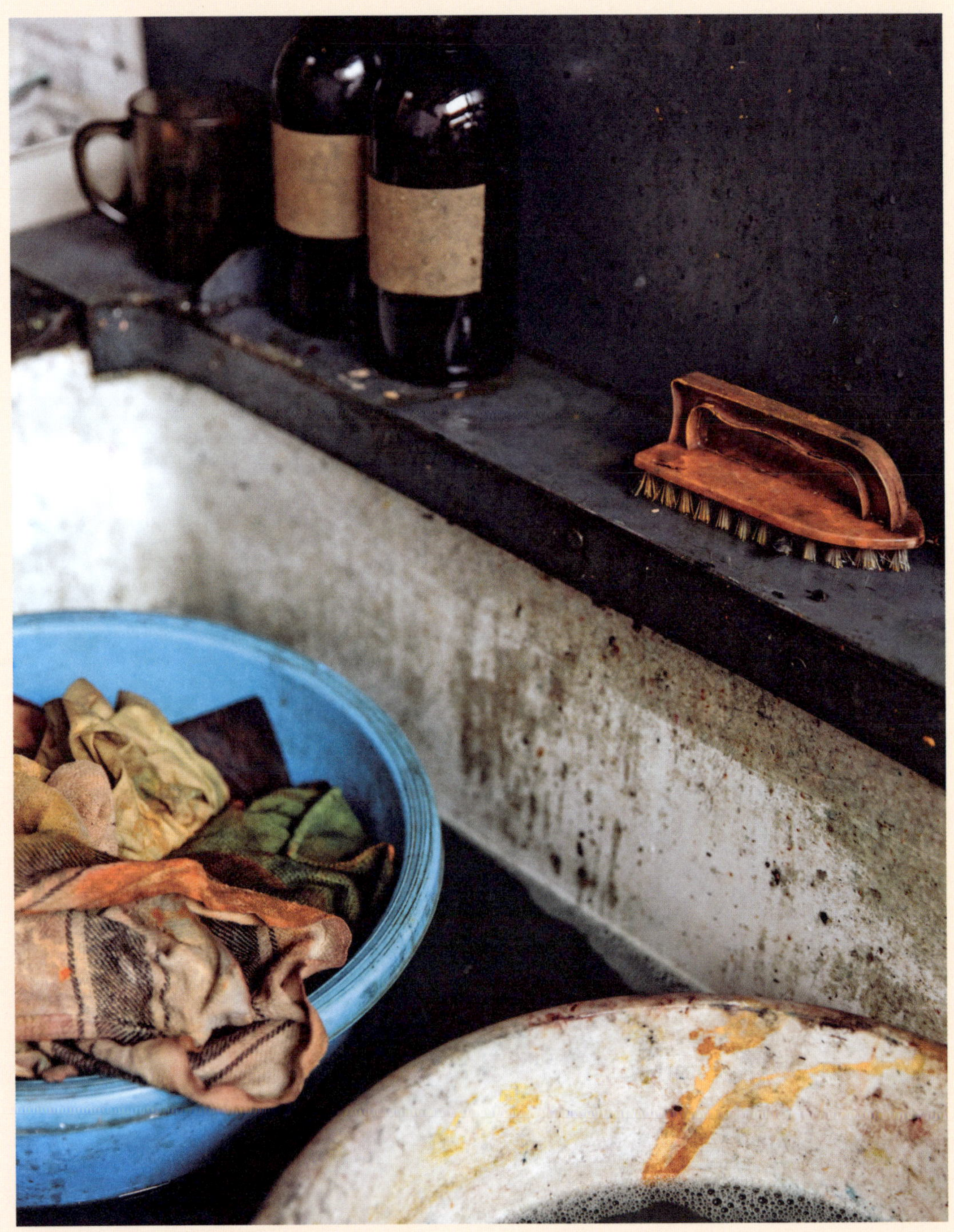

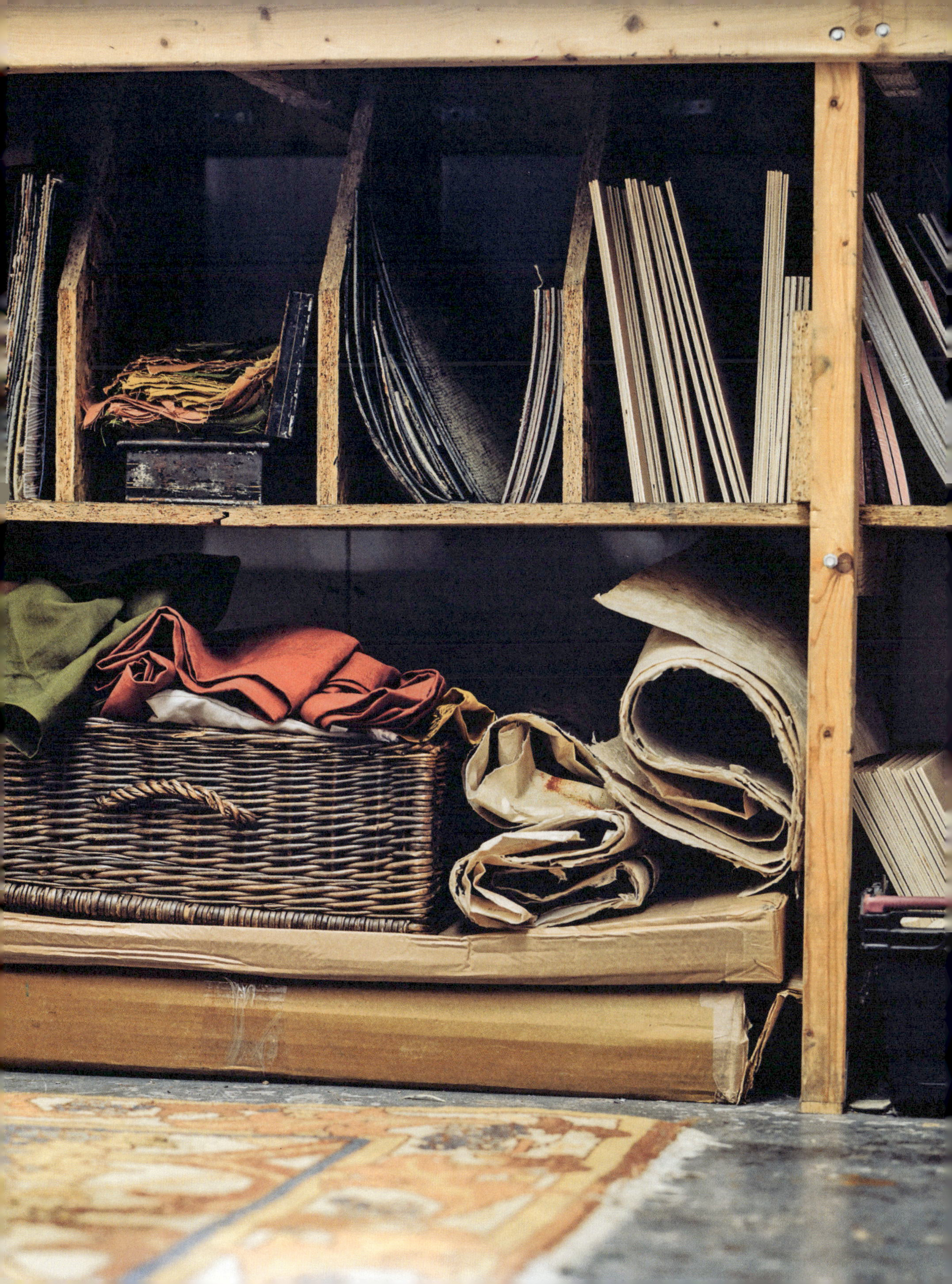

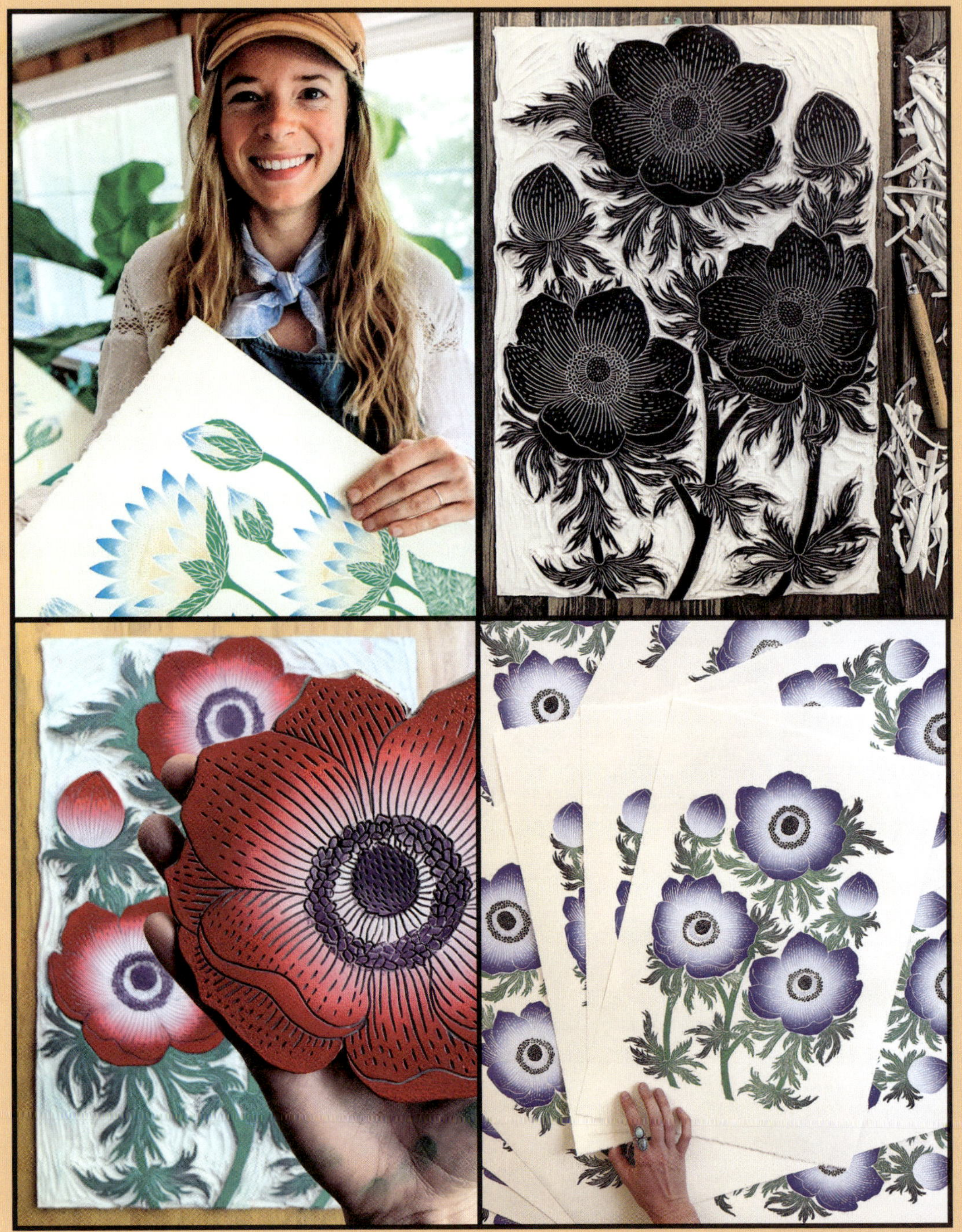

Lili Arnold

Where do you work and what do you work with?
I work in my home studio in the Santa Cruz mountains. I am primarily a block printer, carving my images out of rubber blocks with FlexCut linocut tools and then printing using Speedball brayers, Blick water-based inks, Stonehenge paper, and sometimes a Print Frog glass baren for burnishing. My process begins usually as a Pinterest board, an iPhone note, or a few handwritten Post-its. I usually will begin sketching compositions based on the print size I will be working with, then I slowly refine the sketches until I feel confident about the feel and balance of the composition. Then, I will freehand the image onto my block with pencil, then go over it with pen before starting to carve.

How did you get started making prints?
I stumbled into a printmaking class at the University of California and spent two years refining my technique. Once I entered the working world, I left printmaking behind. After 5 years working in graphic design, I felt a need to work with my hands, so began playing with the medium once again. My first series of prints were ocean inspired; living in Santa Cruz it's hard not to be influenced by the amazing sea life. That year there was a huge pod of Humpback whales that came to visit a local cove and they spent about a week lunge feeding just 30 feet from the shore.

Where do you go for inspiration for your work?
My love for plants was ignited by a visit to our local nursery. I found the most beautiful cactus with bright magenta blooms that captured my gaze. I started collecting books on botanical illustration and wildflower field guides while also visiting arboretums.

Can you explain a little about how drawing is part of your practice?
Drawing is usually how all my pieces take their first form. I sketch in a very rough style with lots of erasing, overlapping lines until I achieve compositions that feel right using a Blackwing pencil in a medium size blank Moleskine book.

What's your favourite botanical piece that you've made?
My Sunflower piece, 'Helianthus Annuus' – Autumn Beauty. I like the feeling of movement and life in the petals. It can be hard to create that feeling in a flat 2D art style, but with the right linework and letting go, it can be achieved.

What does a typical day in the studio look like for you?
Just the excitement of being able to create after having some time away from it (the time when I'm hanging out with my son) gets me in the zone. Each responsibility is amazing in its own way, and keeps everything feeling pretty fresh and exciting. Some days I pack orders, others I make prints, and sometimes I will carve a new piece.

What's the best advice you'd give to a new printmaker?
Follow what feels interesting to you, rather than what you think people want. The artists I admire are those that carve their own path and create something truly unique and authentic. That kind of person is deeply inspiring because it shows that the beauty of one's own interpretation of the world is a powerful road to expression.

IMAGE DESIGN

I'm traditional in my approach to image design; I genuinely believe the act of drawing forces you to truly *see* your subjects, not just pass them by. It encourages you to examine and to concentrate. There are no short cuts – you need to put in the work. If you do, your own voice, style, and unique way of communicating what you see of the world around you will come into its own. In this chapter I'll show you how to develop your drawing practice and search for design inspiration in the natural world.

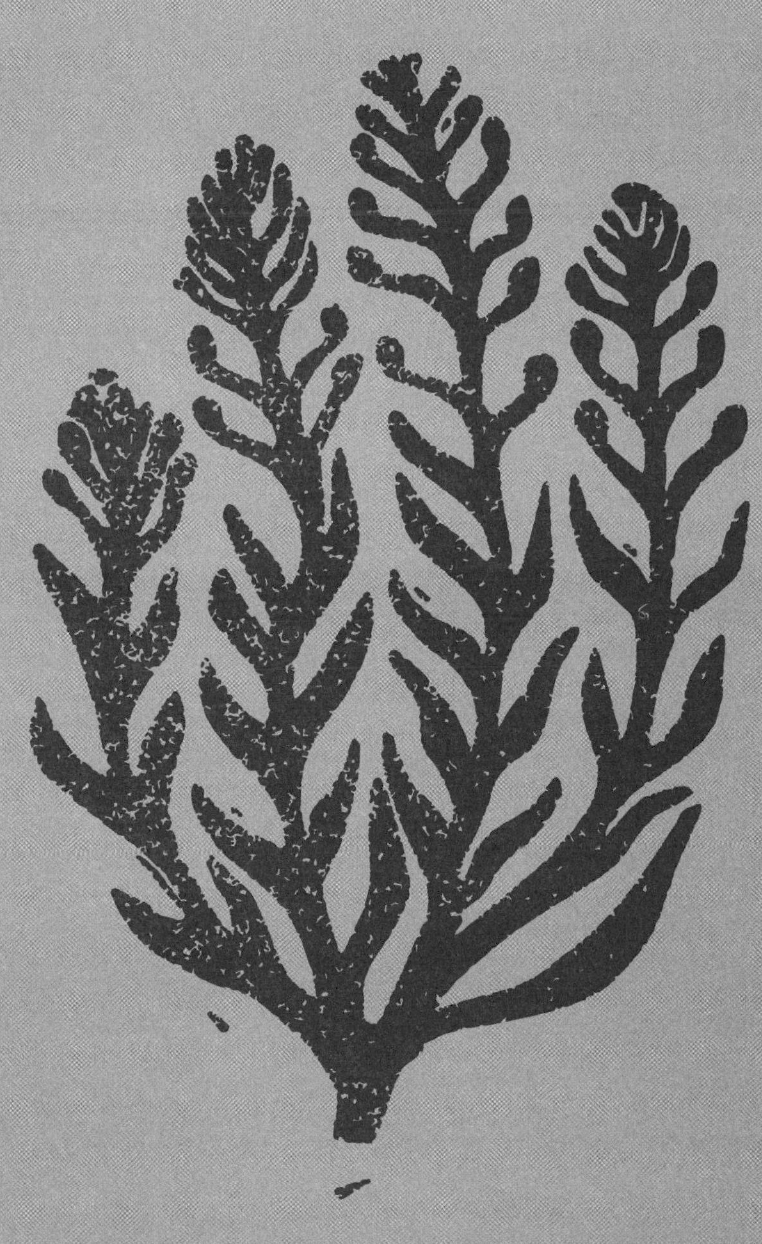

Good Drawing Practice

Many people believe themselves to be 'no good' at drawing. I want to debunk that theory right now – there is no such thing as someone who is bad at drawing. It's just a lack of practice and confidence that leaves you feeling that your image making isn't up to scratch. With consistent and committed dedication to the practice of drawing, anyone can develop the skill. In my own work, when I've fallen out of the practice of regular drawing, I've noticed my image-making ability suffer. But when I put time aside for regular and committed practice, things seem to flow easier, images come together more cohesively.

Keep a Sketchbook

Storing a record of your sketches is essential, whether in a dedicated sketchbook or a bunch of loose pages in a labelled folder. Either way, storing them in an organized system that you can look back on is an excellent habit to get into. Reflecting and looking back on previous work is an important part of developing as an artist.

I once spent a few days assisting the artist Charlotte Mann. She is an incredibly skilled draughtsman with a long history of teaching drawing. On one wall of her studio, she had many shelves lined with black sketchbooks, each one neatly labelled with the month and year. She explained that she had discovered her favourite sketchbook type very early on and had kept that as a consistent backbone in her practice. It was a brilliant archive for her to look back on and she explained that she regularly did so when embarking on a new project. I was fascinated by its uniformity and have tried to employ the same technique.

I always use the same small, green sketchbook. It is small enough to come with me everywhere without feeling too cumbersome. I also find it easy to be scrappy on the smaller pages, which is essential for working things out, whereas bigger, fancier artist's sketchbooks tend to intimidate me and stop me in my tracks.

If you want to draw regularly and make a habit of it, keep your sketchbook in plain sight. Take it with you every day. Whether you choose to use the same sketchbook again and again, or you prefer to vary your designs between different shapes, sizes, and consistencies of paper, keeping some sort of system in place to keep your ideas in order will allow you so much more space for inspiration.

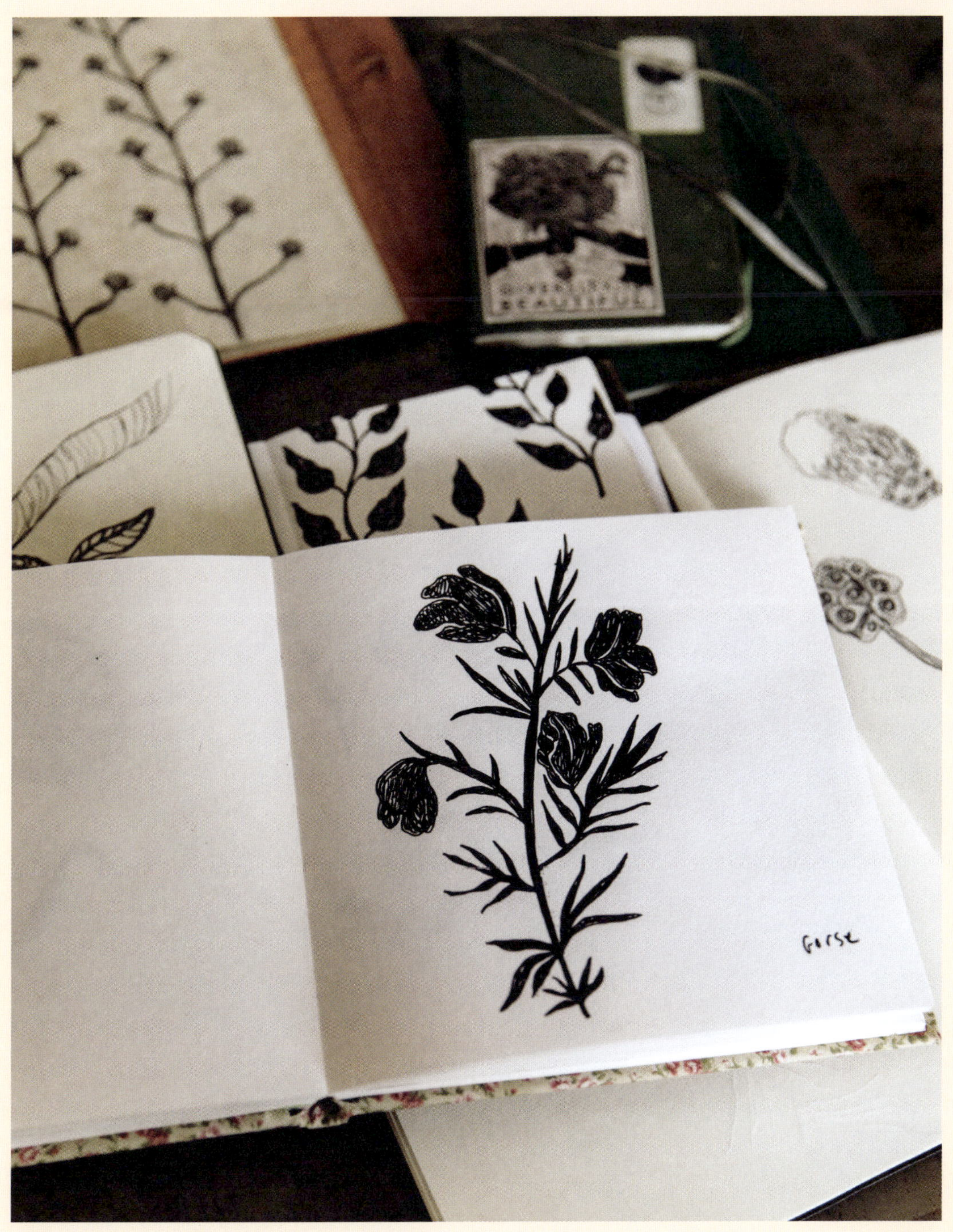
Gorse

Drawing Projects

In this section I have put together multiple short projects to loosen the mind and help you to hone the skill of truly seeing your subjects and making better drawings. When I have been out of drawing practice for a while, it is these drawing exercises that I like to come back to, to warm up my hand and oil the visual cogs in my brain. As exercises, going back to the basics and drawing for the sake of drawing can be so useful in opening your mind and allowing new creative seeds in.

YOU WILL NEED

HB pencil
Sharpener
A sketchbook or several sheets of drawing paper
A leaf

1

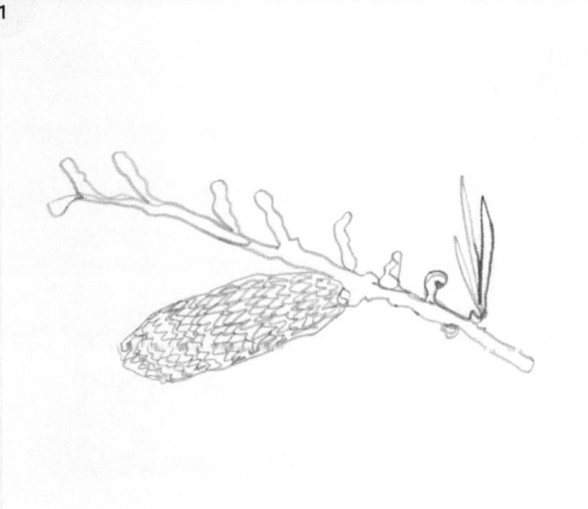

CONTINUOUS LINE DRAWING

Create a line drawing of your image. Trace the outline of the leaf without removing your pencil from the page; notice the movement and shapes your line creates as you journey around the structure of the leaf, committing the whole form to paper without lifting your pencil.

DRAWING WITHOUT LOOKING

Draw the leaf in its entirety without looking at your page. Begin at one end and focus on tracing the outline of the form with your eyes, noting each detail until you get back to the beginning. As you explore the object and focus on its form, let your hand follow suit and trust your natural spatial awareness – don't be tempted to look! This is a wonderful exercise to free up your hand and remove any preconceptions you might have about what is a good drawing. It allows you to concern yourself more with the process of understanding what's in front of you rather than creating something representative.

DRAWING NEGATIVE SPACE

Draw only the negative spaces around the object, not the object itself. Focus on the gaps between the leaves, a table behind the object, the distance between a stem and a bud. Leave the area the leaf would normally occupy blank and focus on drawing all the space around it, to scale and in detail. This is a great exercise in truly looking and drawing what you see rather than what you think you see. Consider where your leaf sits on the page, its composition, the texture of the surface it sits on.

DRAWING THE SPACE WITHIN

Take time to draw the space within the leaf, not the linear edges, but the details of its surface. Focus on the specific elements that make up its form and how your pencil communicates them. Is your leaf rough or smooth? What kind of patterns can you see repeating? Think about how your marks can translate the texture of the leaf to the page.

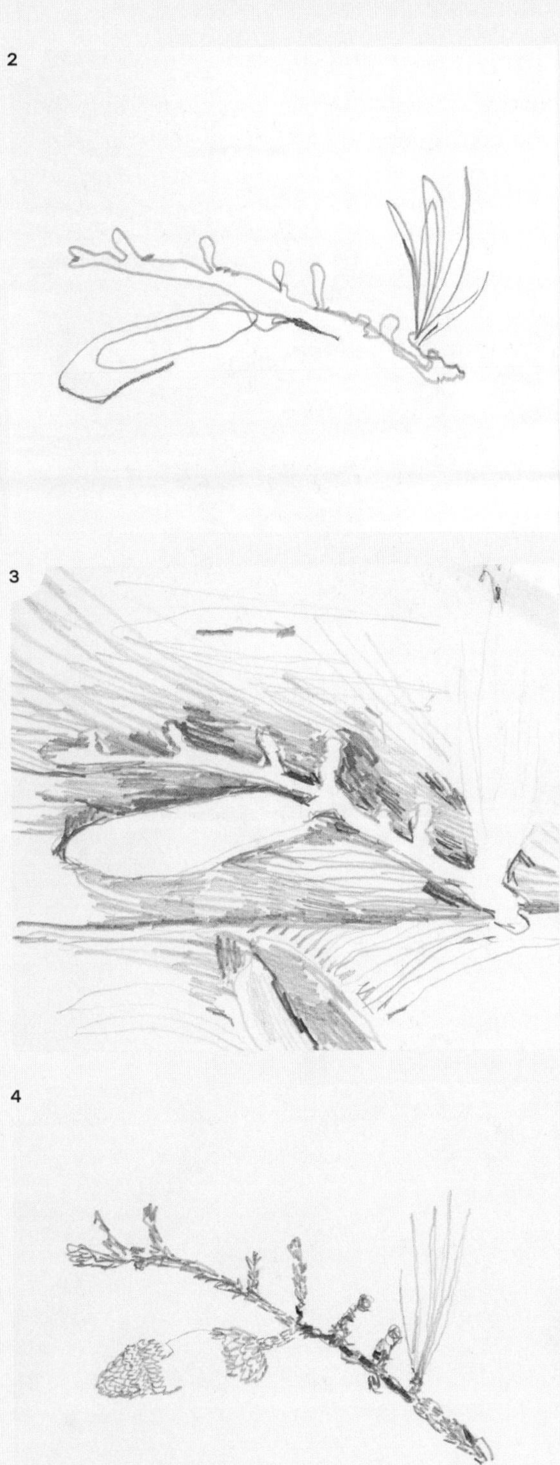

5

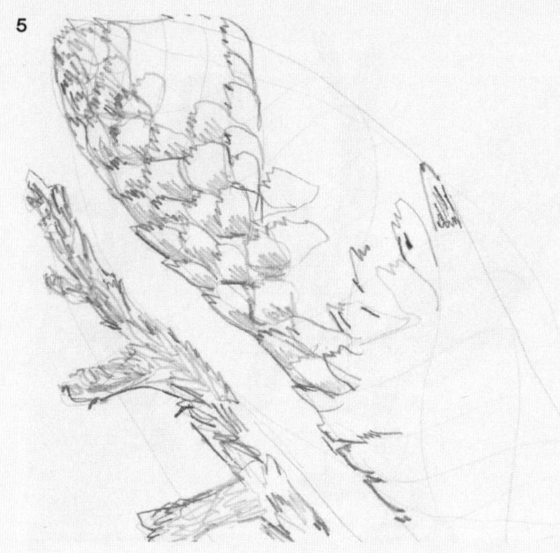

6

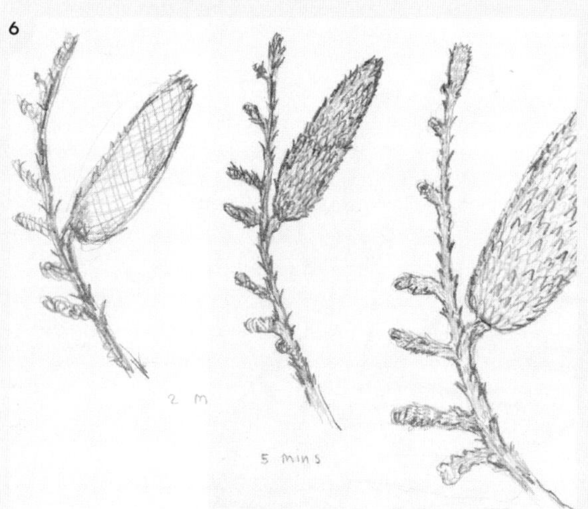

PLAY WITH SCALE

Take a small part of your subject and scale it up to fill your entire page. A small section of the leaf, a bud, or even the stem. Sketch it out to scale and pay attention to the minute details. Sometimes a magnifying glass can be good for this or, if you don't have one to hand, simply get up close and take time to observe all the small details that normally go unnoticed. Think about how you will communicate each texture – smooth, bumpy, hairy, or dimpled. How can you use your pencils to show these marks, are they black, white, patterned, or greyscale? Consider what you choose to draw attention to.

PLAY WITH TIME

Allow yourself 10 minutes to draw a leaf freely, then on a separate piece of paper draw for 5 minutes. Compare the two. Then set yourself the task of drawing for only 2 minutes. Notice the different details that your mind is drawn to capture. What are the differences between the longer image and the much faster drawing? What are the vital elements and what details have you chosen to leave behind?

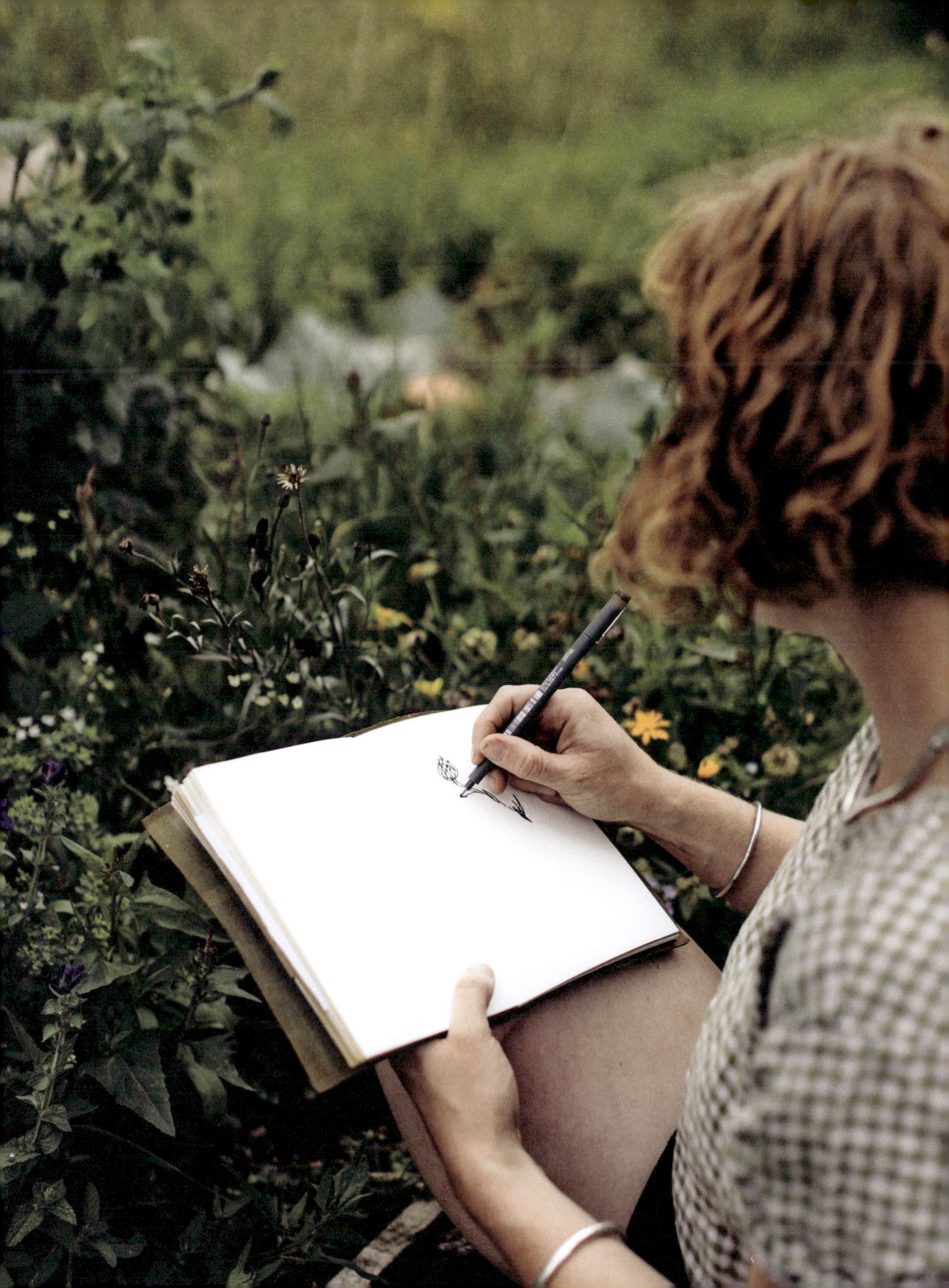

Composing a Good Image

A huge part of what makes a good print 'great', is the composition of the design. I often spend weeks and weeks working a design over, first in my head, later in sketchbooks, redrawing the same image multiple times before I end up with a conclusion that I'm happy with. Coming up with a good idea is just one third of the battle, turning that into a cohesive, balanced, and harmonious image is where the real work is done.

Composition is all about making a lot of choices and deciding where the different elements will go, how they interact with each other, and what we are ultimately drawing the viewer's attention to. When embarking on building on your design there is a lot to consider. I've listed a few ideas I like to keep in mind as I build on a new concept.

Golden Ratio

The golden ratio, also referred to as 'phi' by the Ancient Greeks, is a mathematical equation that is used to explain beauty and balance in natural forms. You can apply the formula to all sorts of objects and formations found in nature that are pleasing to the eye, from acorns to sunflowers, even the patterns whales make in the sea when hunting can be linked back to this simple theory.

Because the golden ratio is approximately equal to a 1:1.61 ratio, it can be illustrated using a 'Golden Ratio Rectangle'. Take a square and multiply one side by 1.618, and you'll get a balanced rectangle. The formula is often linked with the Fibonacci sequence, which is a set of repeating numbers that can be found repeating in nature, with the previous number adding on to the one before: 0, 1, 1, 2, 3, 5, 8, 13, 21, and so on.

For centuries, the golden ratio has been used by scientists and artists alike and can be applied to photography, painting, design, and even music. Leonardo da Vinci employed the technique for his 'Mona Lisa' and the formula has also been neatly applied to 'The Great Wave' by the Japanese printmaking master Katsushika Hokusai.

Although consistently debunked by many in modern times as an accurate or reliable scientific theory, there is still something to be gained and learned from thinking about the golden ratio when designing your images. It's particularly worth thinking about in reference to making images with botanical subjects, as it's something you will come across regularly in the study of plants. Even if it isn't scientifically reliable and infallible, there's no denying that when applied it does create harmonious and beautiful images that are pleasing to the eye.

When I am designing my own images, I tend to hold the golden ratio concept in my head as I work, adjusting the composition accordingly. If that doesn't sound practical to you, and you want to apply it to your own images methodically, you can trace the design out onto tracing paper and lay it over your composition.

Another straightforward way of applying the concept without the methodology, is to off-centre the subject of your imagery, slightly to the left or right of the composition, or slightly above or below the central line. You can also divide your canvas into a grid of thirds, placing elements of your composition at the intersections or on the divisions, either horizontally or vertically.

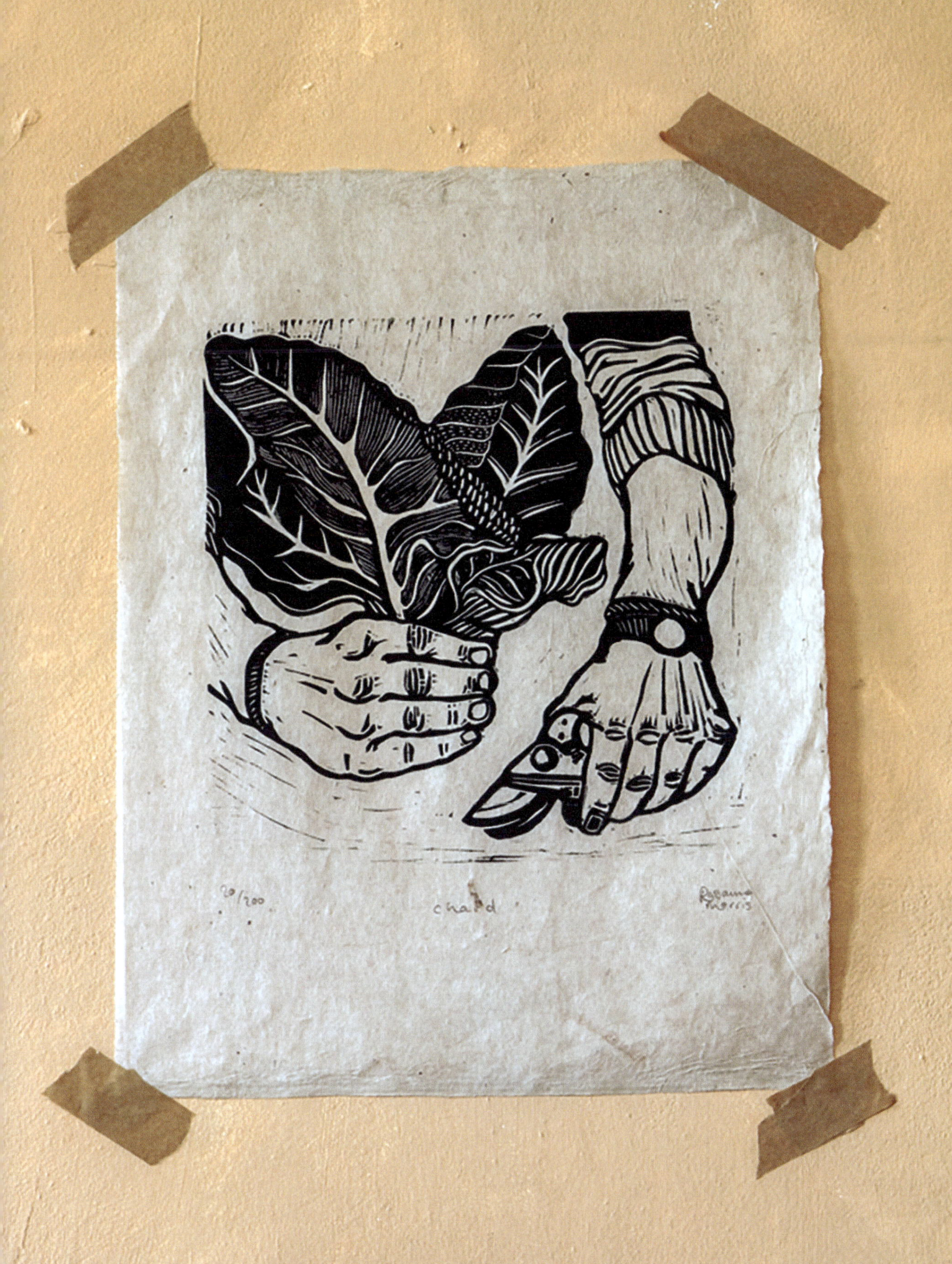
20/200
chard

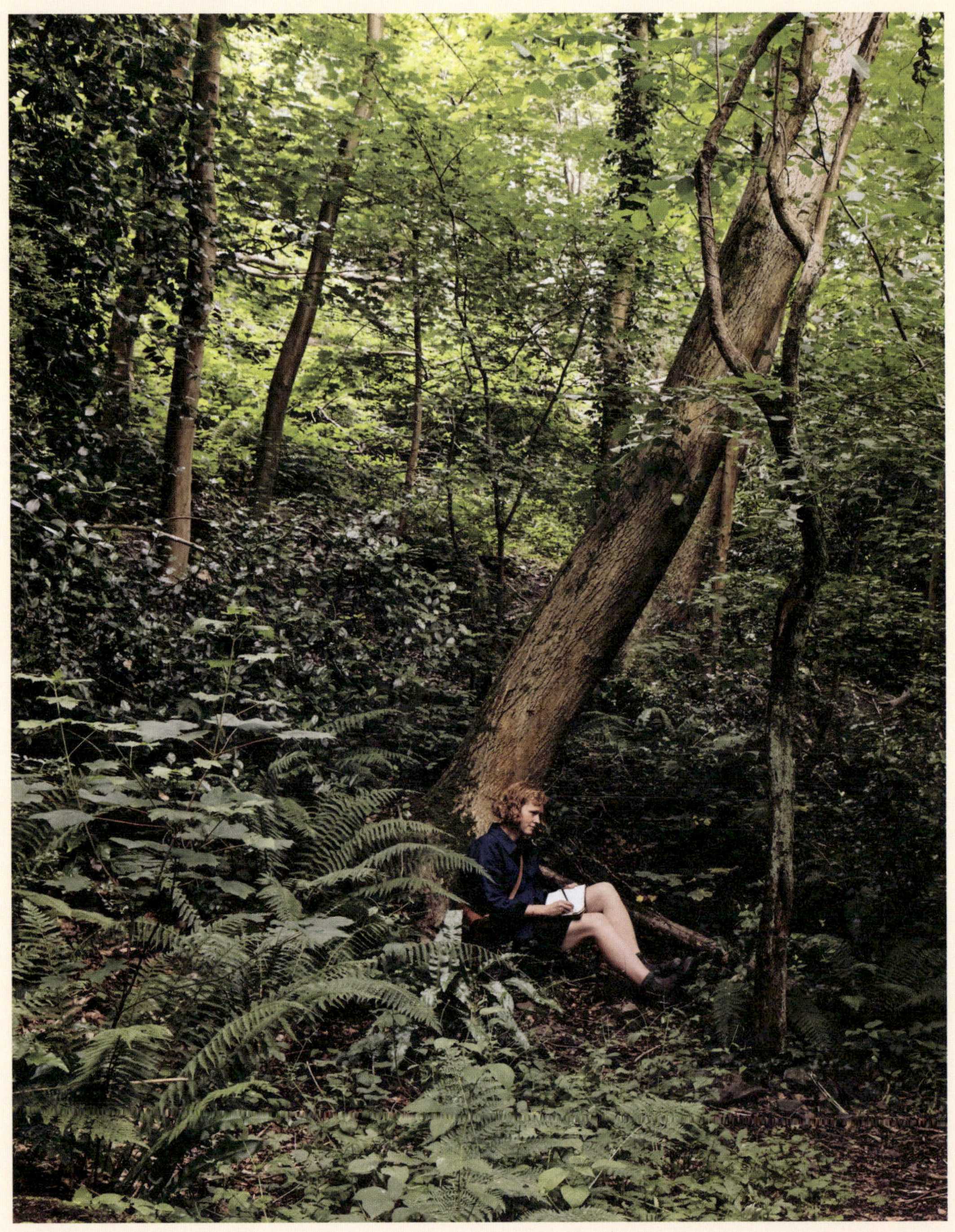

Perspective

Humans are always looking for patterns in nature. These patterns are our way of making sense of the world and when things are a little bit off, we can feel it almost immediately. Naturally, perspective follows a pattern, and our brains recognize where things should be instinctively. Getting our brains to communicate this to our hands, however, is a fine art that can usually only be achieved with consistent practice or, failing that, tracing paper.

There are many formal and mathematical techniques for achieving the correct perspective in a composition, and many books that go into fine detail on this. Linear perspective is a term applied to methods of suggesting depth on a two-dimensional surface. Using converging lines for geometric objects, it gives a sense of recession and depth. I'm personally not great at following formulae myself; for me it's all about drawing what you actually see in front of you rather than what you think you see. A couple of good exercises for honing this technique are the 'Drawing without looking' and 'Drawing negative space' techniques, both on page 75, which allow you to see outside of your subject and map things on the page.

When trying to communicate perspective in print or any kind of image making, a good tactic to follow is to layer your detail: use more detail and fine marks in the foreground and less detail as you move to the background of your composition. This naturally communicates distance to the viewer, as we are used to this experience in nature, where it is known as atmospheric perspective. It draws on the idea that the moisture in the atmosphere makes it harder to see objects that are further away, hence losing the details.

Notan

Notan is a Japanese term and theory for creating balance in an image. It's the idea that to create good images you need to create an equal balance between light and dark, which is particularly relevant for printmaking. To check the *notan,* or balance, tape your drawing to a wall with as much distance as possible, such as a hallway, then stand back as far as you can and squint. From this vantage point with a bit of distance between you and your work, it's easier to assess how the image balances and make changes informed by this view.

Ask yourself: Is the perspective right? Is there balance within the whole? Have I found the perfect weight between the light and the dark? An example of this from my own work is my flower harvest print. There was a point when I took a proof print of the carving just as I had begun to carve away the woman's skirt. I printed the proof and hung the picture on the wall; with distance I realized that I'd lost the weight and that if I kept on carving, the image would be too light and unbalanced. If I hadn't taken that time to step back, I'd have happily carved away much more than I needed to.

TIP *As a rule, I repeat the mantra in my head 'less is more'. Stop before it's too late. You can always take away more later if you need to, but it's very hard to add back once something is gone.*

Composition Practice

Sometimes, when making an image, the temptation is to just go for the first composition that comes into our heads. However, there are many ideas that would benefit from a little more consideration. I use the exercises below to investigate different ways of composing an image, often leading to a much stronger piece.

QUESTIONS TO ASK AS YOU TRY EACH EXERCISE:

- **Perspective** – *What angle am I looking from? Above, below? From the side, or flat on?*
- **Scale** – *What choices can I make about scale in my image? Are the subjects life size, true to scale, or will I play with this and choose to manipulate their scale?*
- **Light** – *Where is the light source for my image? How does the light affect what I eventually cut or leave to pick up ink?*
- **Balance** – *Where is the weight in my image, or how do I find balance in my image between the light and the dark, the notan?*
- **Focus** – *What is the focus of my design, what do I want to draw my audience's eye to within the design, and how will I do that with any of the above?*

THUMBNAIL EXERCISE

Making thumbnails of your composition is a great way to test out lots of different ideas and see what really works.

YOU WILL NEED

Sketchbook or drawing paper
HB pencil

1. Take a piece of paper and divide it into 6 rectangles (or whichever shaped print you are planning).

2. Draw out your first design in a very simple sketch form, being mindful to block off different areas of solid ink, pattern, and so on.

3. Then proceed to explore different arrangements for each thumbnail, really pushing your brain to think outside of its normal restrictions and to create something new with each composition.

1

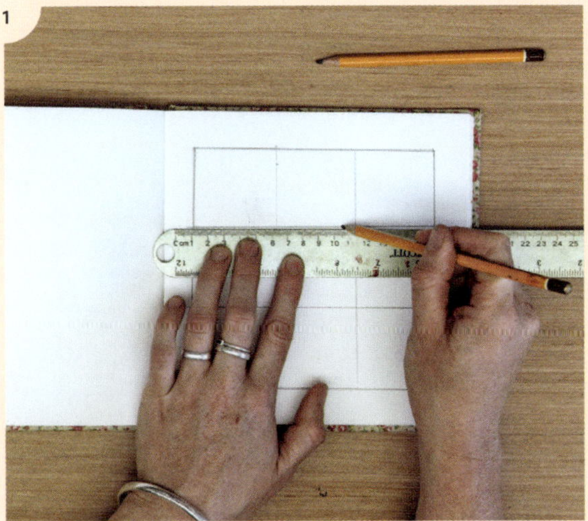

2

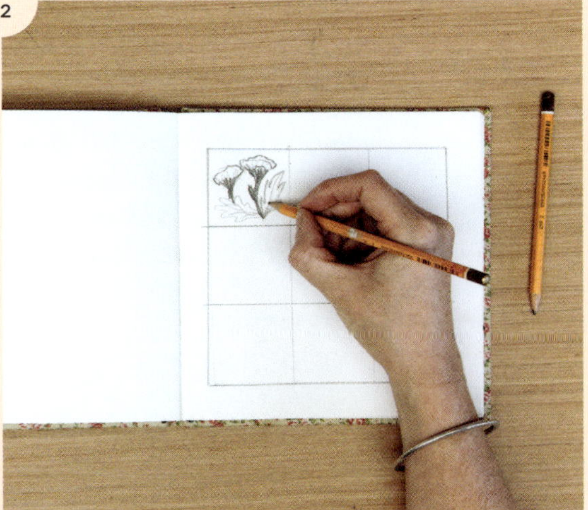

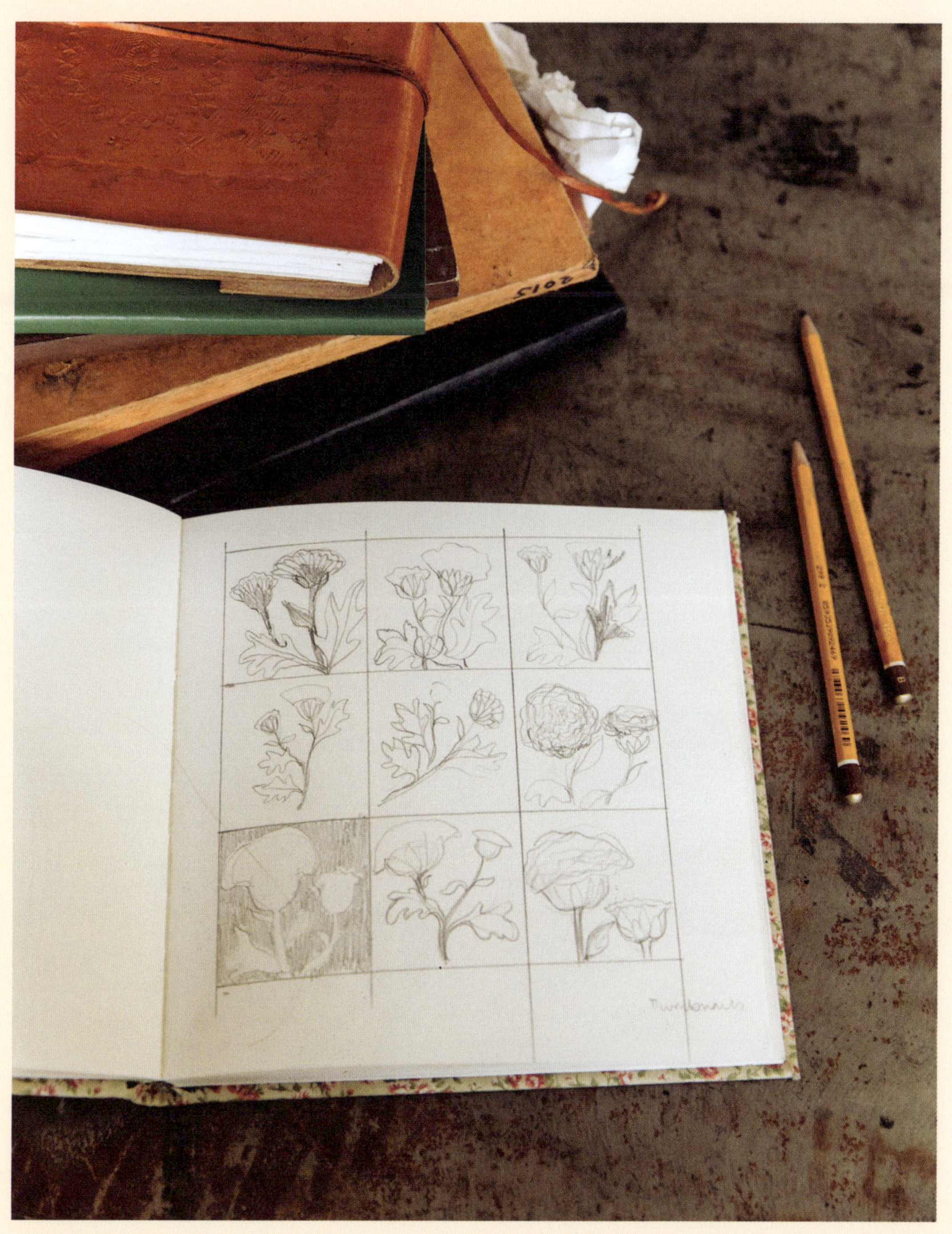

PLAY WITH INK

Transferring a pencil sketch to ink is very liberating after the relatively regimented and focused practice of planning and sketching out your composition. Indian ink has a solid and velvety texture that I love, and when applied with a brush it allows you to bring so much more movement back into your design (see image 1 below, for reference). It is especially good for planning out areas of pattern, details, or solid ink within your print. Use a decent paintbrush and absorbent cartridge paper and create 2–3 versions of your final composition. Have your texture block (see page 40) to hand, as you're playing and testing out ideas for carving later.

Work through the list of questions on page 82 as you make choices in your design, considering perspective, scale, light, balance, and focus. You can also explore more choices about texture and how you choose to represent this with the marks you make. For example, cross-hatching for greyscale or dot work to show the 3D nature of an object as the light hits it from above.

INVERTED IMAGE-MAKING

Another good process to try as you finalize your design, is to try drawing it out on black paper with a good white marker. This practice inverts your drawing process and flips it on its head, creating marks in a similar way to carving, allowing you to conceptualize the carving process (see image 2 below, for reference).

You'll need good black paper and a decent white marker to get the desired effect. Draw out your design in pencil first and then begin to fill in the areas of light that will be cut away. As you make marks on the paper it's important to keep the carving tools present in your mind – consider the cuts and gouges you would use for each mark and refer to your texture matrix as you develop a visual language to describe your subject.

1

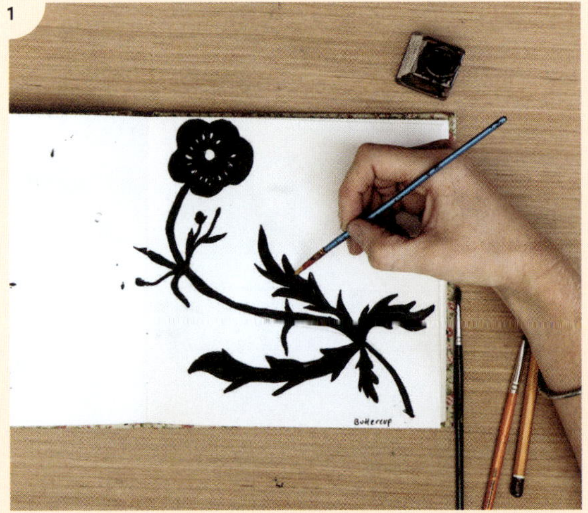

2

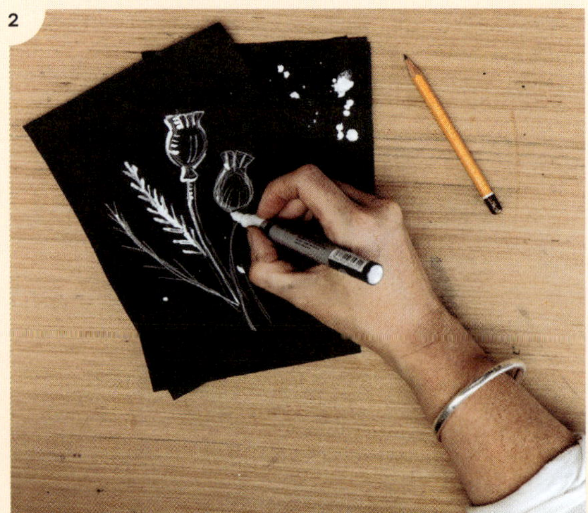

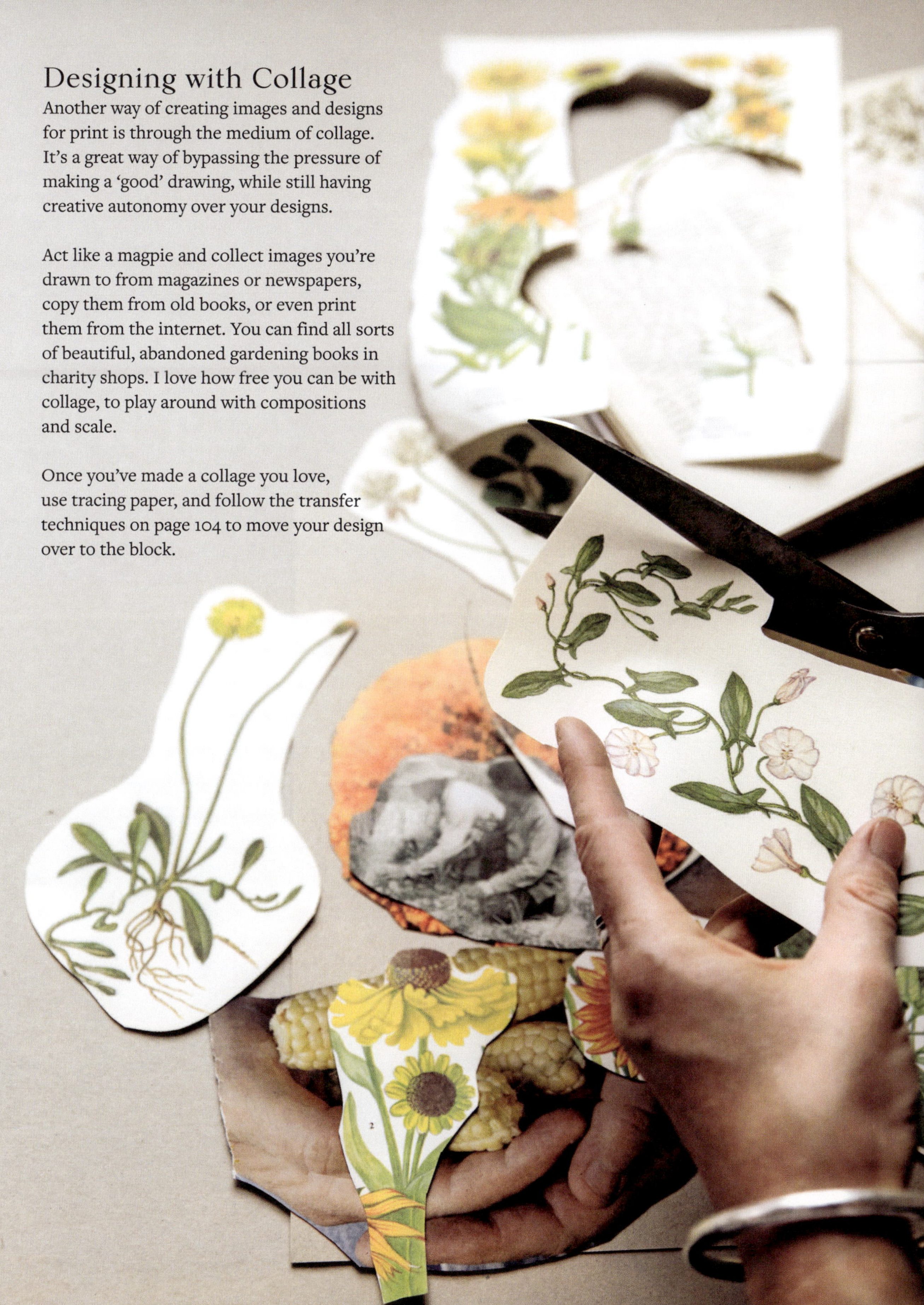

Designing with Collage

Another way of creating images and designs for print is through the medium of collage. It's a great way of bypassing the pressure of making a 'good' drawing, while still having creative autonomy over your designs.

Act like a magpie and collect images you're drawn to from magazines or newspapers, copy them from old books, or even print them from the internet. You can find all sorts of beautiful, abandoned gardening books in charity shops. I love how free you can be with collage, to play around with compositions and scale.

Once you've made a collage you love, use tracing paper, and follow the transfer techniques on page 104 to move your design over to the block.

Connecting with Nature

Drawing on location is one of my favourite things. A day out in nature with only my sketchbook, pencils, and dog for company can lead to the best ideas. Nature is busy, and drawing can feel overwhelming when there's so much to convey in front of you. Take the time to really look at your surroundings and reserve the right of the artist to choose – you are in charge. Drawing is all about choices; it's what you choose to convey and what you choose to leave out that makes a good design.

Taking nature back with you to the studio is also another option and I have included some ideas for foraging through the seasons and how to preserve your finds to use in your image-making and printing practice.

Drawing on Location

There are a few things you can do to prepare yourself for drawing outside:

Pack an efficient pencil case, or tool roll, with a specific set of pencils, ink pens, and sharpeners. I find limiting my palette to just a few pencil colours is incredibly helpful when designing new images. It forces you to think about what you can convey with pattern rather than colour, which also feeds very nicely into the natural limitations of relief print.

Packing for the weather is a must. An umbrella can save you in a quick shower and big bulldog clips work well for holding sketchbook pages open in high winds. Fingerless gloves and many layers in winter for me are essential; don't underestimate how cold you'll get sitting still for hours on end! Also, if you're heading to the woods, bringing something to sit on is useful – it's a shame to be limited to fallen logs when the best angle for your image could be achieved on a pile of wet rotting leaves.

Foraging for Inspiration

Going out and drawing on location is great, but at some stage you're also likely to want to bring some plants home and study them from the comfort of a desk. Wait for a dry and bright day, as collecting plants in the rain means you'll bring them home damp and will have to dry them.

What to take with you?

- Gloves
- Good secateurs
- A basket or bag – give the plants space so that they don't fall apart on the journey home. You can also use a couple of cotton bags to keep plants separate but I find they get damaged more easily when loose in a bag. Avoid plastic, which harbours moisture.

Our eco systems are delicate and with the increase in foraging in recent years coupled with the decrease in wild spaces for the public to access, it's vital that we respect and protect what we have left.

FORAGING RULES

Only pick what you need: be realistic and only take what you're really going to have time to work with.

Be responsible: leave no trace. You want to leave the site as you find it, and avoid trampling delicate plants and leaves as you go.

Do your research: know what you are looking for and leave rare species well alone.

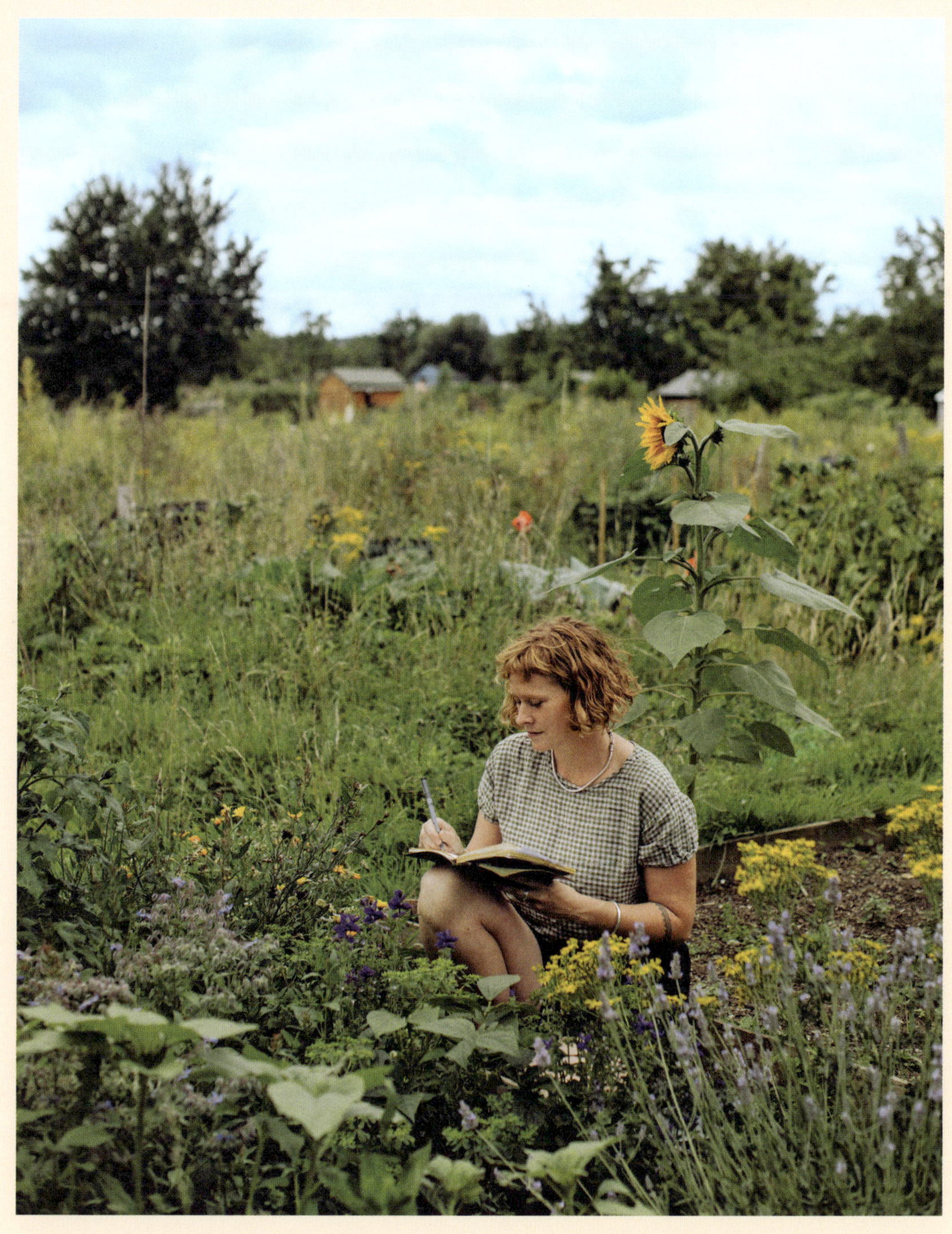

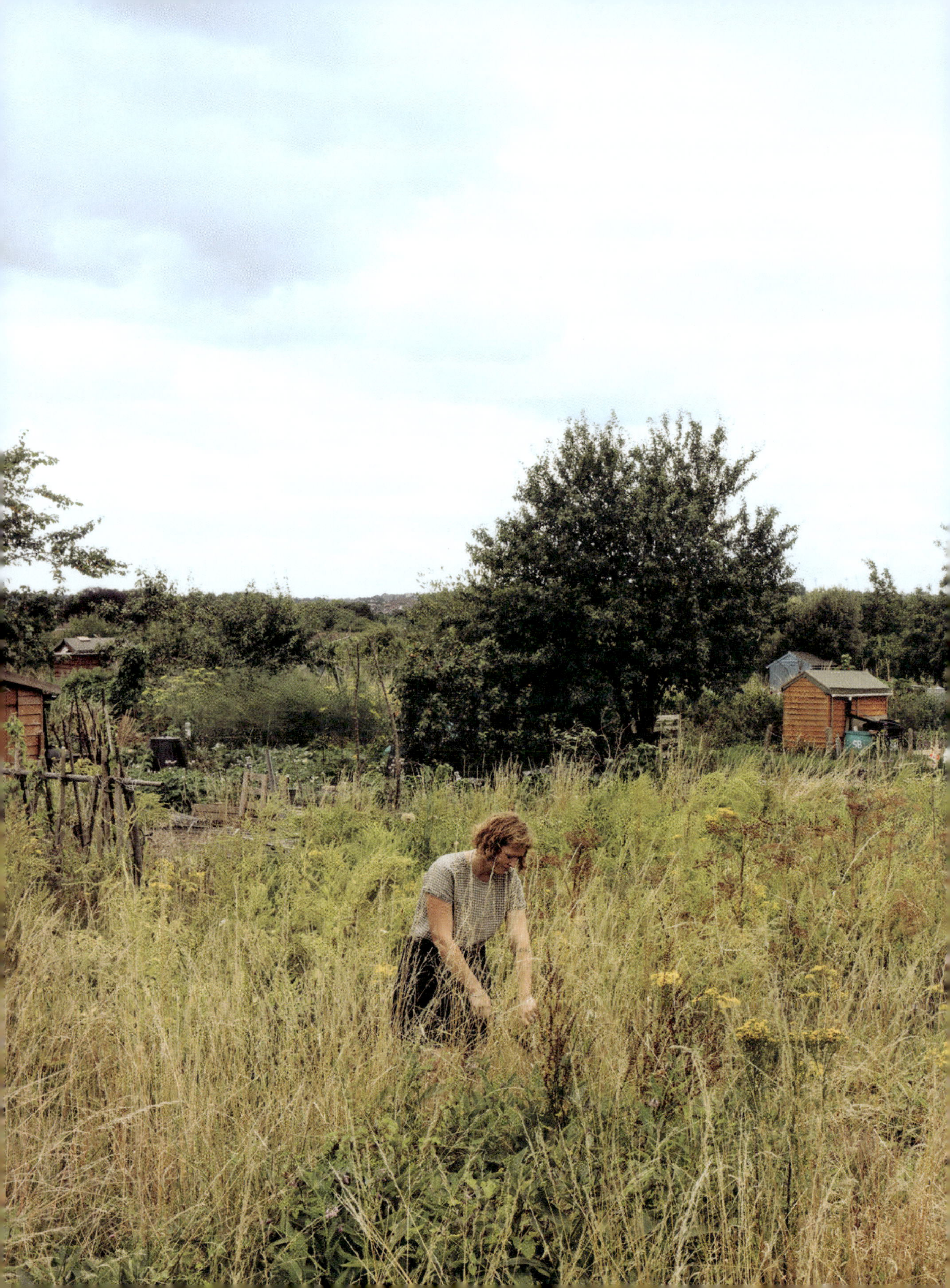

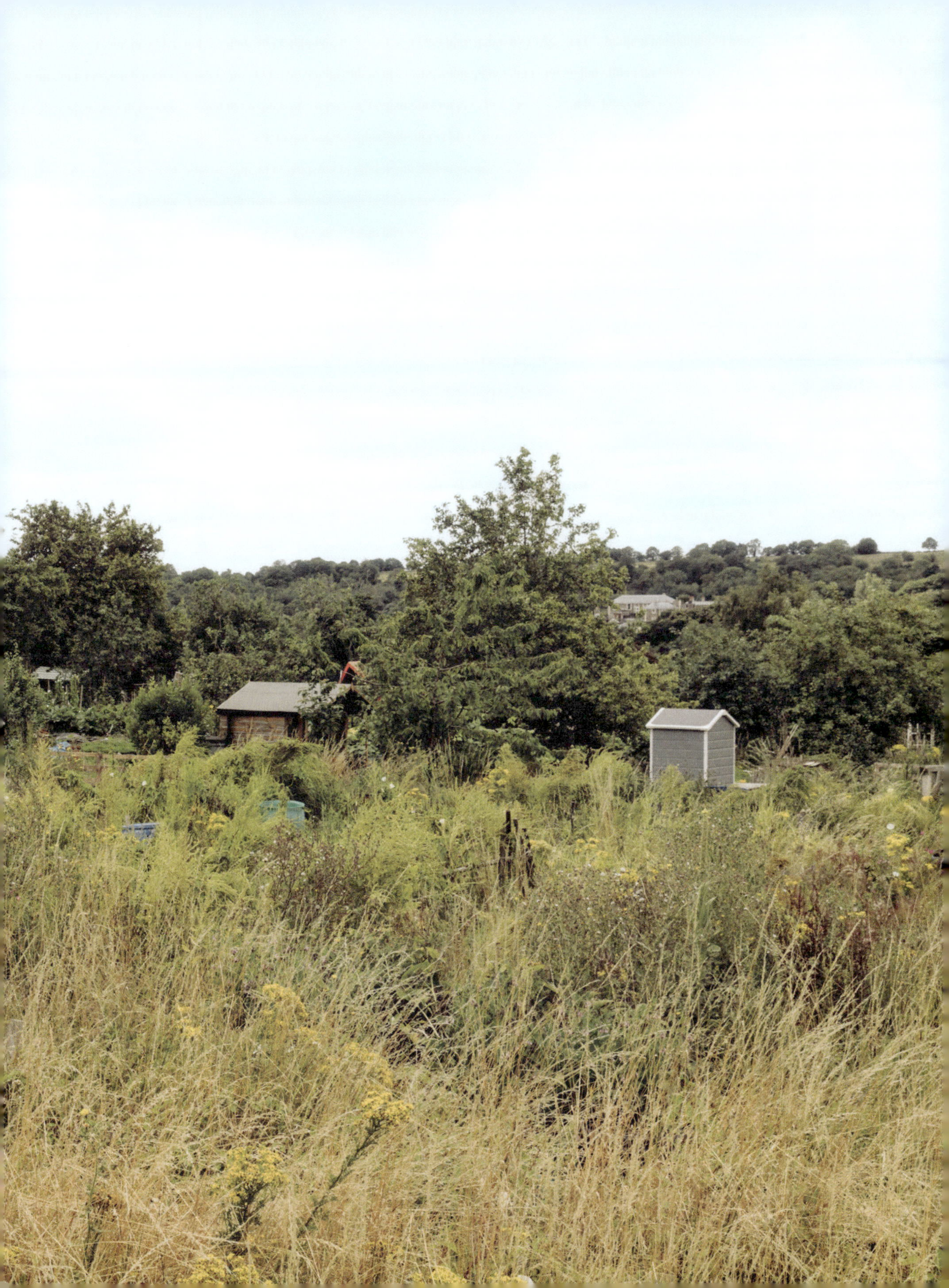

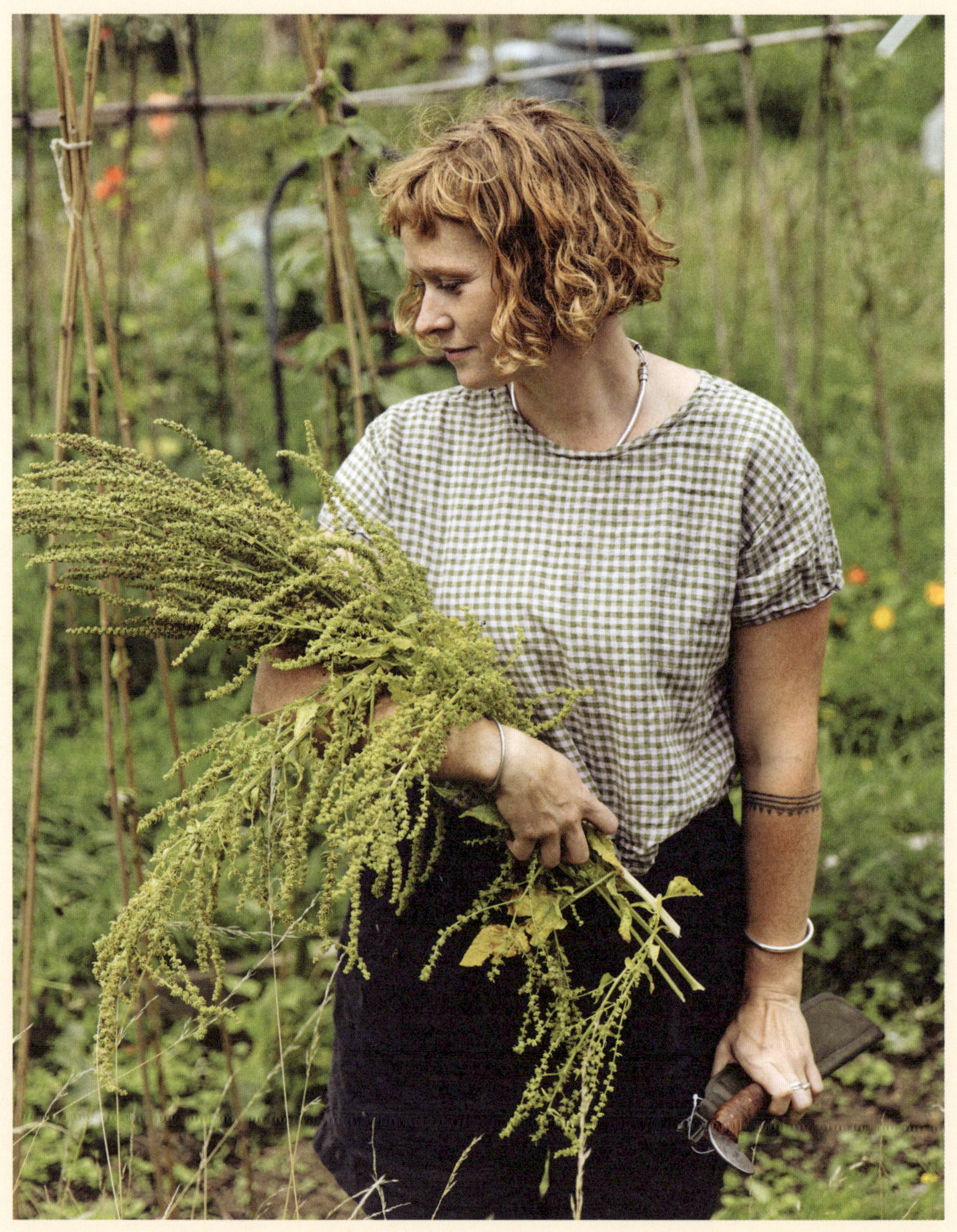

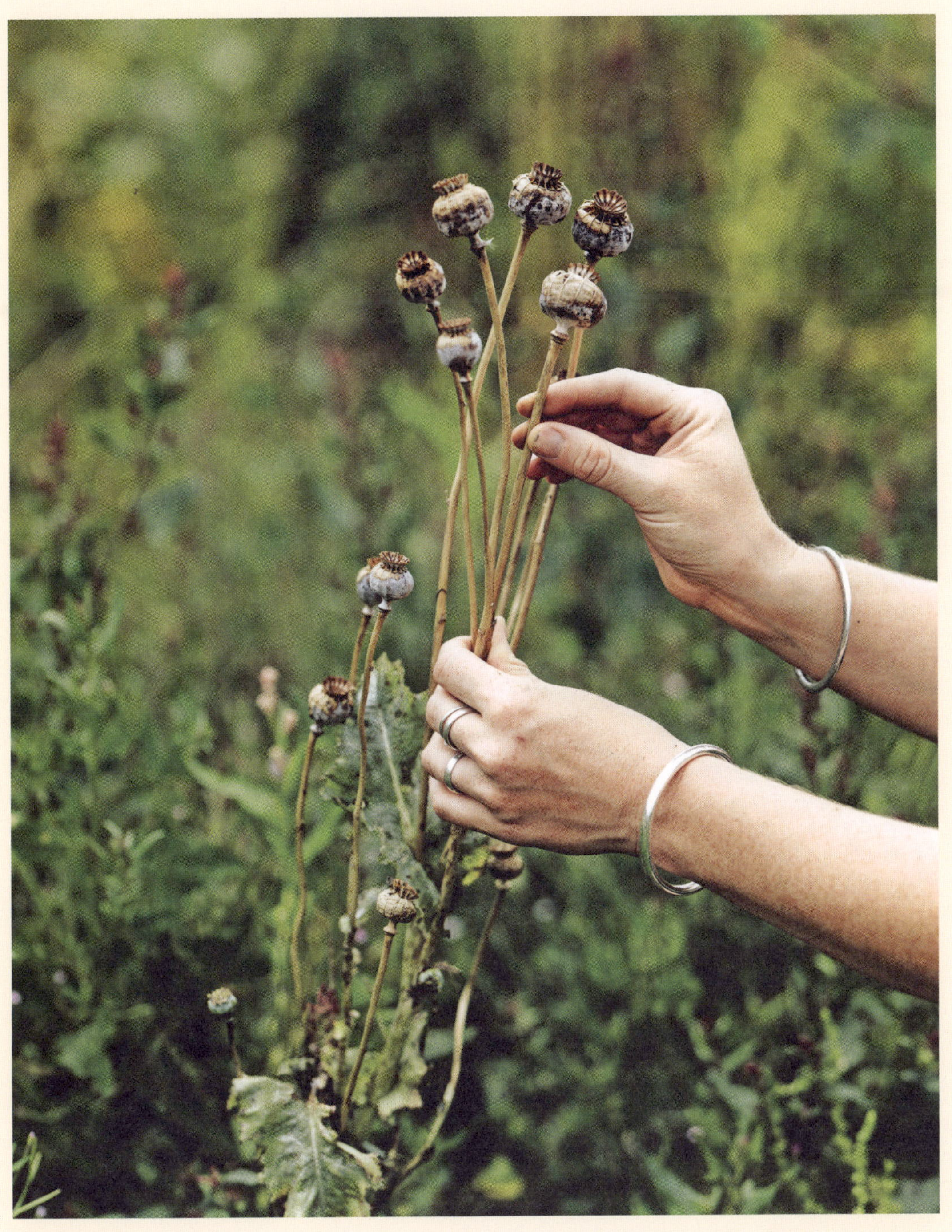

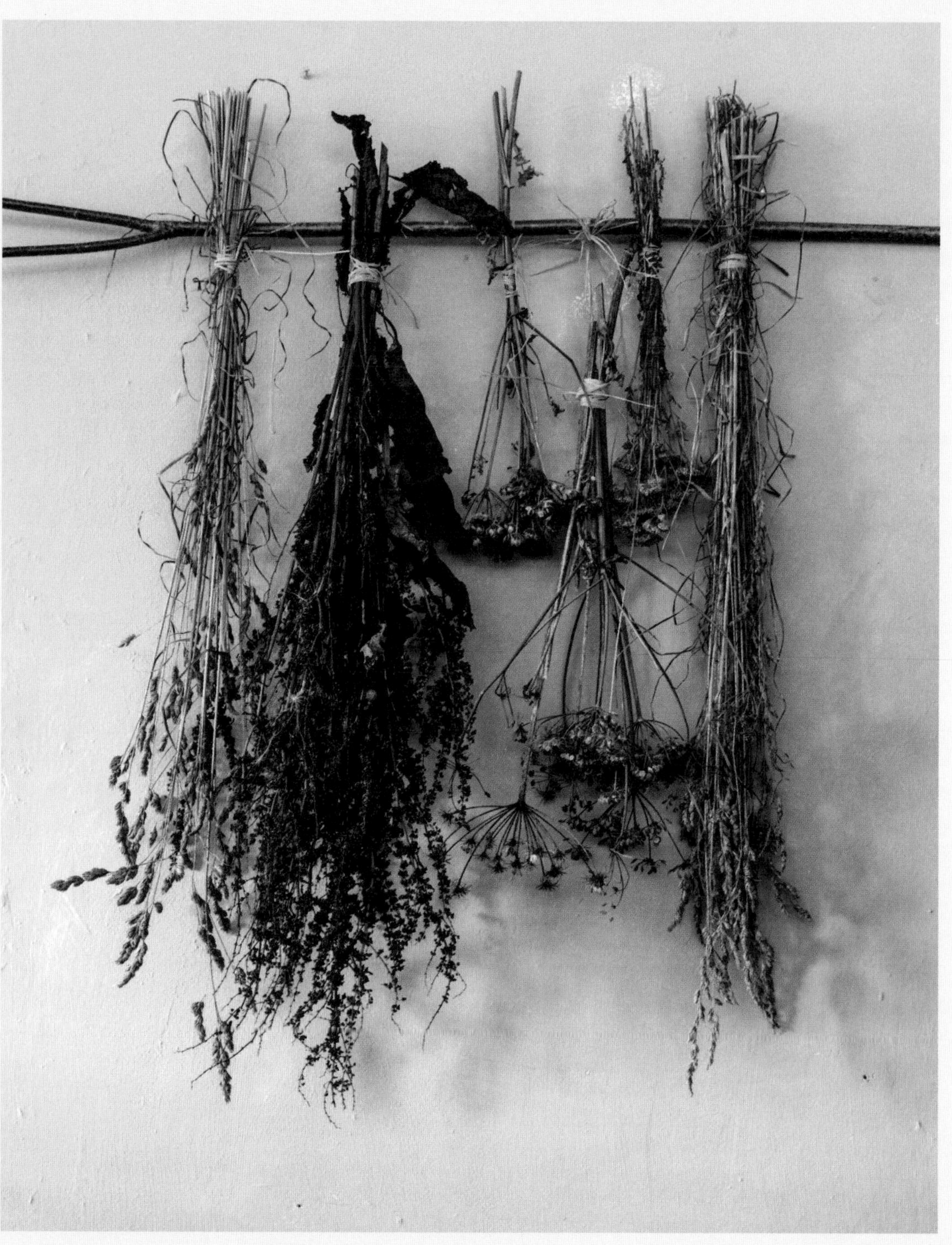

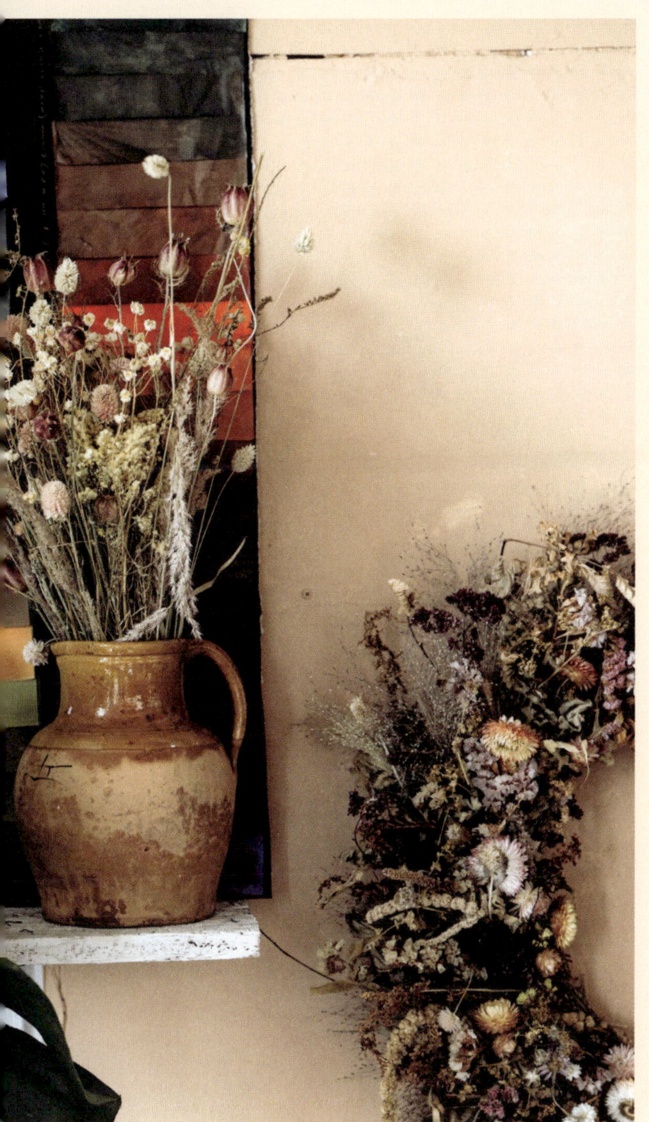

Drying Plants at Home

Once you've collected your inspiration from the wild and brought it home, you're going to want to keep it in the best condition possible while you study it. That means drying it out with lots of air circulation to prevent mould. I tend to have all sorts of flowers and leaves littered about my home and studio in varying stages of decay.

Flower press – A traditional flower press is a brilliant tool for the artist. You can pick them up second-hand, online, or even make your own. There are lots of free tutorials on the internet. If you haven't got access to one, you can always use a large heavy book, with a few sheets of acid-free tissue paper layered throughout to flatten your plants. Just make sure it's a book you don't mind getting a little warped and use lots of heavier books on top to apply pressure. It can take days for large flowerheads or plants to dry, but generally 24 hours is enough for simple leaves to get them flat and ready for printing.

Hanging plants – If you want to keep your plants in their full, beautiful 3D form then hang them up to dry. Tie a piece of string from wall to wall and peg your cuttings upside down by their stems to help preserve their 3D shape. Make sure they don't overlap and that they have as much air circulating around them as possible, to prevent any damp turning into mould. Avoid kitchens or bathrooms where there's lots of steam; position above radiators or near boilers instead. Some plants will dry better than others and it's worth experimenting to get the results you want.

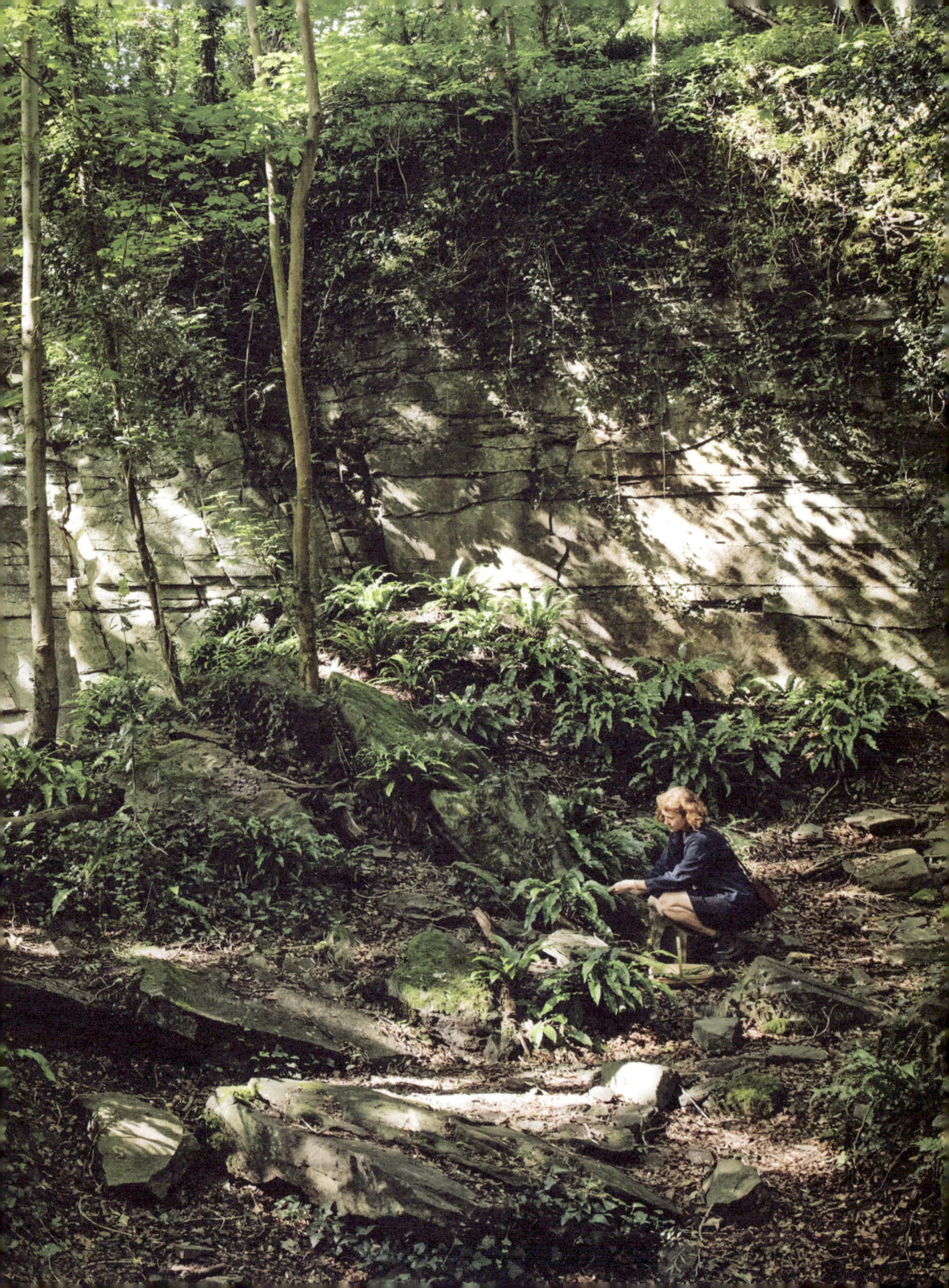

Here's a summary of what I've seen throughout the year on my walks in the southwest of England.

Spring

The best time of year when the earth comes back to life after a long dark winter.

Snowdrops, celandine, wood anemones, daffodils, hellebores, hyacinths, sorrel, and bluebells. Crocuses and primroses, hawthorn flowers, and all kinds of tree blossoms from cherry to pear. Wild garlic and fresh ferns uncurling.

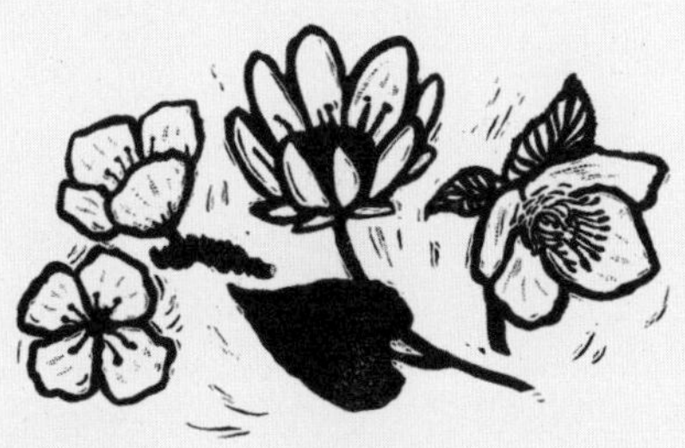

Summer

The number of things in full bloom in high summer makes foraging almost overwhelming.

Flowers: daisies, yarrow, mallow, borage, clover, dandelions, elderflowers, and wild roses. Grasses in their green elements; perennial rye, false oats, and Yorkshire fog. Fresh and juicy leaves, happily on the tree: aspen, birch, and ginkgo.

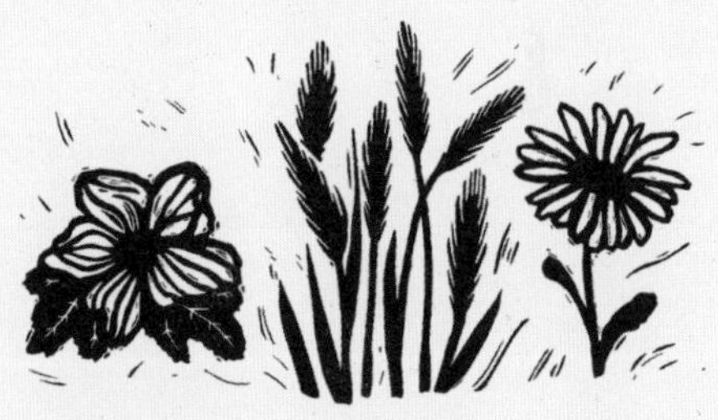

Autumn

The rich red colours of autumn are a great source of inspiration and the leaves are literally falling from the trees all around you; it's hard not to be inspired by the reds, yellows, and browns.

Leaves: all types; oak, beach, maple. Chinese lanterns. Grasses: wheat and ryes. Berries: rosehips, sloes, elderberries, rowan berries, and crab apples. Nuts: acorns, walnuts, chestnuts, cobnuts.

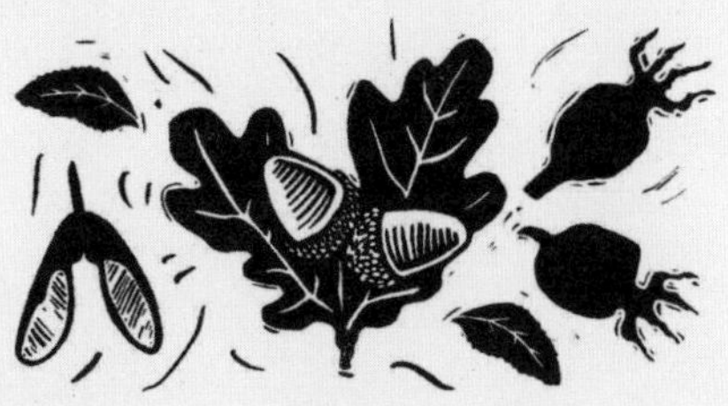

Winter

Even when it feels like the land is barren and there's nothing on the trees, you can still find many beautiful botanical forms to draw inspiration from. Evergreens keep well once harvested – even without water.

Acorns, beechnuts, rosehips, hawthorns, hazelnuts, sloes, rowan berries, ivy, ferns, eucalyptus, lichen, moss, fungi, holly, pine leaves, pine cones, chickweed, common sorrel, nettle, and wild chervil.

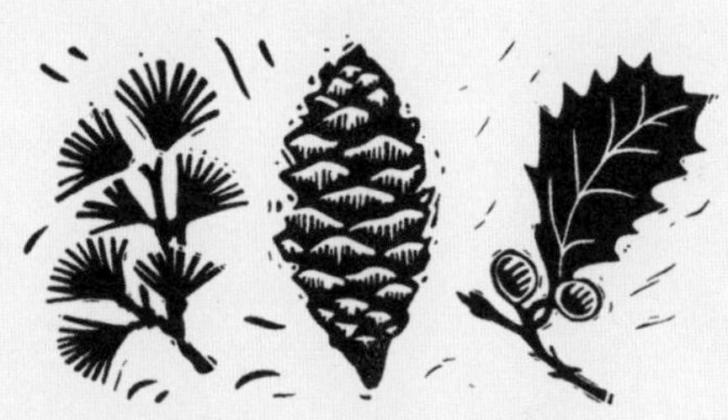

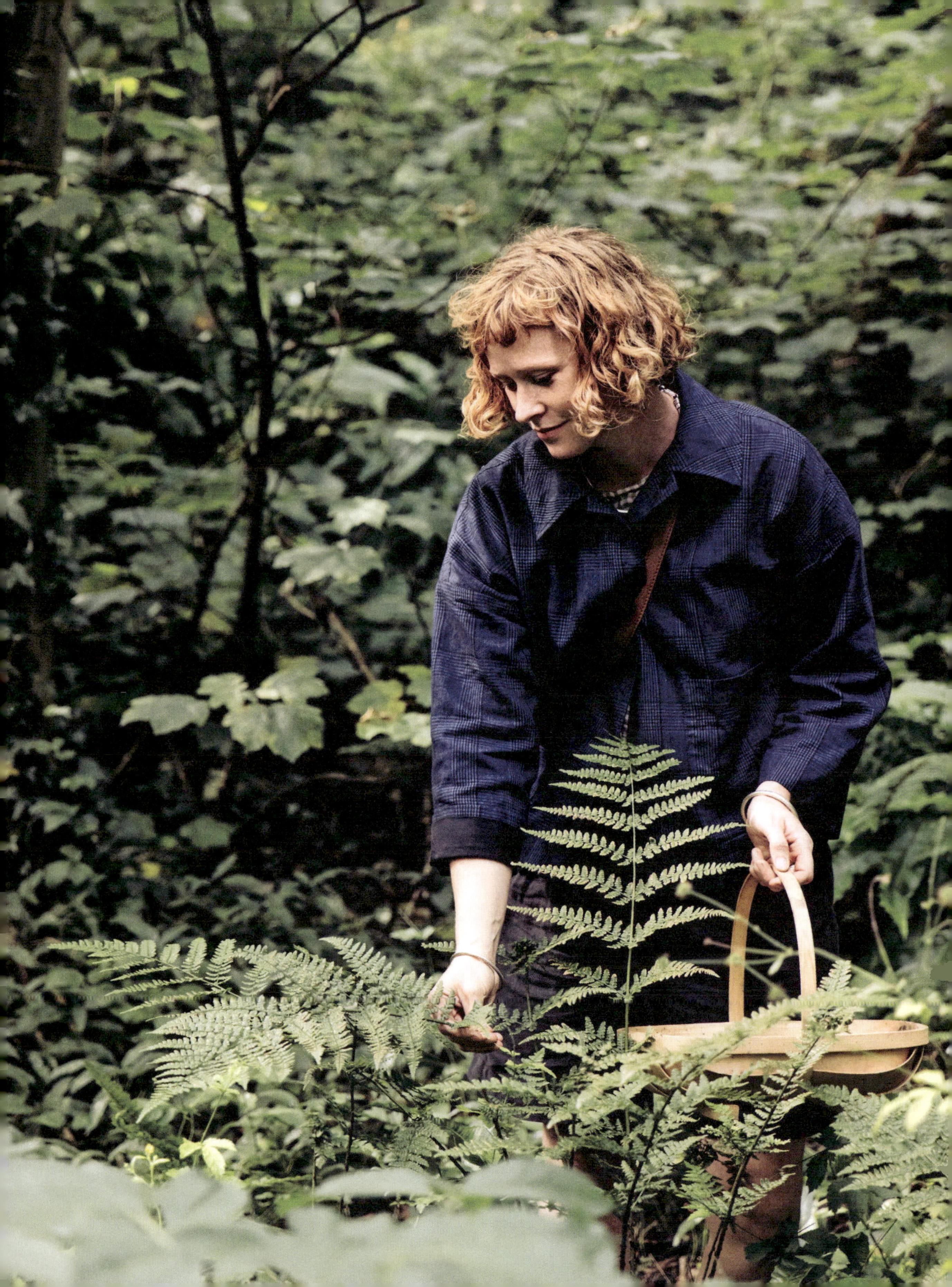

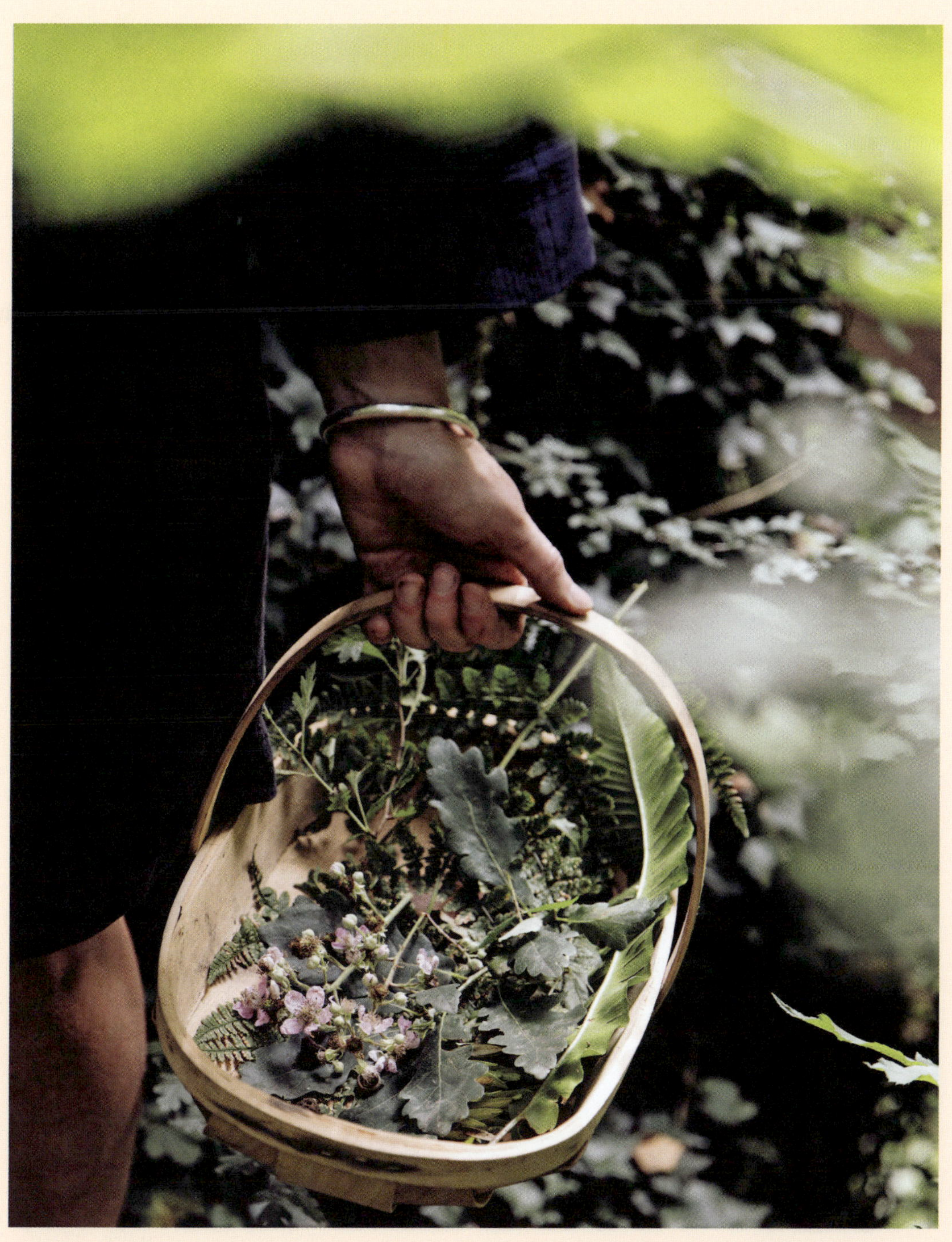

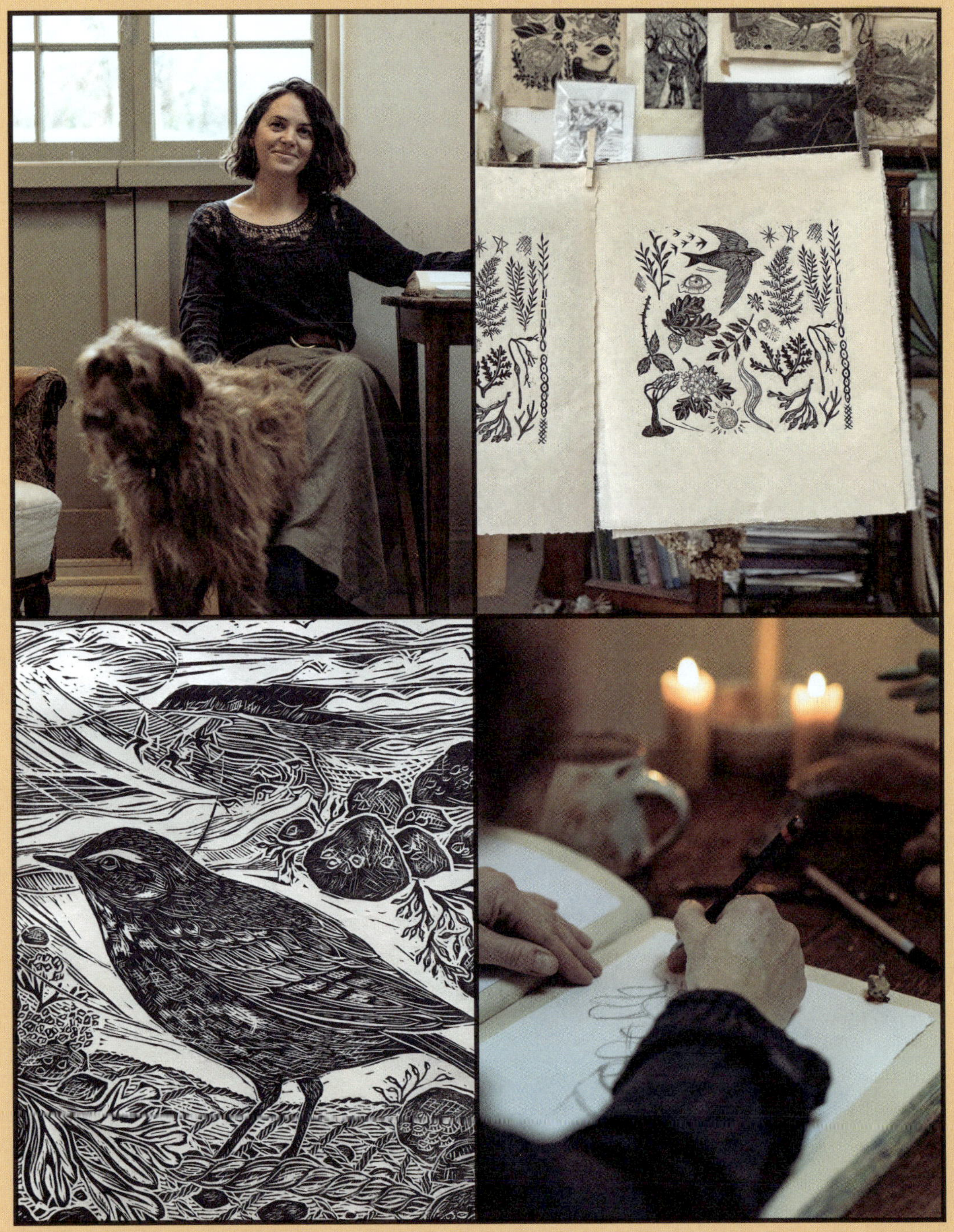

Lou Tonkin

Where do you work and what do you work with?
I work either from my garden studio in Cornwall, or more commonly from the kitchen table. I'm very much a lino block printmaker. I use the traditional lino and I work with traditional wooden handle tools, tubes of ink, and lovely Japanese paper. With a lot of my work, the planning is done outside or in my studio van. I've always got a sketchbook with me. I'm really not fussy about my drawing materials; I sketch with anything from an old biro, beautiful pots of ink with a sable brush, or mud from the ground with a stick or my fingers – depending on what I have to hand.

How did you get started making prints?
I should say when I studied illustration at Falmouth Art college, but actually my love for lino print started a long time before then, probably when I was doing GCSEs at secondary school. I remember doing a tiled lino project and really feeling the joy of that process.

Where do you go for inspiration for your work?
My inspiration comes almost exclusively from nature. I walk every morning, and every day I'm greeted with something new or a change in our hedgerows or the path from our village by a creek. I'm inspired by the weather; the elemental experience of it, seasons, birds. All interaction with nature is so inspiring.

Can you explain a little about how drawing is part of your practice?
I try to draw every day. I have a huge sketchbook which is an antique book ledger, which I started a few years ago. It's so thick and heavy that I'm only two-thirds through! I draw straight over the lines and use all sorts of mediums in this sketchbook. As I've said, I have no bias for my drawing material – so it's all very accessible. I also have a mini sketchbook which lives in my coat pocket, along with a portable ink well and a travel paint brush. I often have lots of sketchbooks open in the studio at the same time to study different subjects. Drawing is absolutely the foundation of any artwork; all my prints are better for the drawing practice that I put in between them.

What's your favourite botanical piece that you've made?
It's impossible to choose just one piece, maybe my old leaning hawthorn tree.

What does a typical day in the studio look like for you?
I go for a walk first, always. I make a big pot of Rooibos or Tulsi tea in my Matthew Foster tea pot from Leach Pottery. I take a few minutes to choose the right mug (this is a real daily ritual). Then, I settle down wherever I'm working and put on an audiobook. I find my work is often inspired by emotion, or the emotion of a place. Music can change my mood too much.

What's the best advice you'd give to a new printmaker?
To test lots of different paper types, choose one that you love, or that means something to you. Get good ink – ink is such a joy when it works well! Find your own inspiration, don't compare, and feel the process deeply.

PRINTING ON PAPER

Now that you've explored all the basics of what you need to print, how to use your tools and how to set up your printing space, you're probably raring to get your hands inky. In this chapter, I'll run through all the basics of creating print runs: transferring techniques for getting your designs onto your blocks, registration techniques for pulling the perfect print, and how to go about creating editions.

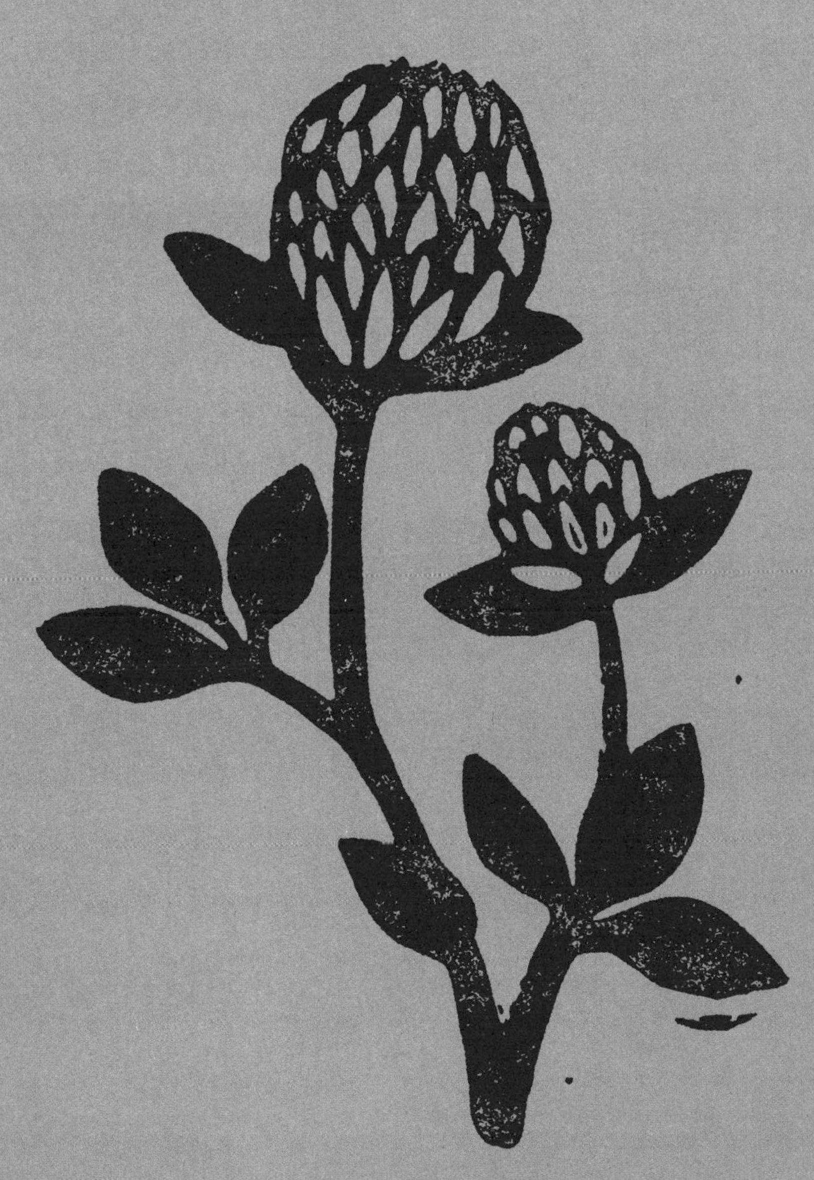

Transferring Techniques

Once you've come up with the perfect design, you'll be ready to transfer it to your block and begin carving. Lots of people love to draw straight onto the block and go from there but it's also useful to be able to transfer your drawings from your sketchbook or computer.

Before you start, remember that what you're carving will be a mirror image, the reverse, of your final print, as the printing process flips it. So, if you are including text or a design that needs to go in a specific direction, it's important to plan for this and consider which technique you use to get the result you want.

TIP *Some relief blocks take to the transferring techniques better than others. Generally, I recommend using the grey battleship lino (see page 14), instead of the rubbery easy-carve linos, which can smudge easily when marked up.*

PREPARING YOUR BLOCKS

Sanding *– Some printmakers give their blocks a light sand before carving. This helps to take off any ink, dirt, or residue that may have built up and which might interfere with the printing later. Personally, I don't tend to sand my blocks, but naturally I'm a bit slap-dash in my making and enjoy the happy mistakes that come from a bit of grit and grime.*

Ink staining *– Staining the surface of your lino or wood blocks before you begin designing on them is a great technique for improving visibility when you are deep into the carving process, and makes it easier to differentiate between what will pick up ink and what you have already carved away. To stain your blocks, use diluted acrylic or printmaking ink in any colour – most printmakers prefer to use red – and rub it evenly across the surface with a cloth.*

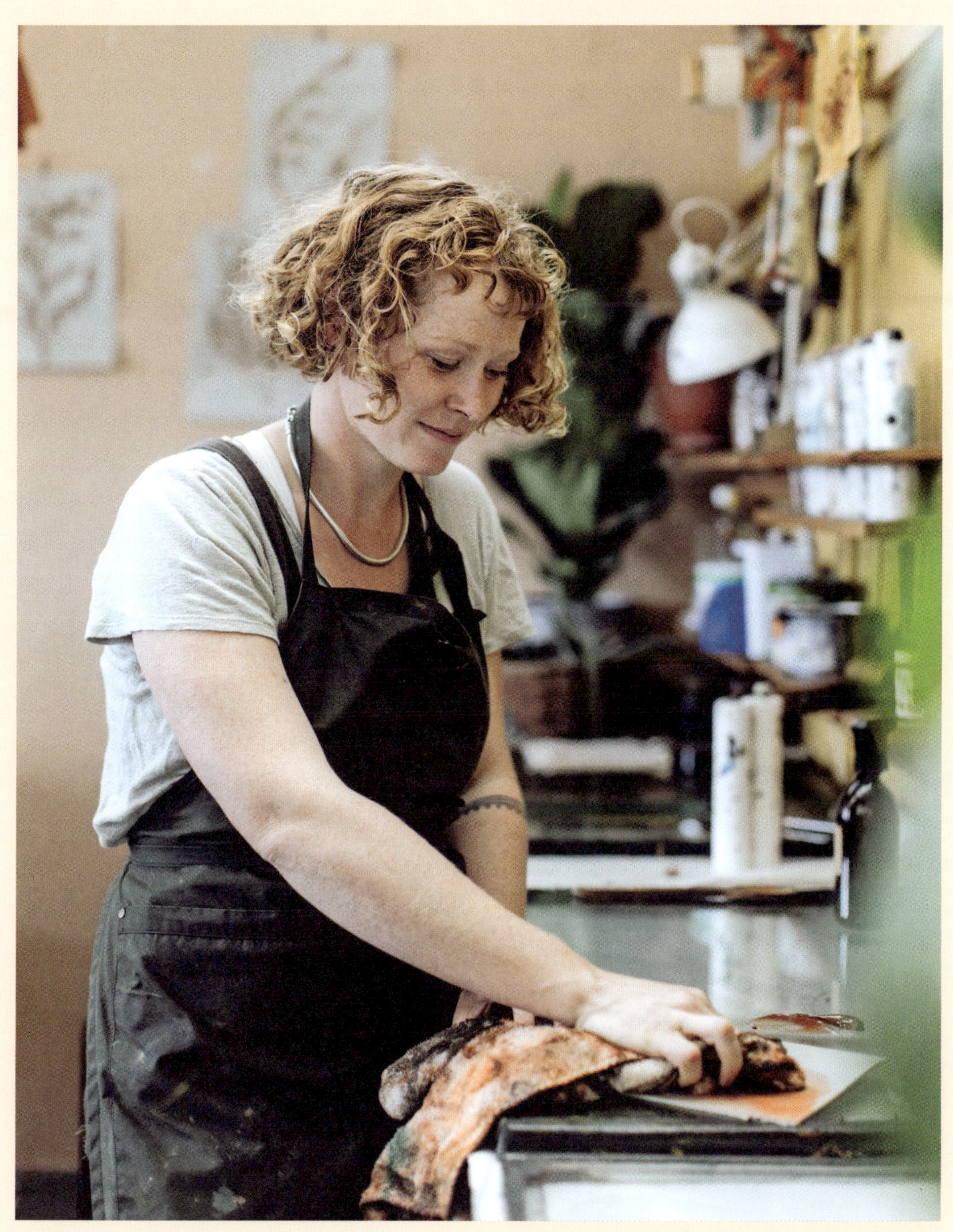

Tracing Paper

Tracing paper is one of the most straightforward methods for transferring your image to your block and also has the added benefit of flipping your design for you. This means that when you come to carve and print, your final image will align with your original sketch.

YOU WILL NEED
Original sketch or design
Prepared lino or wood block
Tracing paper
Masking tape
2B pencil, or softer
2H pencil

3

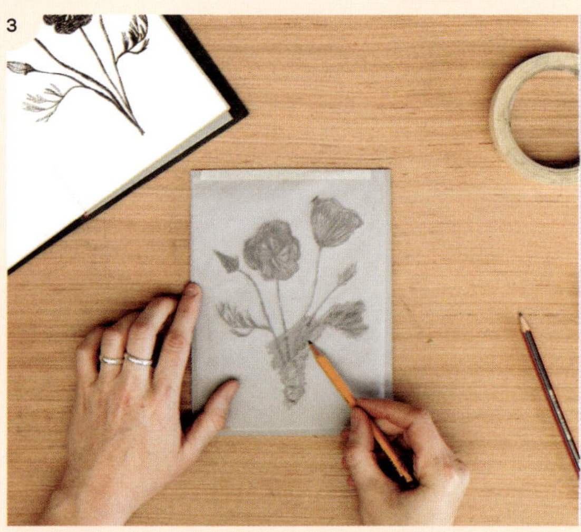

4

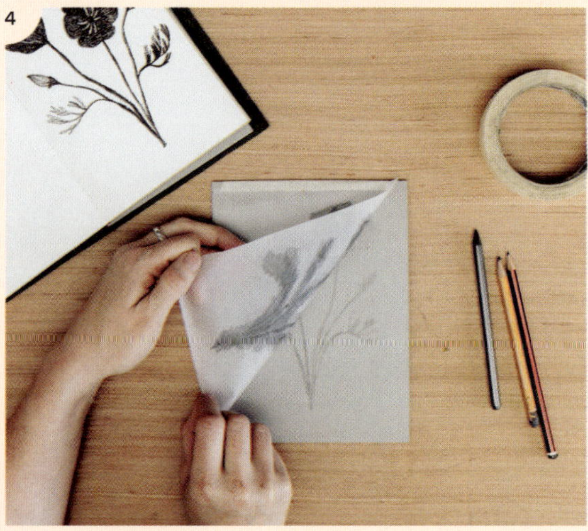

1. Line your tracing paper up on your drawing or design and tape in place. Trace over your design, carefully following the lines without moving the paper.

2. Flip the tracing paper over and attach it to your block with a tape hinge at the top.

3. Shade over the lines you've drawn with a hard pencil. You want to apply pressure as you go over the lines to help the graphite transfer to the block beneath.

4. Keep checking that the graphite is transferring properly by lifting a corner of the tracing paper, and take care to lay it back down in its original position.

Carbon Paper

I love carbon paper – it reminds me of Nineties offices: franking machines, beige carpets, and old colour-coded folder systems. It is the method I use most in my work and I think it's great, not just for the nostalgia but also for how straightforward and efficient it is, as you only draw the image once.

TIP *Unlike tracing paper, carbon paper will replicate your sketch as drawn, so bear this in mind when designing, and flip your image if necessary for your final print.*

YOU WILL NEED
Original sketch or design
Prepared lino or wood block
Masking tape
Carbon paper
Coloured pencil

1. Attach your sketch (or if you're particularly attached to it, use a photocopy as you'll be tracing over the design) to the block with a tape hinge along the top so that you can lift regularly to check progress.

2. Slide the carbon paper into position underneath, carbon side down. It doesn't need to be attached necessarily, but it is worth checking it's covering all your design. Carbon paper has two sides, do a quick check by rubbing on some scrap paper on both sides to see which side releases the carbon marks.

3. Begin to trace out your drawing. I like to use a different colour pencil here to keep track of where I've drawn. You need to apply a fair level of pressure to help the carbon come off onto the block – no light shading here.

4. Check your marks are transferring correctly every now and then by lifting a corner. Be sure to realign the sketch to its original position, however, or you'll get a wonky final image.

3

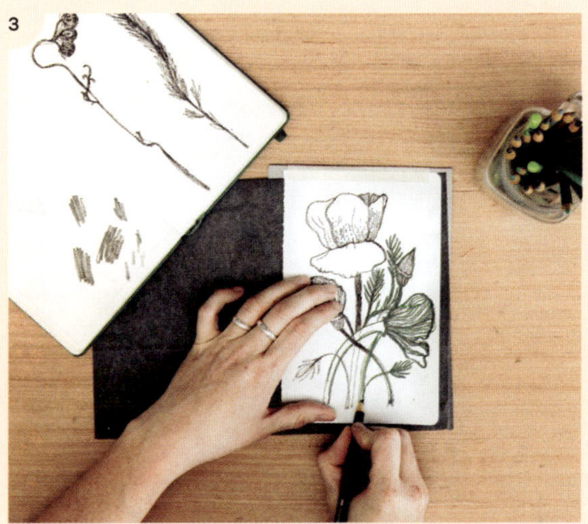

4

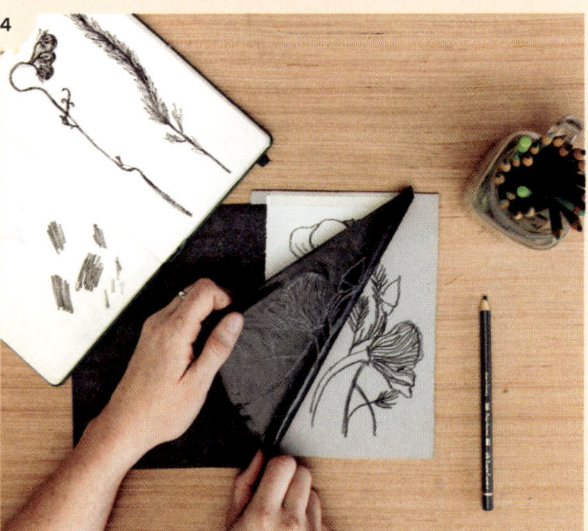

Inkjet and Wood Glue

This technique is an accurate way to transfer your image to the block. It's great when you've got lots of detail in an image that would take an age to copy out by hand.

YOU WILL NEED

Wood glue
Large paintbrush
A bowl of water
Inkjet printer
Lino
Sponge
Masking tape
Heavy item for press (e.g. pile of books)

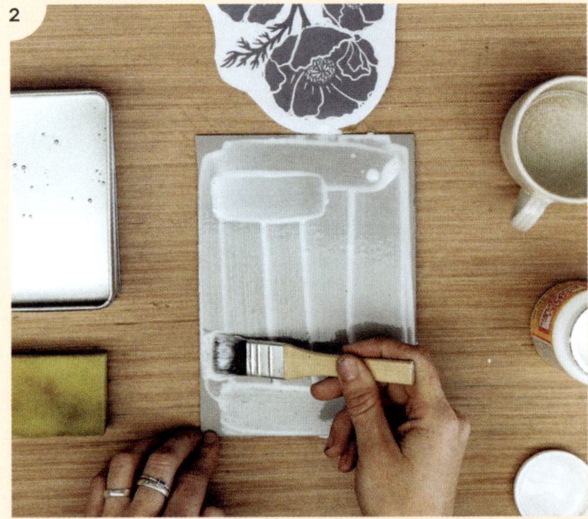

2

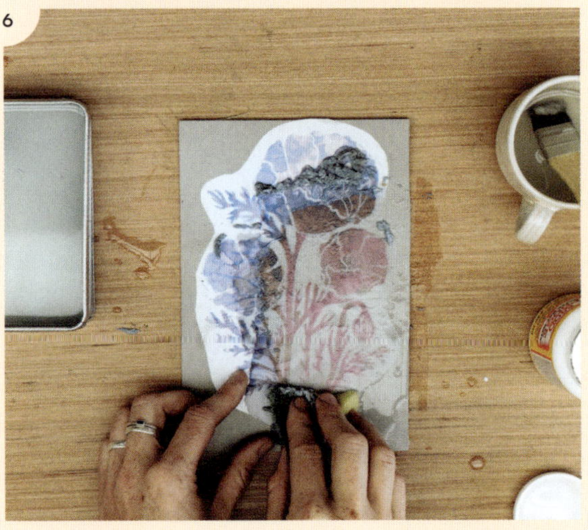

6

1. Prepare your sized image on the computer. Use masking tape to attach the printout to the top of your block with a hinge, to make placing easier.

2. Cover the surface of the lino with an even, thin layer of wood glue. Use a paint brush to wipe away any streaks.

3. Lay your inkjet print face down onto the block and smooth out any creases.

4. Wipe away any excess glue that may come out of the sides with a dry sponge.

5. Using a couple of protective layers of scrap paper, lay your prepared block under a heavy item to flatten overnight.

6. The next day, after it has fully dried, remove the heavy weight and, using a wet sponge, gently rub away the paper. Don't scrub away the ink, which will have adhered to the block.

7. If all goes smoothly, you should be left with a perfect transfer of your image, ready to carve.

OUTLINE YOUR DESIGN

Once your image has been transferred to the block, I suggest going over with a black permanent marker in areas that haven't fully transferred. This helps to get an idea of where the ink goes before you start carving.

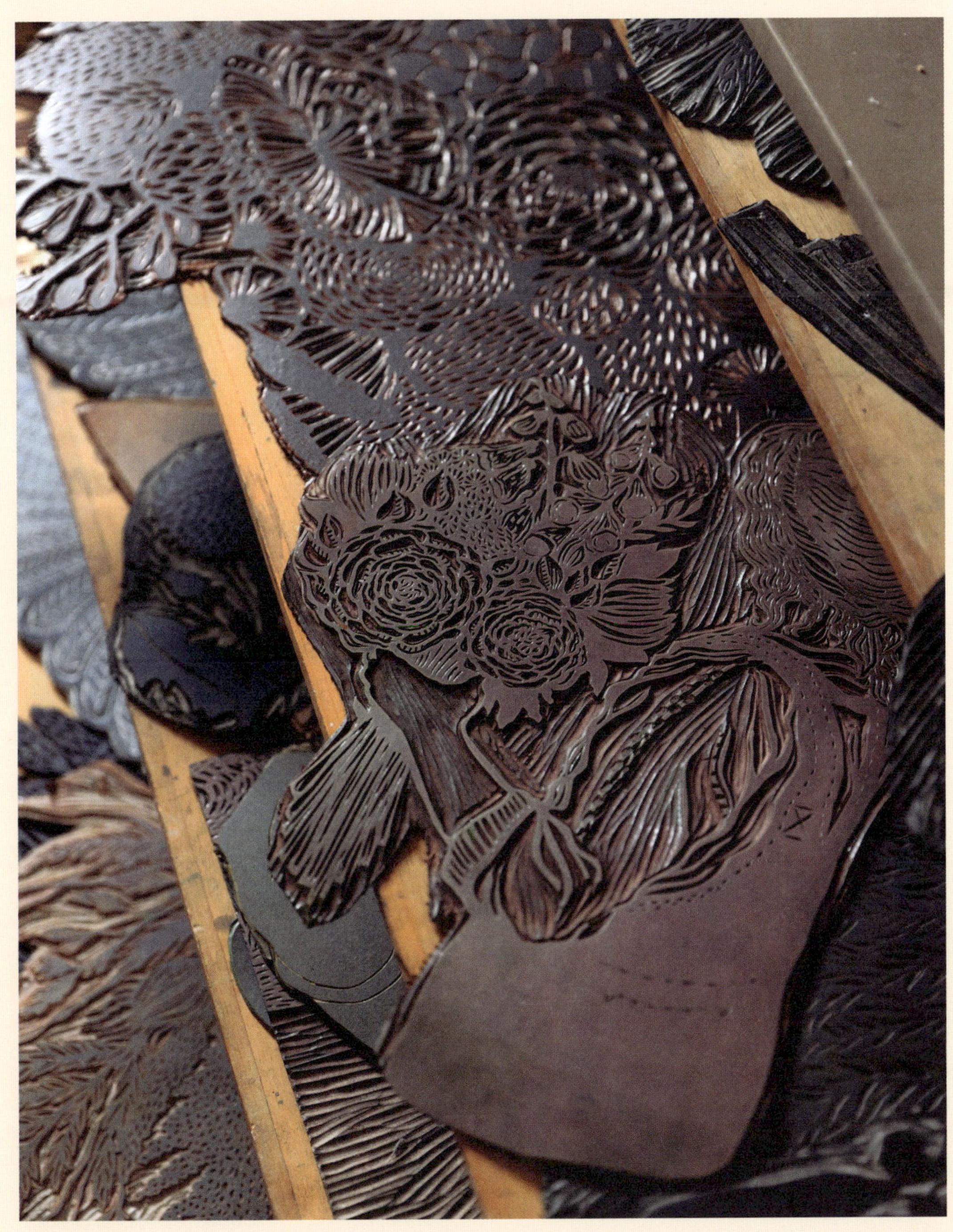

Registration

Mastering the fine art of registration – where you ensure your paper and print block are aligned – is a big part of pulling the perfect print. Registration is particularly important when you start making colour prints, but it is also helpful to get these techniques in your repertoire for single-colour blocks. There are a lot of things you can get away with in print, but bad registration is generally not one of them.

However, it is worth noting that sometimes mis-registered prints can look brilliant – it's just important that it's a choice rather than something you can't control and something you can't repeat even if you want to.

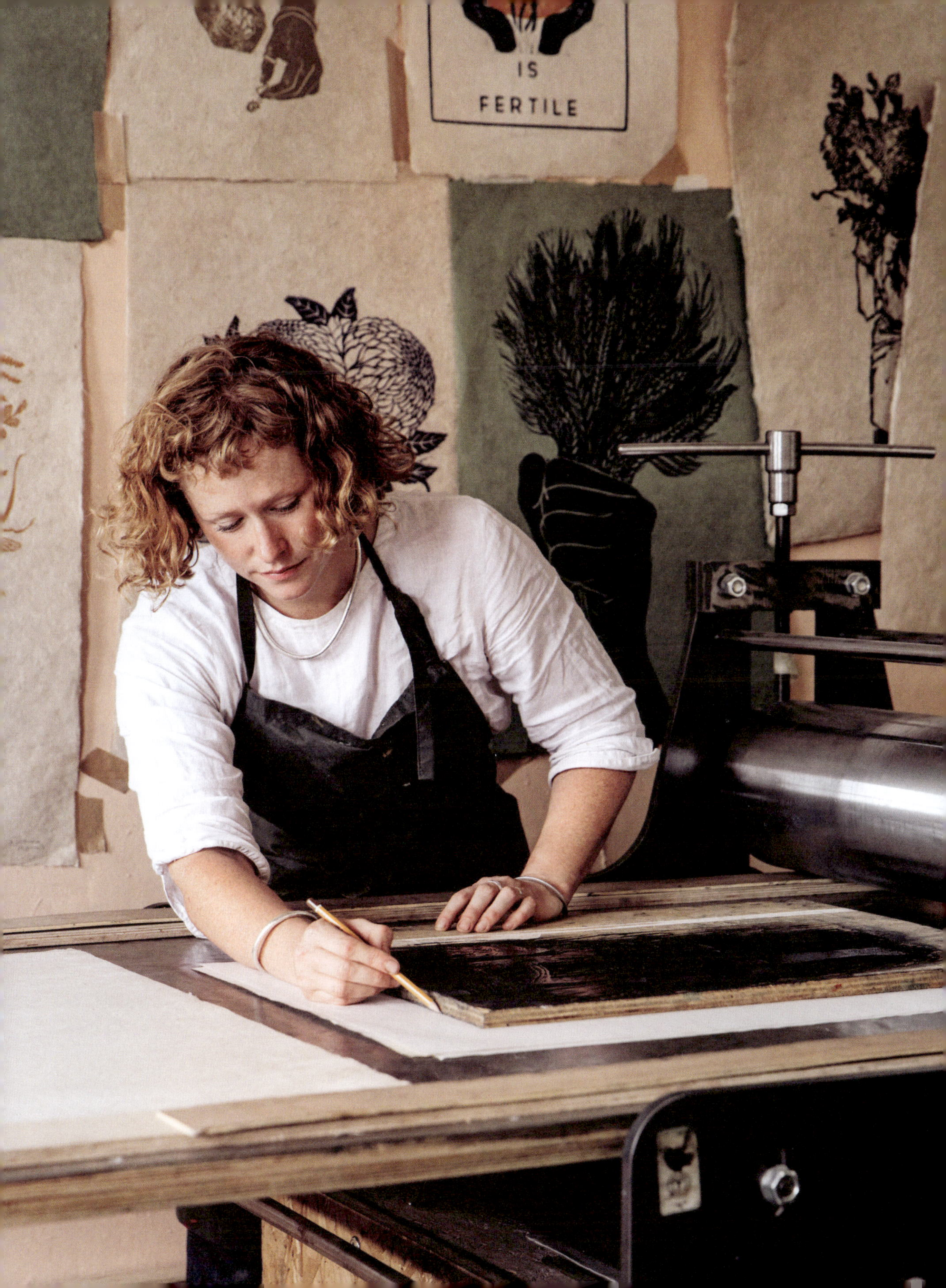
IS
FERTILE

Paper Template

The simplest of registration techniques, this is the one I use most in my studio as it only takes a minute and is relatively accurate.

YOU WILL NEED
Newsprint
Paper for printing
Pencil
Prepared lino or wood block

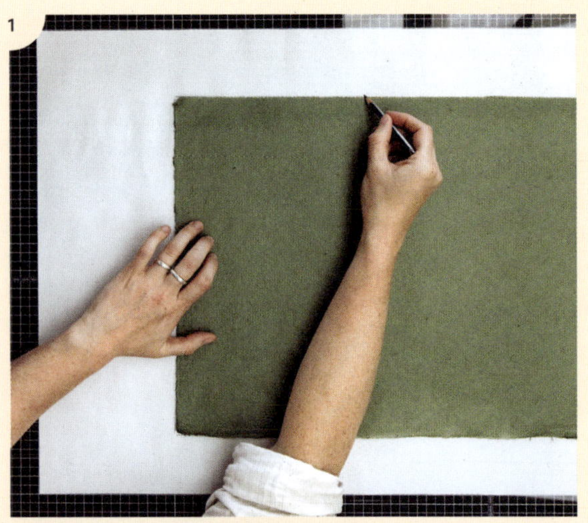

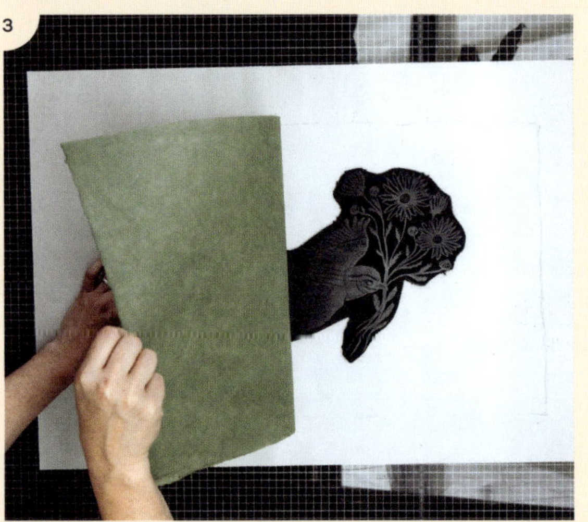

1. Using a sheet of newsprint, place a piece of the paper you will be using for your edition in the centre. Draw around it with a pencil.

2. Then take your block and place it where you would like it to sit on the page within the pencil outline. Draw around it. I also find it helpful to note which way up everything is at the beginning.

3. For every print all you need to do is centre your block and line up each piece of paper within the pencil outlines on the newsprint.

Ternes Burton Registration Pins

A genius invention and well worth the investment if you want perfectly lined-up prints or plan to move into colour. These pins take the labour out of multiblock printing and make it kind of fun. There's something so satisfying about clipping the pins into place and the trust in the process, as they really do work.

YOU WILL NEED
Ternes Burton registration pins and tabs
Sheet of hard cardboard
Parcel tape
Pencil
Masking tape
Two thin pieces of card

1

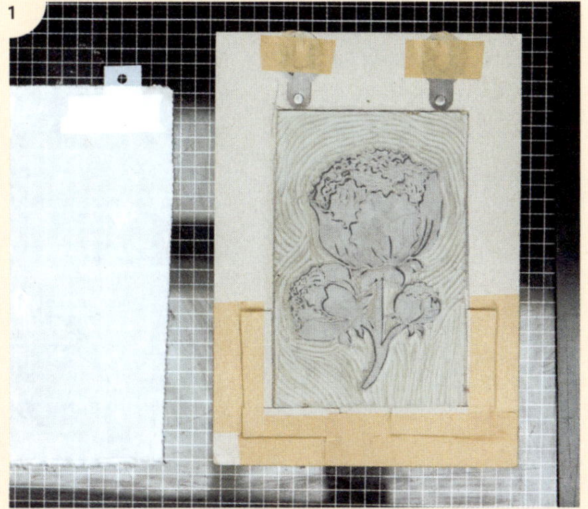

1. Line up a pair of pins and stick them to the top of your cardboard with parcel tape.

2. Line up your paper on the board and click a pair of stripping tabs in place onto the pins, then attach the tabs to your paper with masking tape. Remove the tabs from the pins and the paper is ready. Repeat with a pair of tabs for each sheet of paper in your edition.

3. Pin a sheet of paper in place and draw around the edge onto the cardboard. Remove the paper so you can work out where you want your block to sit on the page.

3

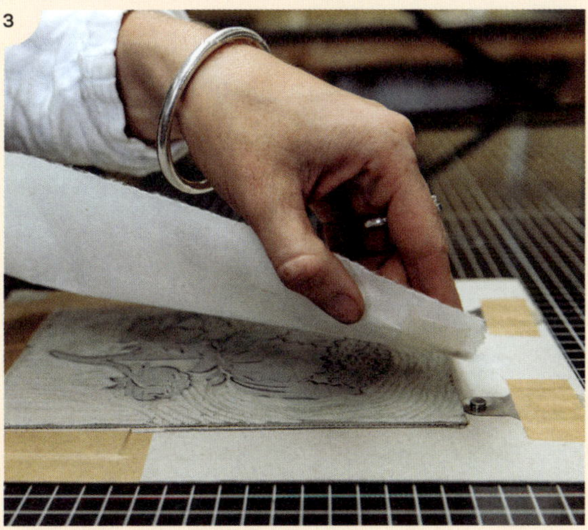

4. Make a little corner slot out of two pieces of thin card taped in place for your block to slot into. This way it goes back into the same place each time you ink up and bring it back to print; just be sure they are lower in height than your lino.

5. To print, snap the tabs to the pins and lower the paper onto the inked block. Keep the tabs in place if you are printing in multiple colours until you are finished.

Making a Jig or Print Window

This is a highly effective and tidy way to make a neat print, using materials that you'll likely have in the studio already.

YOU WILL NEED
Two sheets of thick card
Two pieces of thin card
Pencil
Ruler
Stanley knife or craft knife
Parcel tape
Palette knife

1
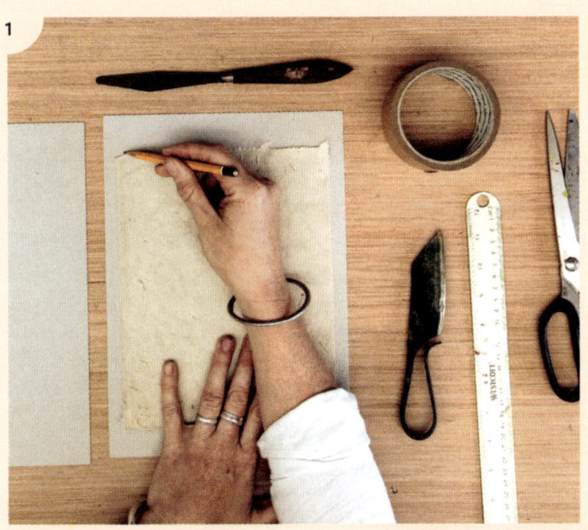

1. Take two pieces of sturdy thick card. They need to be larger than the paper you're using for your edition. Centre a piece of your paper and draw around it onto the card with pencil.

2
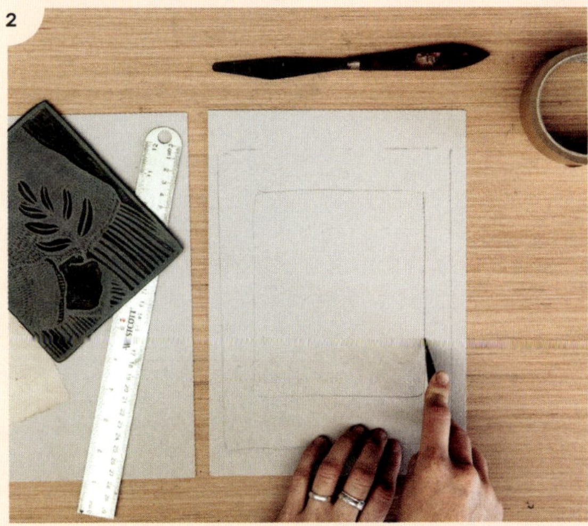

2. Place your block and work out where you want it to sit on the paper within this box. Draw around it and cut it out with a Stanley knife. You want your lino to fit in the box snugly, so use a ruler to keep your lines straight.

3. Using parcel tape as a hinge, stick the two pieces of card together at the top. This backing piece isn't essential but helps if you need to move the jig around when printing.

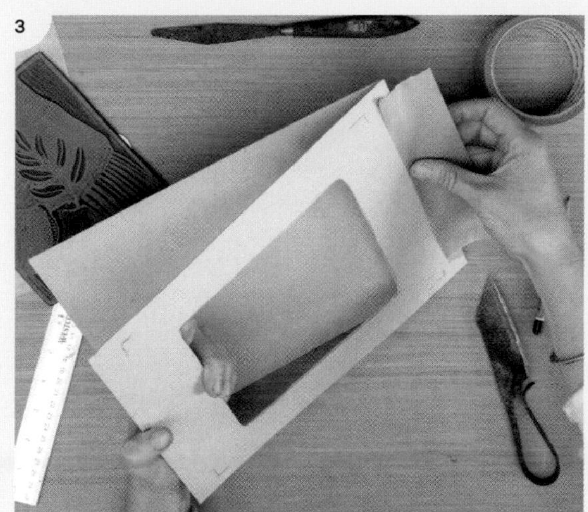
3

4. Now cut out two small strips of card and line them up with where your paper will sit to make a corner. Tape them in place neatly, making sure they are lower in height than your lino.

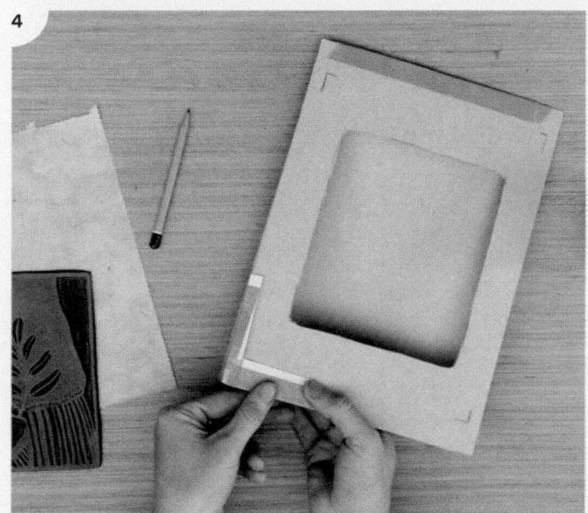
4

5. Each time you come to use the jig, you will place the inked lino block into its frame and line the paper up with its corner to print.

6. Removing the block for re-inking without making a mess is tricky, so use a clean palette knife to help get it out of the box.

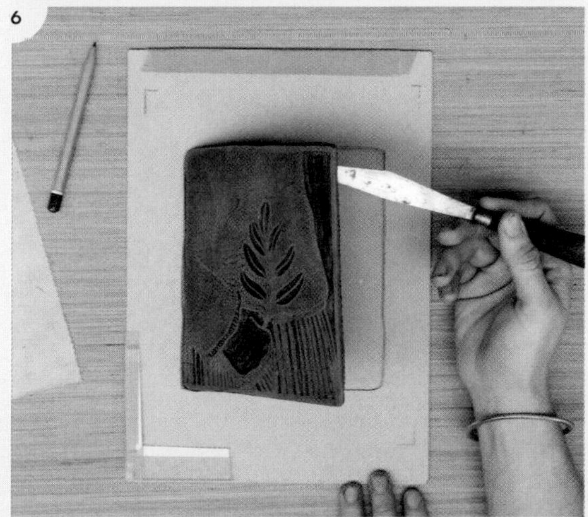
6

Editioning

An edition is a series of identical prints taken from the same block. The number of prints made are usually limited, which adds value to them, hence the term 'limited edition'. The concept of an edition of prints was developed by artists and art collectors in the nineteenth century, to help sell more work and make more money. Originally, the number of copies in an edition would have been mainly practical; the print run would contain as many prints as possible before the original print plate began to degrade.

How Many Editions?

How many editions you make is up to you. You can technically vary colours and papers indefinitely – there is no secret editioning office in the sky keeping track of how many copies you make! Because it is generally accepted that the higher the edition the less value assigned to a print, artists tend to limit these numbers to give more value to their work.

When I started out, I would make editions of ten, limited to how many I could print in one session. But as I have become more established and demand for my work has grown, my edition sizes have grown too. I tend to print around thirty in each printing session and usually limit my editions to around 100–200.

An edition is usually signed with the number on the lower left hand side, the title in the middle, and the artist's signature on the right. The edition is usually displayed as a fraction of a number, for example, 3/300 is the third image printed in a run of 300.

PRINTMAKING TERMS

Printmakers love an acronym, and there's a whole array of old printmakers' terms that can be used in an edition. I've detailed some of the most-used below, but there are even more obscure ones out there to discover.

AP (Artist's proof) – Artist's proofs are usually the first prints in an edition and are separate from the numbered prints that make up the rest. They are generally thought to be the best and most sought after. Firstly, because they are made from the block in its newest and least worn-down state. Secondly, because they were usually kept by the artists themselves for their own collection. This makes them much more desirable for collectors and generally a bit more expensive than other prints in the edition. There is a general rule among printmakers that APs do not make up more than ten per cent of an edition, so for an edition of 50, you'd be limited to five APs.

BAT – An acronym for the French 'Bon à Tirer' which means 'good to go'. This is a term more commonly used in bigger printing studios, but if you feel like being fancy you can use it yourself. BAT prints are usually the first proof and approved by the artists as the standard they must go by for the rest of the edition. They are usually limited to one and can often be the most prized of an edition.

PP (Printer's proof) – These are proofs specifically for the printer. They are separate from the numbered edition and usually limited to one per person helping print the edition. These old terms and traditions aren't as relevant to most solo printmakers today, but if you have a friend helping you out, it can be fun to give these old traditions a nod.

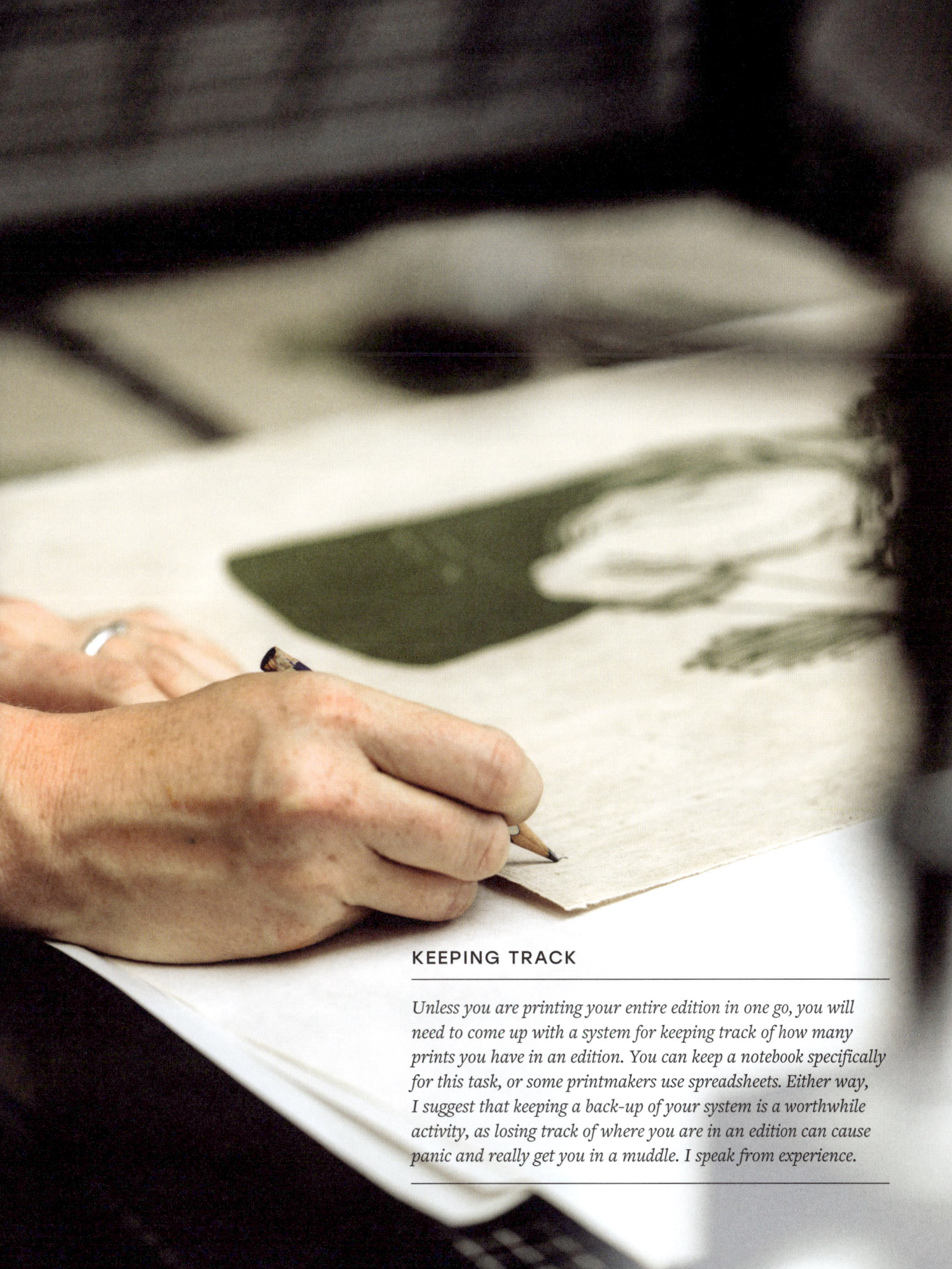

KEEPING TRACK

Unless you are printing your entire edition in one go, you will need to come up with a system for keeping track of how many prints you have in an edition. You can keep a notebook specifically for this task, or some printmakers use spreadsheets. Either way, I suggest that keeping a back-up of your system is a worthwhile activity, as losing track of where you are in an edition can cause panic and really get you in a muddle. I speak from experience.

Printing on a Press

Printing with an Albion Printer

These beautiful top-pressure presses are specifically designed for printing relief prints and they make the whole process a joy. However, when printing large blocks, you do have to be able to exert a good amount of power to pull the handle across the bed, and with a big edition this can add up to a proper workout, so be prepared.

HEALTH & SAFETY

Make sure any jewellery, hair, or loose clothing is secured or removed before working on any printing.

SETTING THE PRESSURE

The beds of these presses are designed to be used at 'type height', so you may have to add layers, such as ply or card, to get the correct pressure for your block. Before you start printing you can test your packing pressure by doing a 'blind' print, which is essentially your block, paper, and packing run through the press with no ink. The resistance you feel will help you determine whether the pressure is correct. It also allows you to inspect the paper after it's been through the press for any indents and embossing you may not want, and adjust accordingly.

USING A VERTICAL MOTION PRESS

The type height on an Albion is 23.32mm and linoleum is generally 3.2mm, so you'll need lots of extra bits of ply and packing paper to reach it.

YOU WILL NEED
Carved and inked lino or plywood block
Edition paper
Newsprint

1. Place your inked block in the centre of the bed with a registration template (see pages 110–113). Lay the paper from your edition on top and add a sheet of newsprint to protect the press.

2. Lower the tympan and wind the bed in to sit under the platen.

3. Stand to the left of the press and pull the bar towards you across the bed.

4. Hold the bar in position for a second before gently releasing back to the original position.

5. Wind out the bed and lift the tympan to reveal your print.

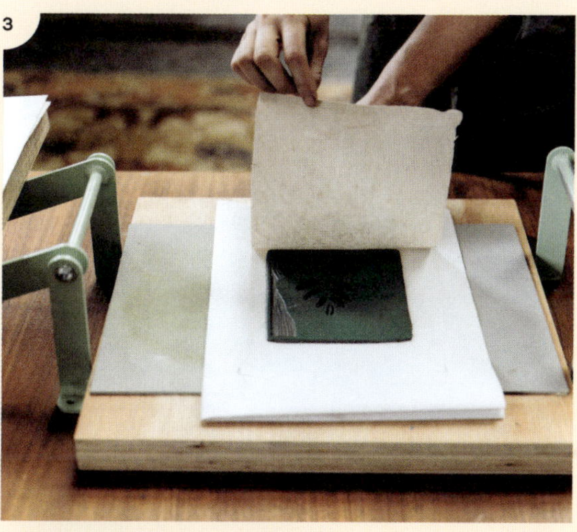
3

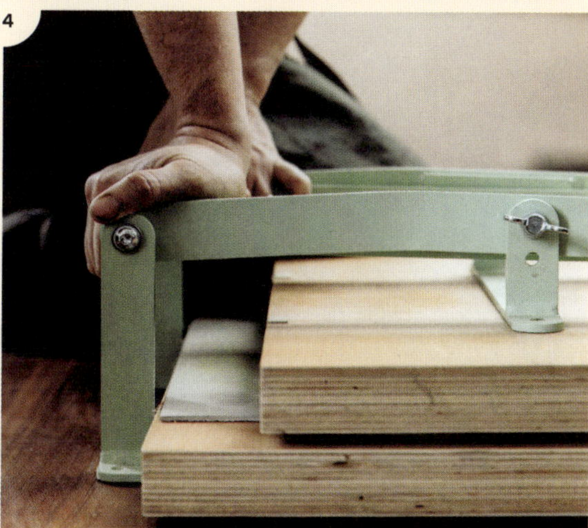
4

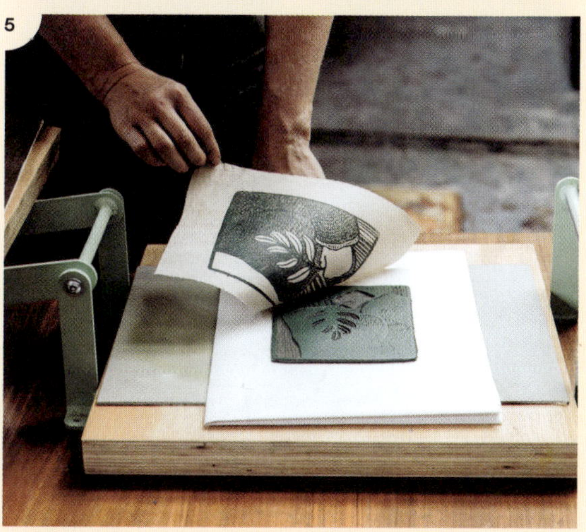
5

Relief Printing on an Etching Press

It's important when setting the pressure on an etching press that you turn the two handles simultaneously so as not to create too much imbalance and damage the mechanics of the press. Most presses work with screws either side that are turned by two small handles to adjust the roller height.

For relief prints, you don't want the pressure to be too tight, or to be struggling to push your block through the bed. I tend to set my press to 'just catching' on the runners and find that gets the best results. Setting the pressure for each press varies, some have rings you can count, or measuring points in place. I find it tends to be a bit of an intuitive process, but with a bit of experimentation and practice you'll find you get used to achieving the perfect pressure and print.

TIP *If, like me, you often struggle to remember which direction to turn the handles, you can use the sweet phrase that applies to most presses and screws in general – 'lefty loosy, righty tighty'.*

BLANKETS OR NO BLANKETS?

Most etching presses come with etching blankets. Generally, they are very expensive, woven from wool, and made especially for etching. You can use these blankets for relief prints, but they aren't always necessary. Blankets create a cushioning effect between the block and the paper, which can cause the paper to emboss or to pick up more ink from the carved-away areas of the block.

Instead of wool blankets, I often use thin lino or even a cutting mat, to sandwich my block between the press bed and etching rollers. This helps to apply even pressure across the surface of the block and also protects the rollers from ink seeping through.

RUNNERS

When printing relief on an etching press, it is important to make yourself a set of runners for all the different block thicknesses you plan on working with. This allows you to set the press height correctly and protects the inner workings of the press over time. In my studio, I have both lino and wood runners of all different thicknesses sitting on a shelf next to the press ready to be called on. If I have salvaged ply of different thicknesses, I just layer these runners up to reach the required height.

USING AN ETCHING PRESS

YOU WILL NEED
Newsprint
Carved and inked lino or plywood block
Edition paper
Blankets, cutting mat, newsprint, or similar to protect rollers

1. Lay a sheet of newsprint down to protect your press bed.

2. Place your inked-up block and registration sheet (see pages 110-113) on top of the newsprint in the centre of your press.

3. Line up your paper and lower it onto your block. Lay your blankets or newsprint on top of your block and paper.

4. Turn the wheel to move the press bed through the rollers.

5. Once out the other side, remove the blankets and newsprint and reveal your print.

3

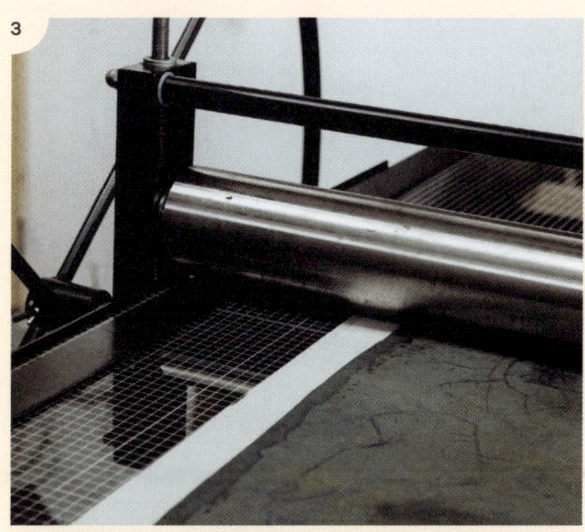

4

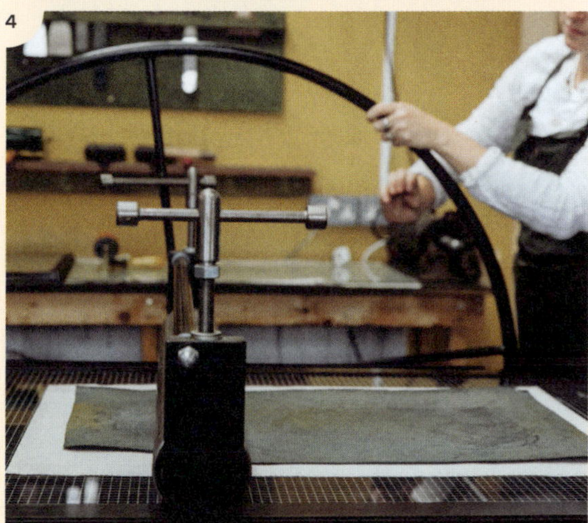

5

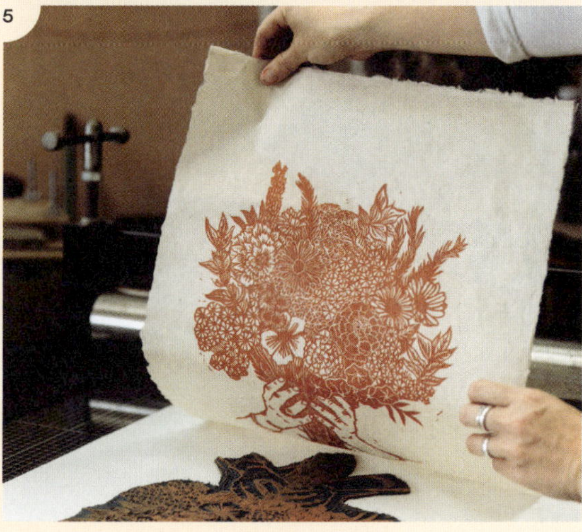

HEALTH & SAFETY

Make sure any jewellery, hair, or loose clothing is secured or removed before working on any printing.

Collaged Botanicals Print

Now that you are up to speed with all the processes involved in making a print, it's time to begin printing your first collaged botanical print. This is a great starter project that will get you exploring different shapes, textures, and compositions within one block. If you have other plans and don't want to follow the specifics shown here, you can use the step-by-step instructions as a starting point to explore your own ideas.

YOU WILL NEED

Foraged botanicals (see pages 86, 95)
Prepared lino or wood block (I've used A5)
Sketchbook and pencil
Paper for printing
Tracing paper or carbon paper
Permanent marker pen
Ruler
Basic print set-up or press

TIP *If you don't have access to physical leaves and blooms, consider making a collage of elements from old magazines, books, or printed material.*

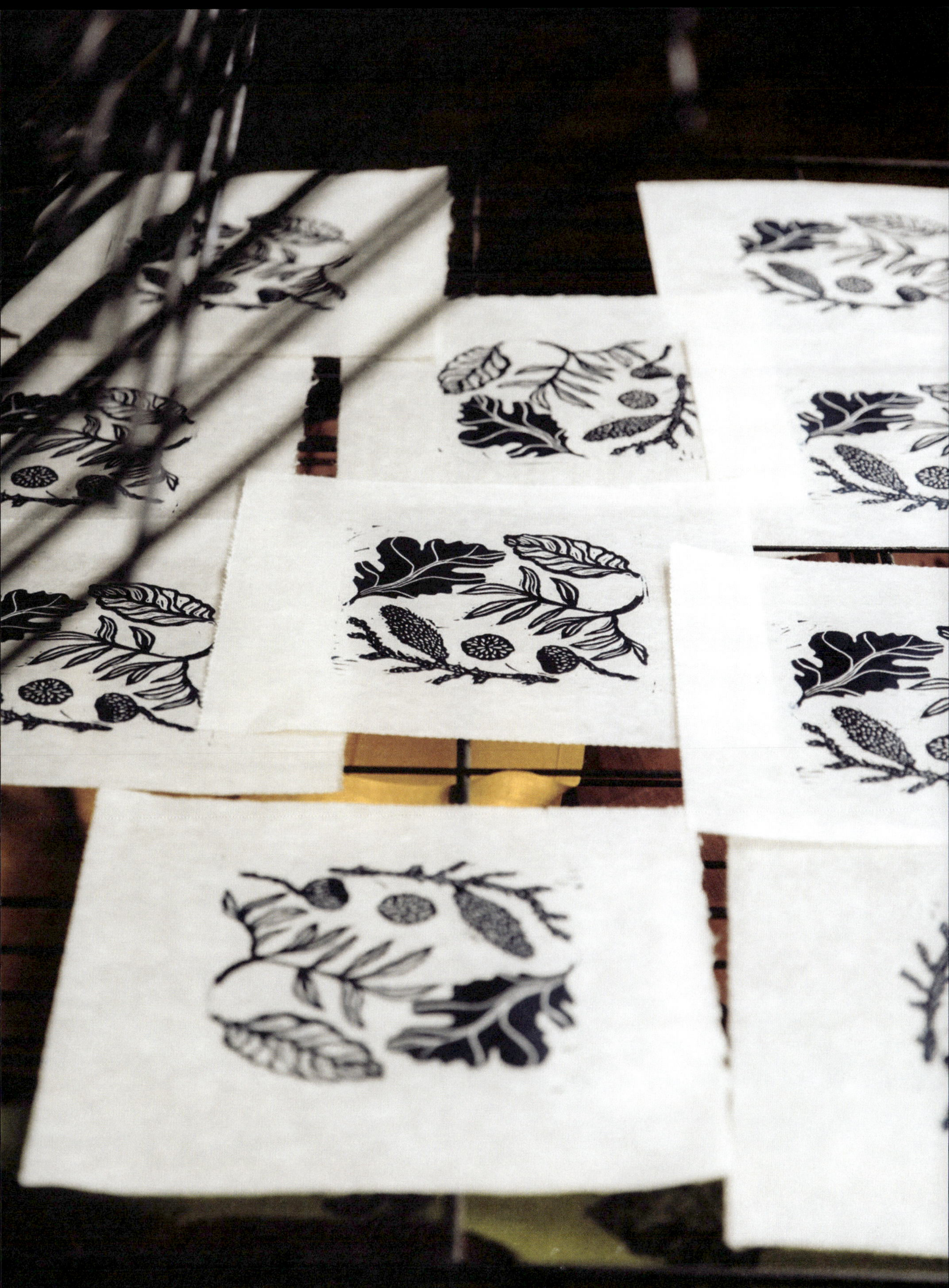

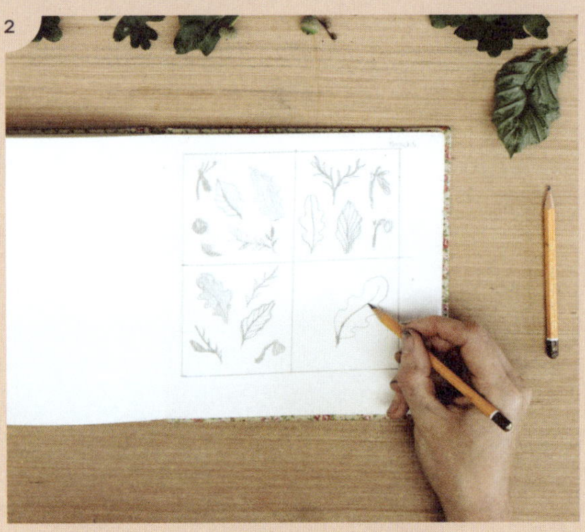
2

1. Collect a selection of botanicals: leaves, branches, berries, and flowers, or just one of these themes. Aim for between four and seven items to create a nice, varied composition.

2. Using the design concepts on pages 82–85, create a selection of thumbnails of different compositions and find the best of these; aim for balance.

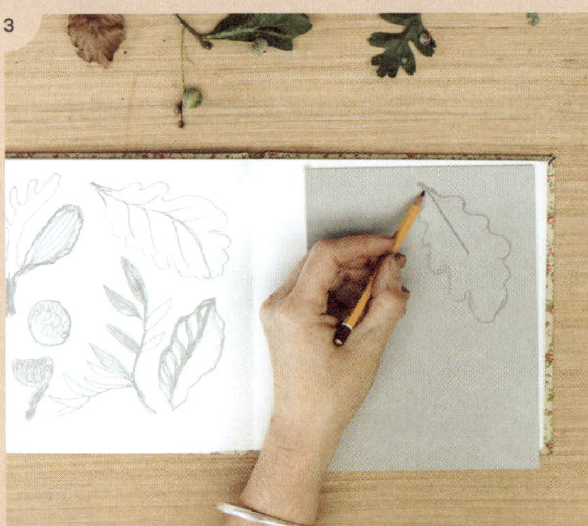
3

3. Draw out your design on the prepared block, either using a transfer technique (see pages 102–107) or draw straight onto the block with a pencil.

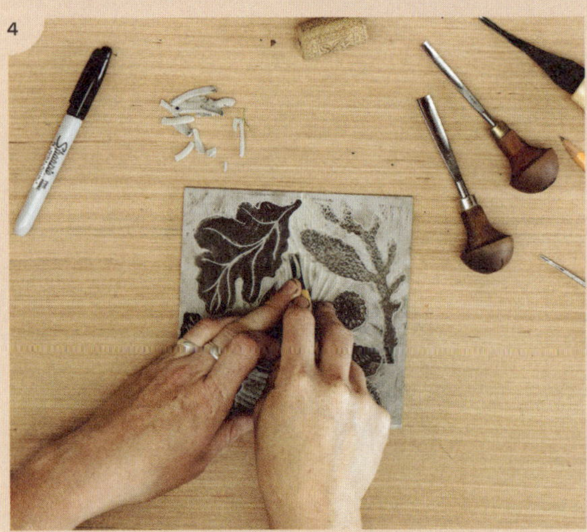
4

4. Mark up your design with a permanent marker to make it easier to plan and see what you want to keep and what you plan on carving away. Begin carving, using your texture block for reference (see page 40).

5. Check your carving and make a proof print on scrap paper. Prepare your paper by cutting it to size (see page 26) for your first edition; aim for five to ten prints for your first run.

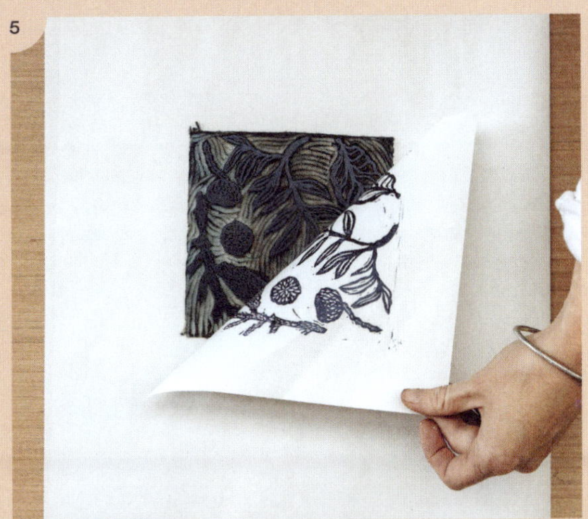
5

6. Create a simple registration template (see pages 110–113) to position your print on the page. Now you're ready to print your first edition by hand (see pages 46-53) or on a press (see pages 116–119).

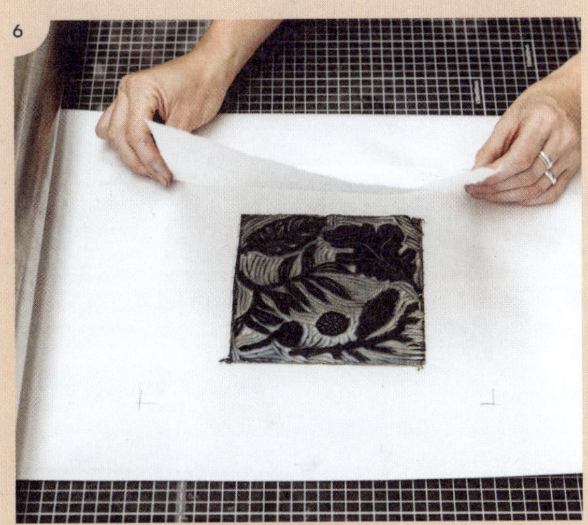
6

7. Once they are dry, name, sign, number, and record your edition in your notebook or spreadsheet.

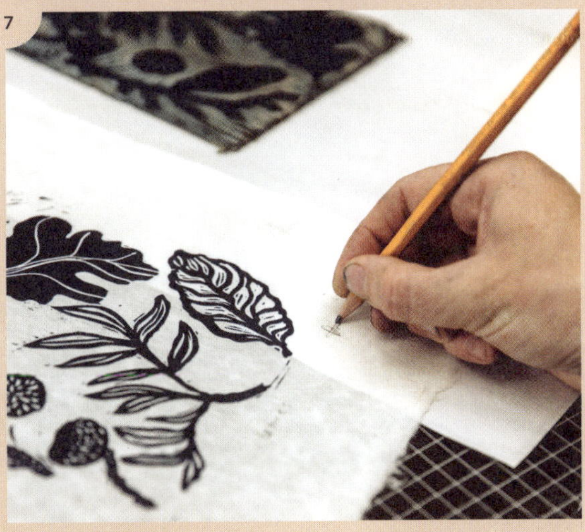
7

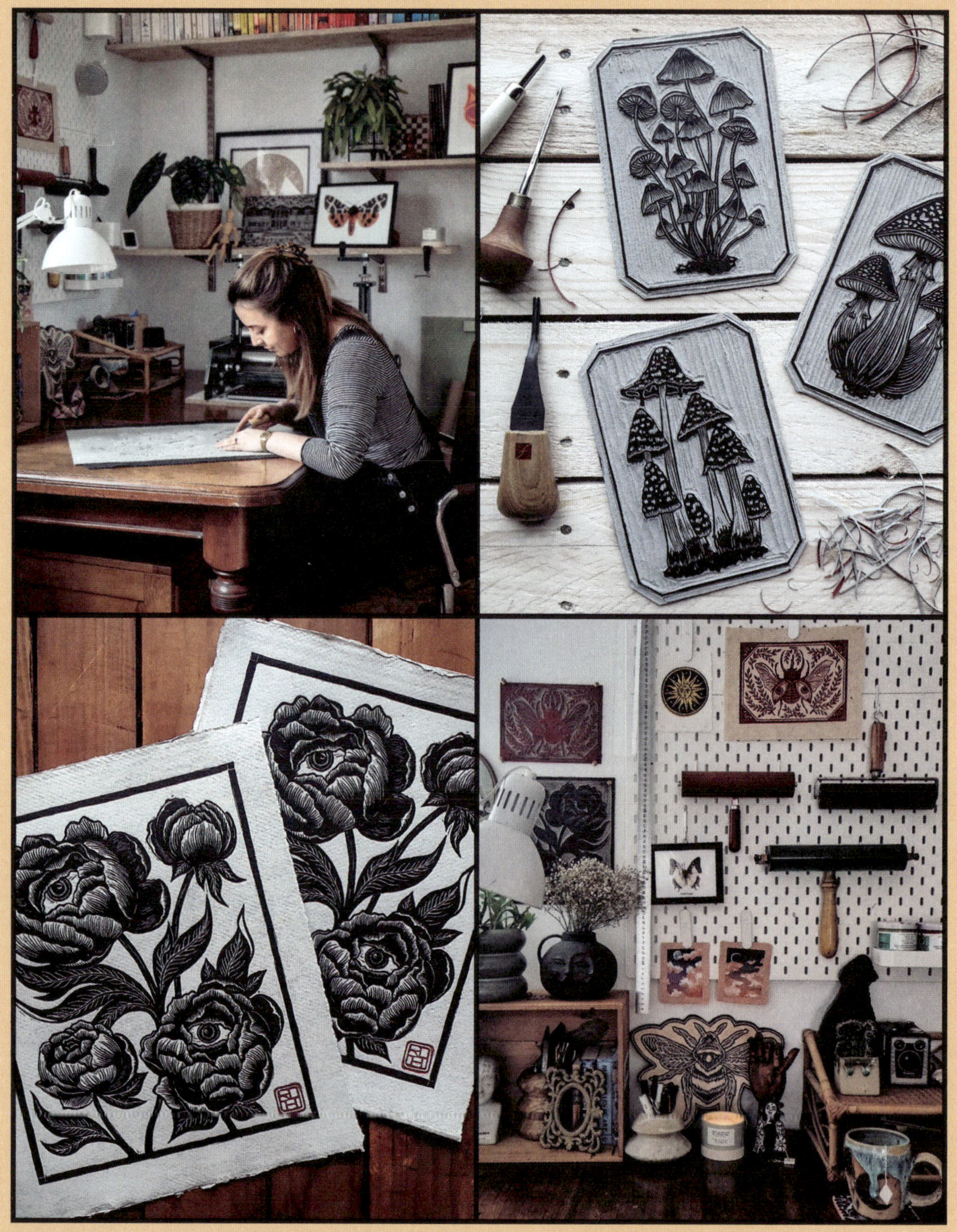

Rachael Hibbs

Where do you work and what materials do you work with?
I split my time working between my small home studio, where I have a small table top etching press, and the print studio of a university. I am very fortunate to get to use the facilities there, which is great if I have a larger scale project that requires more space and bigger equipment. I work primarily with the medium of block printing, more specifically linocut. I have tried many other forms of printmaking, but I always come back to linocut as I love the bold graphic outcome of the prints.

How did you start making prints?
I studied Fine Art at University, but it wasn't until I left the course that I developed my printmaking practice. I started working as an art technician at a private school and they had an etching press that I had access to. Linocut was an easy process that I could develop at home over the next few years and, eventually, it became more than just a hobby.

Where do you go for inspiration for your work?
I take a large amount of my inspiration from the natural world and that is often my starting point for developing my practice. I have a catalogue of photographs from specific hikes or national parks that I have visited. I also tend to draw inspiration from things like old botanical illustrations, historic folk tale drawings or sometimes scientific diagrams. I also watch a lot of nature documentaries and was especially inspired by the *Fantastic Fungi* film by Louie Schwartzberg that was released on Netflix.

Can you explain a little about how drawing is part of your practice?
Sketching plays a huge part in how I develop a piece of work. I used to draw straight onto the lino without predetermining the outcome of the piece. Now, I often use my iPad and sketch my designs on there, but I do think it's good to break out of the digital side of things and go back to basics. I am also experimenting more with using Indian ink to make my pieces feel a little more fluid.

What's your favourite botanical piece that you've made?
My 'Mindcelium' block print. As I said before, I am very inspired by mushrooms, so I wanted to create a piece that captures the delicate balance between man and nature and how we communicate with our ecosystem.

What does a typical day in the studio look like for you?
A typical day in my home studio starts with making myself a coffee and sitting in the studio room so I can get into the headspacc of working. I water all my plants and play with my cat before putting on a podcast, lighting some incense and starting my day. This helps me get into the zone with minimal distractions from the outside world.

What's the best advice you'd give to a new printmaker?
Have patience with your practice and to make sure you map out all your lines before you start carving. I really struggle to see the lines that I have carved, so I often stain my linoleum a contrasting colour with watered-down acrylic. Keep your tools razor sharp and clean as you go. A messy space makes for messy prints!

PRINTING ON FABRIC

There is something magical in hand-printing your own fabrics; designing them to be just as you want them is an exciting prospect with many possibilities. In this chapter, I'll introduce you to the techniques of creating botanical pattern repeats before the practical techniques of printing your designs onto fabric. In my own work, I tend to make repeat patterns when working with fabric, so it felt right to include the design principles alongside fabric printing here, too.

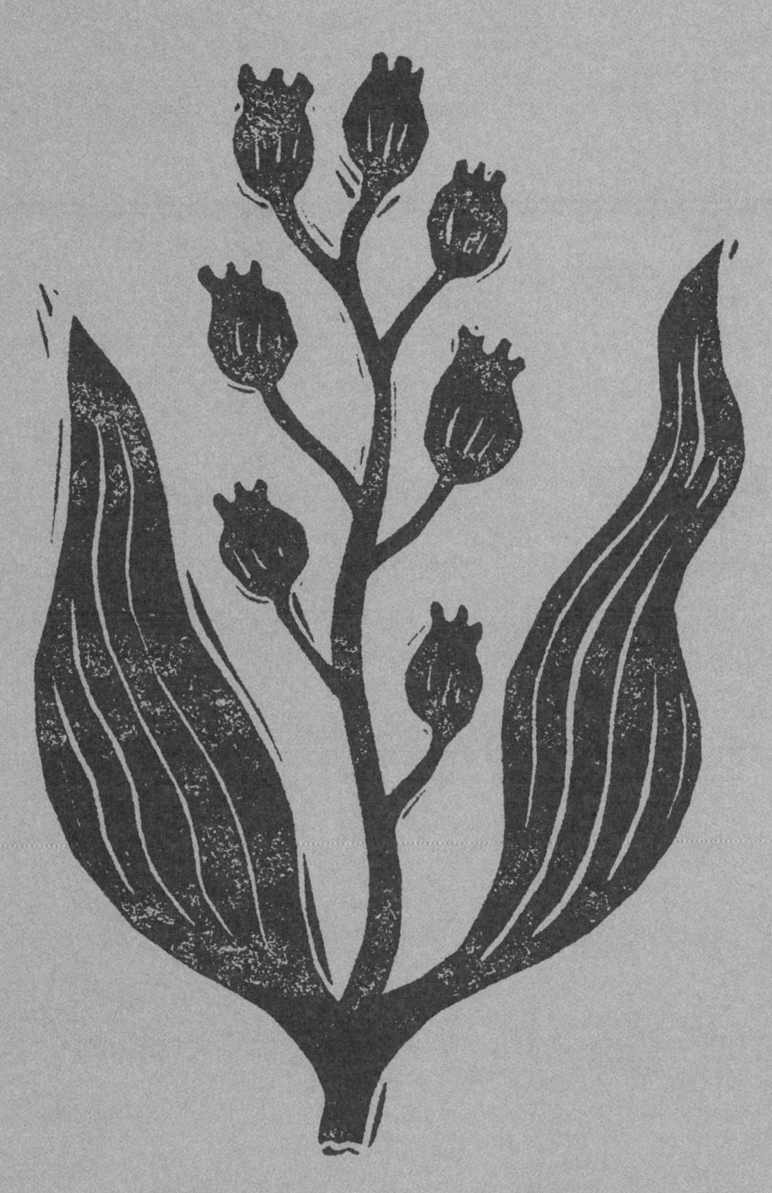

Creating Botanical Repeats

For pattern inspiration, consider contemporary designers like Marthe Armitage or Jen Hewitt, or masters such as William Morris. Creating repeat patterns isn't exclusively for fabric; they're essential for paper products, like wallpaper. Below are a few recognized techniques for creating repeat patterns that flow for you to replicate and explore.

Uniform Repeats

It can be daunting knowing where to start. I've put together some simple botanical patterns below, which you are free to trace and try out as a springboard to your own designs.

A NOTE ON SIZE

When hand-printing, smaller/simpler blocks are a lot easier to print. The bigger your block, the harder it is to get an even consistency. Unless you plan on using a press for each part of your pattern (a highly laborious process) then I recommend working on a smaller, palm-sized scale.

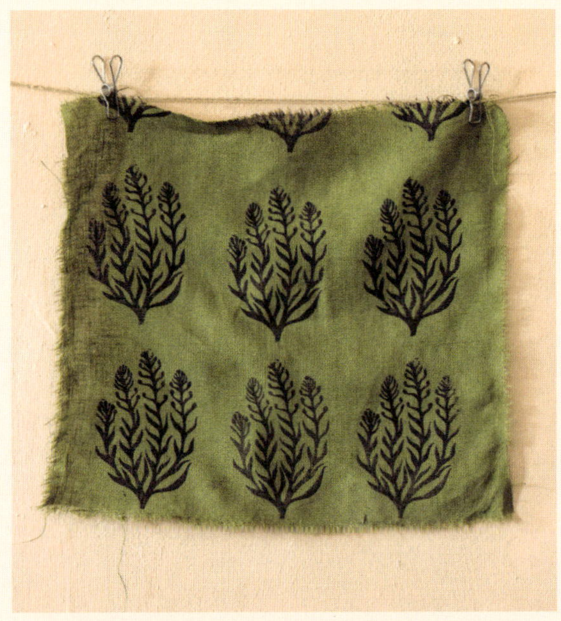

CLASSIC REPEAT
Side-by-side placement with the same design repeated again and again in a uniform grid.

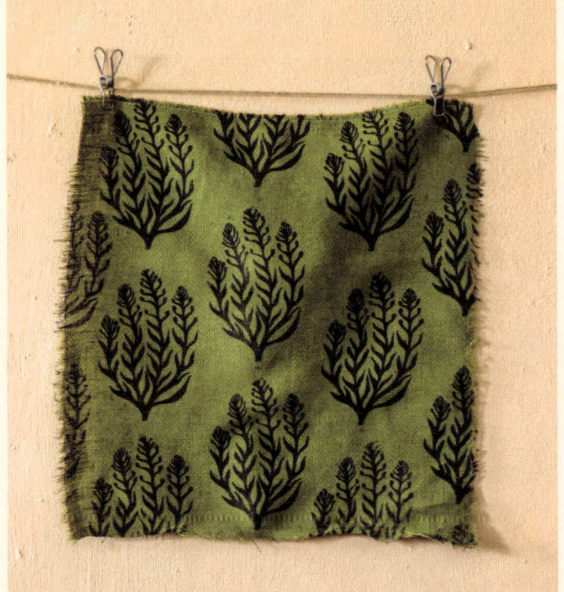

HALF DROP
Repeated design in vertical columns with a half drop between rows. This is a great way of making your design look less uniform and formal.

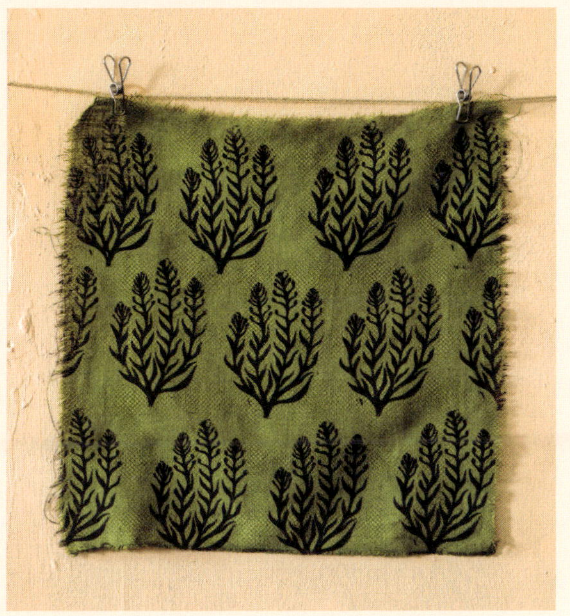

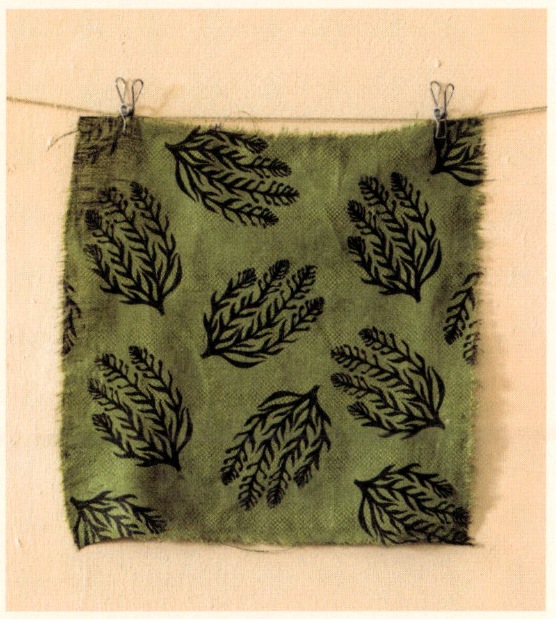

BRICK PATTERN

Similar to the half drop but this time you're working horizontally across your fabric in a similar way to how bricks are laid in a wall.

RANDOM OR TOSSED

A layout with a variety of different blocks or images placed at random throughout the design.

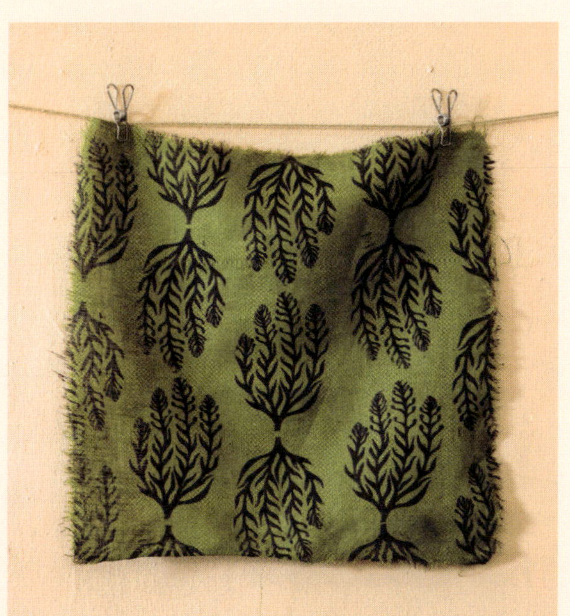

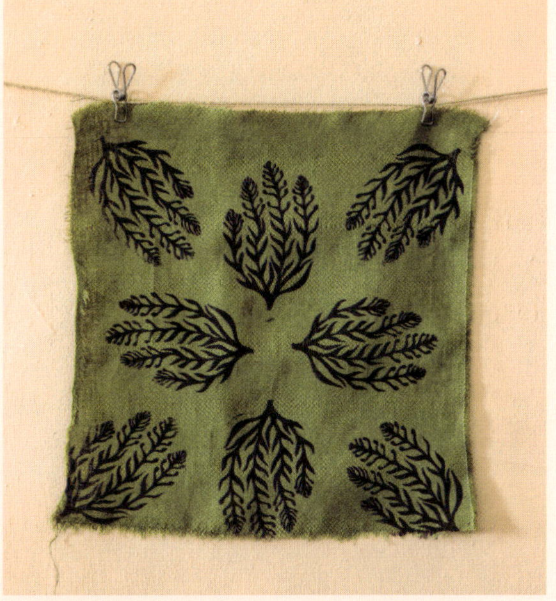

DIAMOND

The design is laid down in a diamond shape, corner to corner, working vertically down the surface. This works well for square designs.

MIRROR REPEAT

Placed corner to corner, much like the diamond style, but turning the block on its head with each alternate line of the pattern.

Flowing Patterns

Once you've explored the simple block techniques, you may want to try creating patterns that flow across your fabric. Below are two of my favourite techniques for achieving this.

TIP *Consider using a leaf or bud at the point that the block ends to hide the slightly different inking from block to block.*

CUT-THROUGH

This is a straightforward technique for creating a repeat pattern with multiple elements. The benefits of a design like this are that, once it comes to printing, the irregular shape of the block makes it easier to line up each print by eye.

YOU WILL NEED

Intended print block
Sheet of paper
Pencil
Scissors

1. Draw around your lino block onto a piece of paper and cut to size. Begin filling in with your designs of botanical forms. The idea is that you draw around the elements so that it's at random and makes a more seamless final design.

2. Draw a line from edge to edge top to bottom through the centre of your design without cutting into any of the forms. Cut along this line.

3. Flip or rotate one half, then tape the two straight edges together from behind and you should have something that looks step 3, below.

4. Fill in any gaps either with more motifs or extend the ones you've already drawn to fill the empty space.

5. Repeat the process horizontally, cutting a line through your design, rotating one half, and sticking the straight edges together.

6. You should now have an irregular and seamlessly flowing design that is ready to be transferred to your block and carved.

2

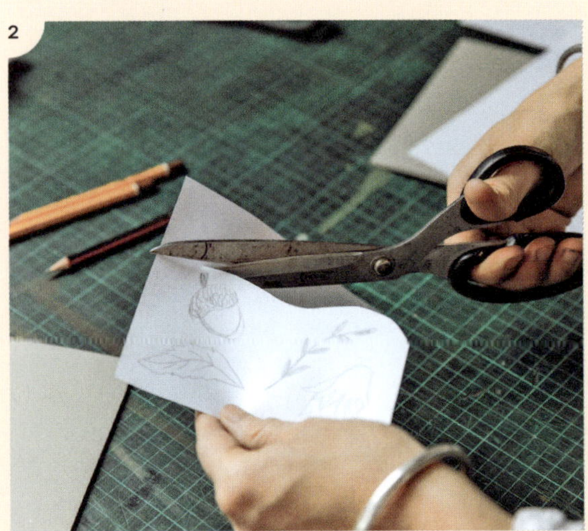

3

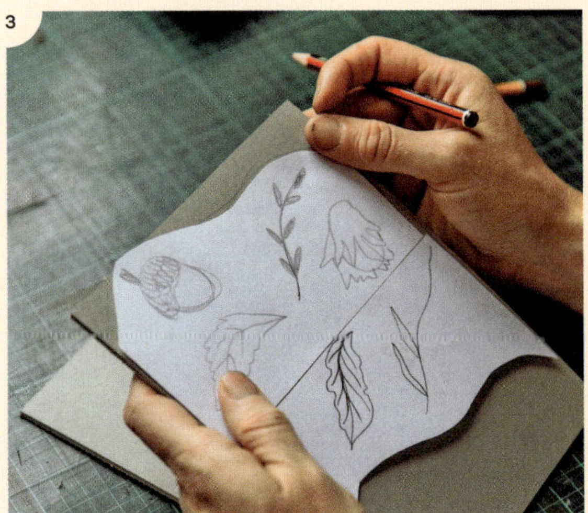

PAPER FOLDING

This simple technique is brilliant for creating balanced repeat patterns. Once you have the hang of it, it opens up so many possibilities for design. It's ideal for creating tile blocks that flow beautifully – great subjects to try are rambling brambles, ivy, and rosehips.

YOU WILL NEED

Intended print block
Sheet of paper
Pencil
Scissors

1. Cut a piece of paper down to the same size as your lino block. Draw the main part of your design in the centre, then turn the paper over so the design is face down, and fold the top and bottom edges in to meet in the middle.

2. Connect your design together across the join where the edges meet and fill in any gaps that may become apparent. It can be useful to place a bud or leaf at the connection point in your design as this shows up the edges less when you come to print later.

3. Repeat the process vertically, folding the outer edges to meet in the middle, connecting the design across the join again and filling in any gaps if you wish.

4. Once complete you should have a seamlessly flowing pattern ready to transfer to your block.

1

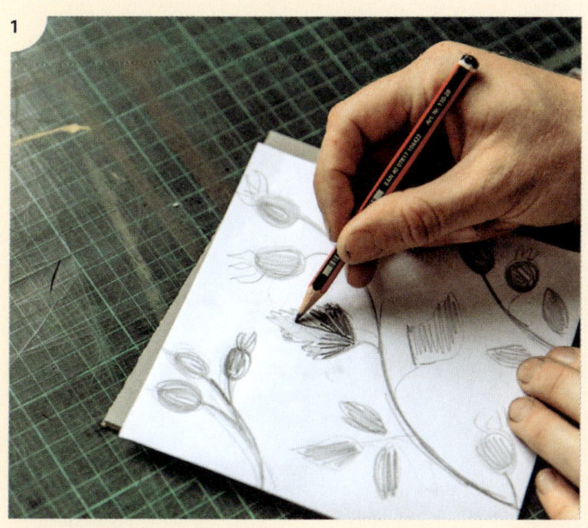

2

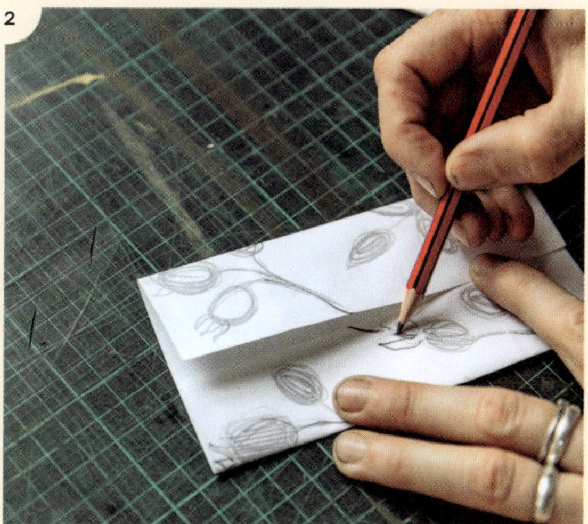

Fabric Printing

Once you have created your fabric design and carved your block, you are ready to print. I have explained two techniques below for inking and printing onto fabric, and given you a couple of projects to encourage you to transform your beautiful designs into everyday objects.

Once mastered, all the skills and techniques outlined in these projects can be applied to pretty much anything fabric based, from a pillowcase to tea towels, t-shirts, bags, and more. For each of the projects it is possible to interchange both techniques – block printing and hand-printing with a roller – for similar results; it just depends on which set-up you prefer. If you'd like to try the techniques without worrying about making your own designs just yet, feel free to simply trace and transfer the designs used here.

Preparing Your Fabric

Before printing, wash all fabric with a simple detergent at a recommended temperature for the fabric type, avoiding fabric softener as it leaves a residue. You want to remove anything that could form a barrier for your print, such as dirt or oil stains, as these can get in the way of your ink or can cause it to spread.

Ironing is also an important step that is easy to skip, but will save you time when printing. Creases and folds in your fabric can so easily mess up all your hard work, so take the time to prepare and iron before you begin.

PRINTING BLOCKS

For all the fabric printing projects in this chapter I recommend using pink speedy carve blocks (see page 17) for their washability and hardwearing nature. However, you can also print on fabric using traditional lino – just make sure the hessian backing doesn't get too wet as it may warp. Similarly, wood can be effective, but it may benefit from sealing before use to prevent it from warping.

TIP *Natural fabrics are generally more absorbent than paper. When block printing on fabric I find applying more ink leads to a better print. This is also another reason to aim for bolder designs, as detail won't be lost in the inking.*

Block Printing

For this technique, we are replicating an Indian block print workshop and creating our own inking pad for our blocks rather than using a roller. It's a faster technique for covering a wider surface area quickly. Doing it this way around also allows us to make multiple prints on the same surface without smudging and to accurately line up our prints by eye.

TIP *When printing large pieces of fabric, I like to use a clear ruler, or a piece of paper, with the spacing between blocks pre-marked out to keep me on track.*

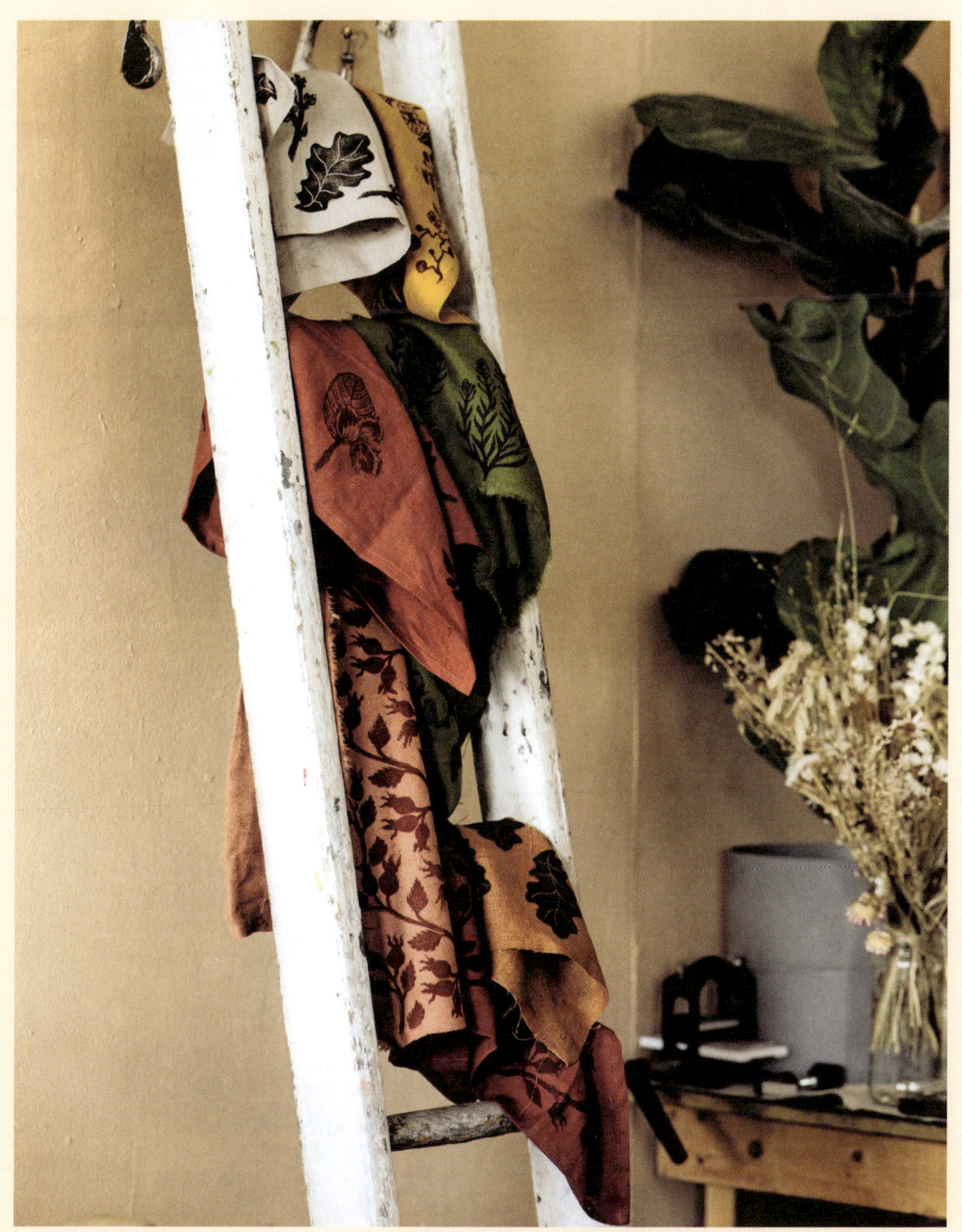

Using a Stamp Ink Pad

For the stamp pad to work, it is important you water down your inks a little. Most printmaking inks are very thick, even those designed especially for fabric printing. I keep my diluted inks in squeezy bottles so that they don't dry out in between uses. A ratio of 70 per cent ink to 30 per cent water usually works well, but you may have to play a little to get a good consistency, depending on which ink you choose.

YOU WILL NEED
Prepared lino block or stamp
Paper for design
Tracing paper/carbon paper
Permanent marker pen
Scrap fabric for inking surface
Felt or cotton for ink pad
Tray for ink pad
Ink - Speedball or Cranfield inks are great for fabric
Felt or cotton for ink pad
Scrap cotton for testing
Fabric for printing
Baren, hammer, or roller for printing
Metre ruler

4

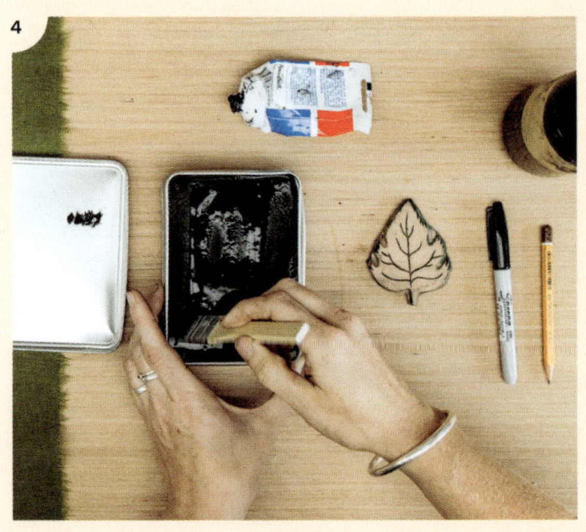

1. Design a simple and bold stamp. Transfer to a lino block with your chosen transfer technique (see pages 102–107), mark out with permanent marker, and carve (see page 39). Remove any cleared corners with scissors to help with placement when repeating.

2. Prepare your surface by laying down scrap fabric. Remove folds and clamp if necessary.

3. Prepare your ink pad. Take a piece of felt, or layer some thick cotton and cut down to size so that they fit snugly in a tray. The fabric pad absorbs the ink and creates bounce for your block as you press to pick up ink for each impression.

4. Apply ink to the stamp pad in the tray; err on the side of caution here, start with just a little at a time until the fabric is fully saturated.

5. Take your block and press it on the surface of the felt stamp pad; aim for full coverage without it seeping into the carved areas. Getting the ink quantity-to-felt ratio right is a matter of trial and error.

6. Place the block face down on your fabric and apply pressure to the back. It will require some pressure from your palm in order to print consistently. You can experiment with using a hammer, baren, or a clean roller to add a little pressure and help get even coverage. Make a few test pieces on cotton scraps.

7. For each print you will have to re-ink your stamp pad and realign your block on the fabric. You can use a ruler to aid you with this, or paper with the spacing marked out.

8. Play with layout patterns described on pages 128–129, such as brick, half drop, or diamond. You can use a large metre ruler to help you line your blocks up as you go, by measuring out the spacing you want in between each block and repeating.

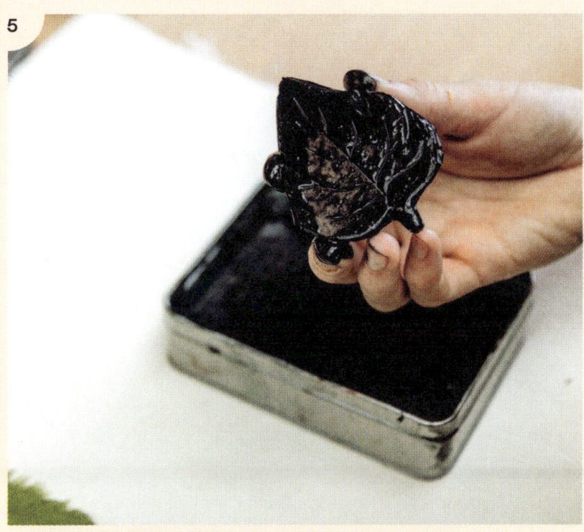
5

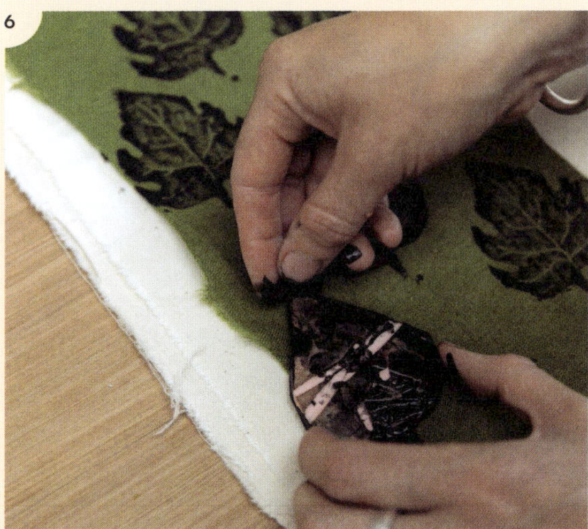
6

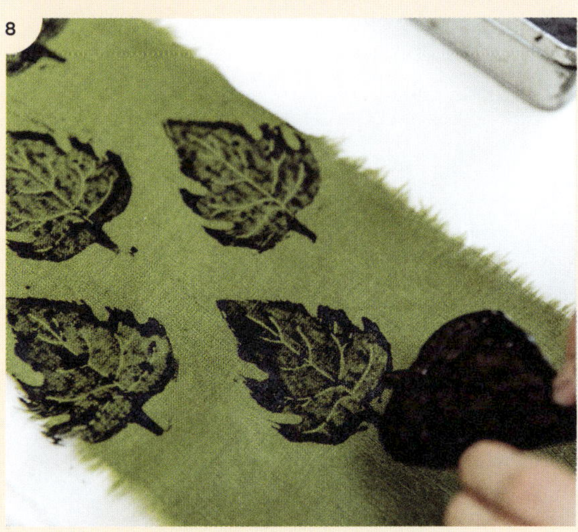
8

Block Print Runner

There's nothing nicer than inviting friends over for a big feast! Make it even more wonderful by using the block printing method to create a beautifully hand-painted talking point for the centre of your table.

YOU WILL NEED

Prepared speedy-carve carved lino block or stamp
Scrap fabric for inking surface
Felt or cotton for ink pad
Tray for ink pad
Ink - Speedball or Cranfield inks are great for fabric
Scrap cotton for testing
Linen runner
Baren, hammer, or roller for printing
Metre ruler

FABRIC CHOICES

You can buy pre-sewn table runners easily, but if you've got the hang of a sewing machine, they are simple to put together. For this project I've suggested using linen, but bear in mind that the thread count for linen can vary massively and the looser the thread count the harder it will be to pull a decent print because of gaps between the threads. Cotton and hemp are also great options.

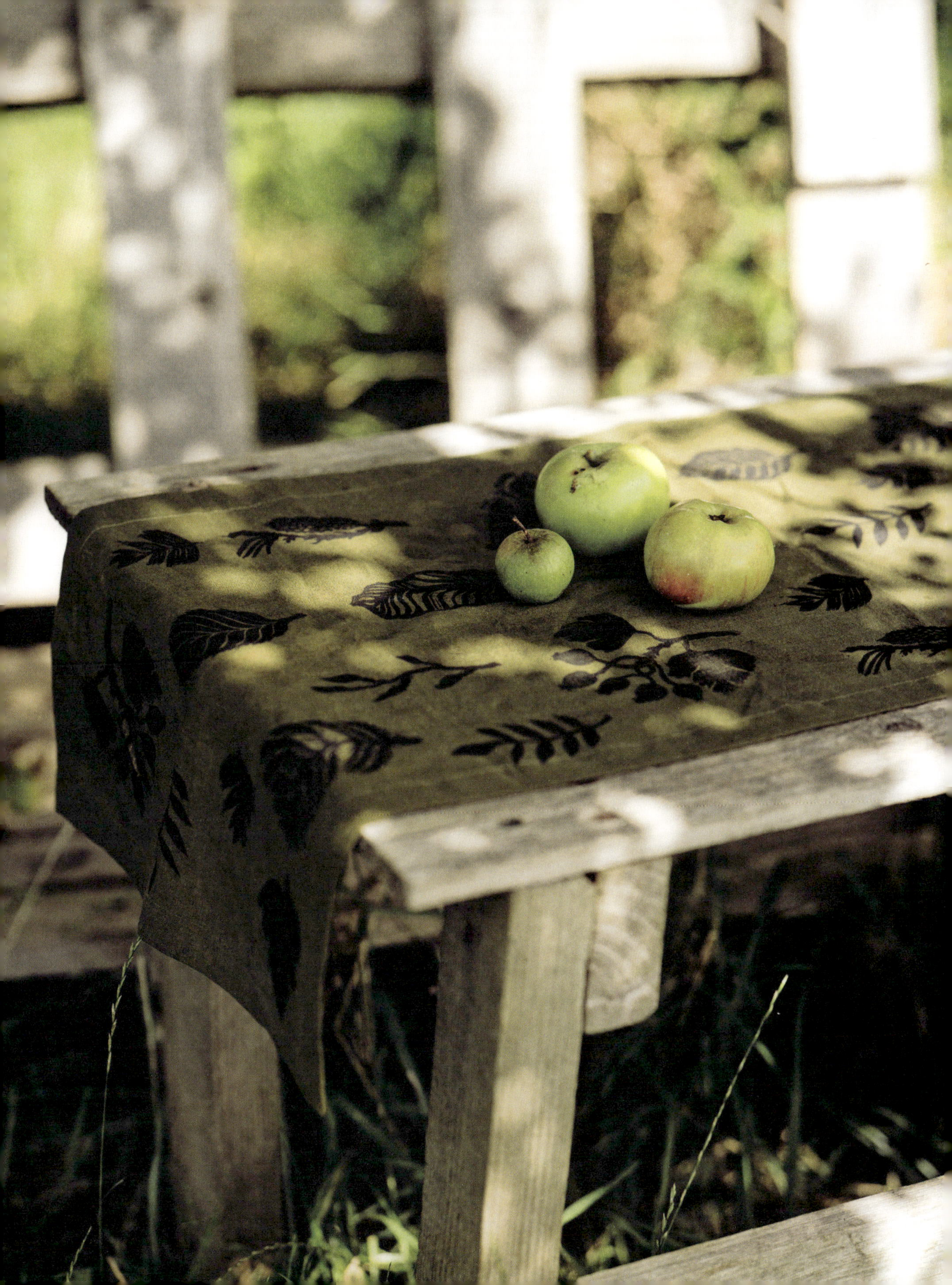

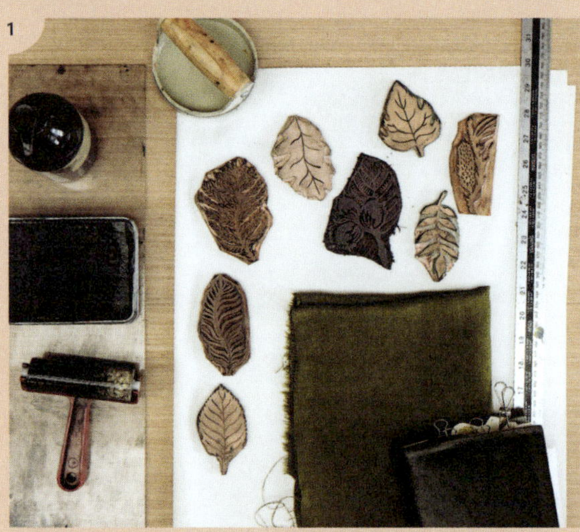

1. Prep your surface area and ink pad following the instructions on pages 134–135.

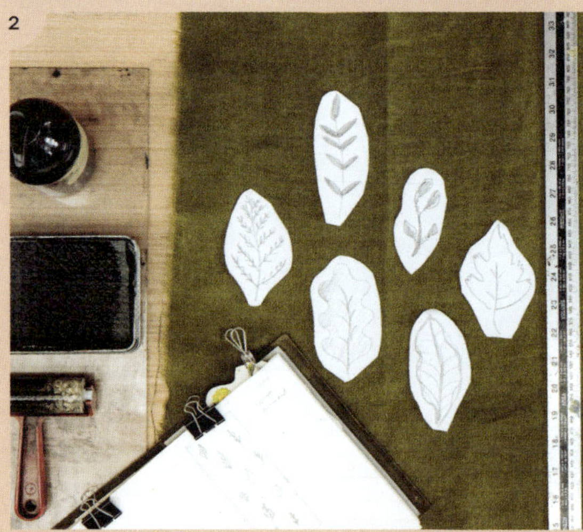

2. Create a plan for your block placement on your runner, either in your sketchbook or by using cut-out drawings of your blocks laid on the fabric.

3. Begin to ink up your block and work from left to right across your fabric, or the opposite way if you're left-handed. Be mindful of smudging the ink and keeping your hands clean as you work.

3

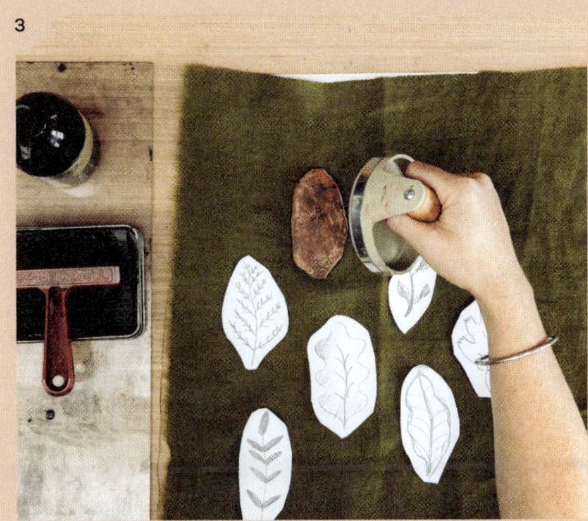

4. Once dry, iron to set your ink in place.

5. Set a beautiful table with a feast and invite your friends to enjoy it.

4

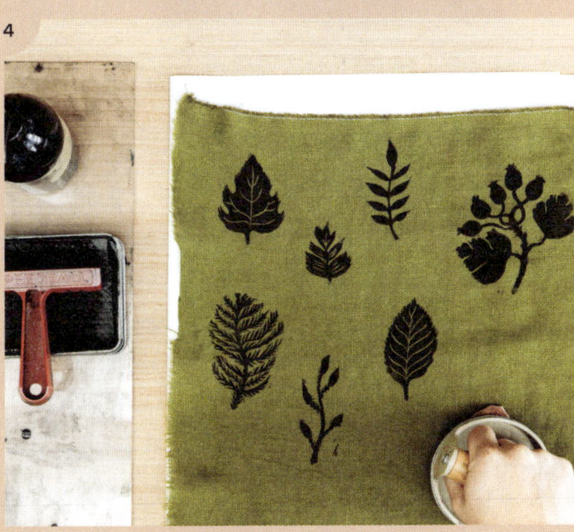

Hand-print Napkin

I love a traditional hankie or napkin in my pocket to catch all that life as a mother of three throws at me. They are so versatile, and a simple bold print really lifts them up. I use napkins I find in charity shops but if you prefer to start with the raw fabric and sew the edges up later, you'll have an easier time getting an even surface coverage and more flexibility with your design.

For this project we are going to use the traditional inking and roller set-up and printing by hand. Printing with the roller is a slightly more labour-intensive process, as for each small block print, you are hand-rolling your block with ink rather than simply stamping it. However, I find that this technique gets a better ink coverage and more solid final print.

YOU WILL NEED

Prepared A5 speedy carve lino block
Pencil
Paper for design
Tracing paper or carbon paper
Permanent marker pen
Ruler
Carving tools
Fabric inks
Scrap fabric for testing
Felt pad for inks
Baren, hammer, or roller for printing
Washed napkin or handkerchief, or square
of unsewn linen for hemming later

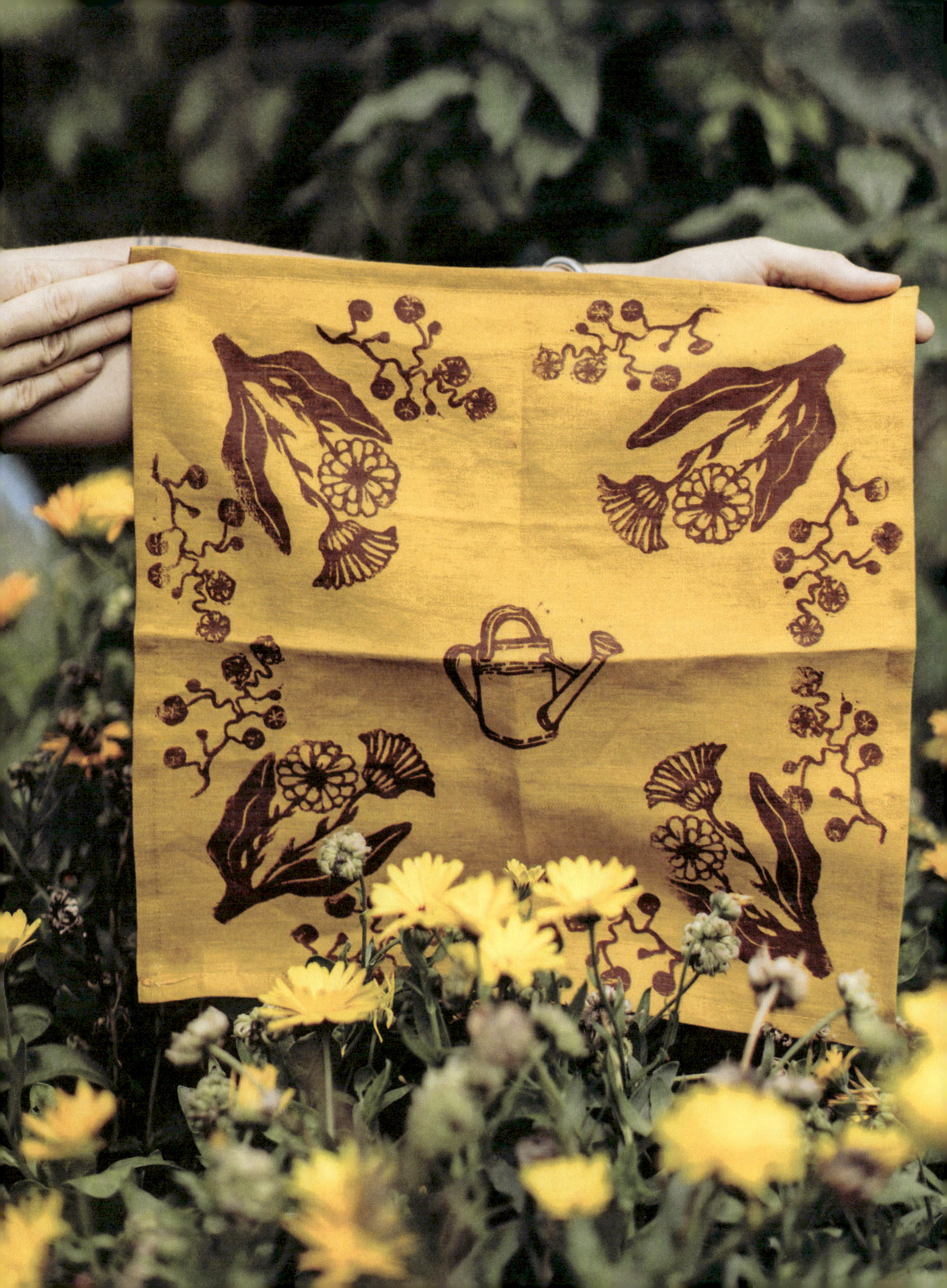

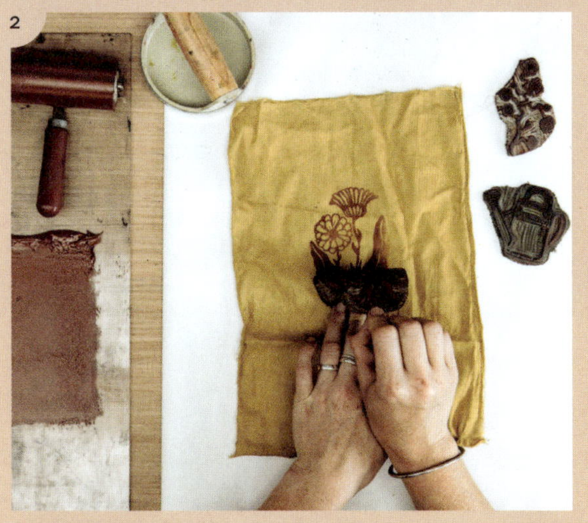

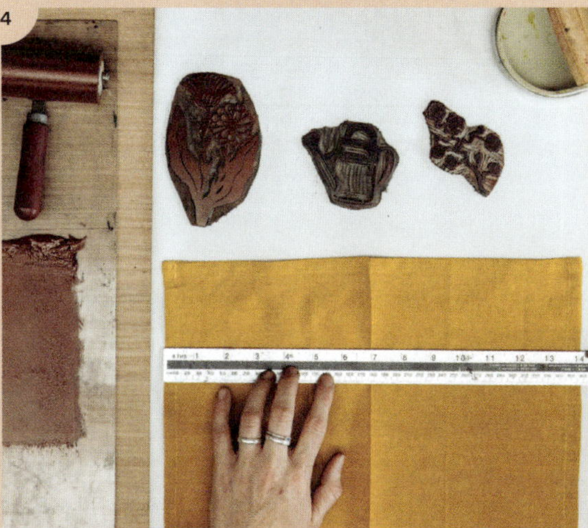

1. Design your fabric stamp: think bold, simple, and straightforward to repeat. Transfer to your lino block with your chosen transfer technique (see pages 102–107), mark out with permanent marker, and carve (see page 39).

2. Ink up and flip your block over to test print on scrap fabric or paper to see if there are any areas you've missed. It takes a bit of pressure from the palm of your hand to print properly, or alternatively use a baren or clean roller on the back to apply pressure.

3. Once you're happy, test out the block repeat (see page 128) or one of the other techniques, and choose the one you prefer.

4. Measure out your napkin and find a central point. Alternatively fold the napkin in half and use that as your starting point. I find that starting in the centre and working out from there helps to balance the pattern.

A NOTE ON ROLLERS

The type of roller you use when fabric printing depends on the ink. If you are using a more liquid-viscosity ink, such as Speedball fabric ink, then it's wise to invest in a tight foam roller. If you are using traditional printmaking inks that have been approved for fabric printing, then a normal printmaker's roller will work perfectly well (see page 20).

5. Use a ruler or pre-marked paper to keep your placement even.

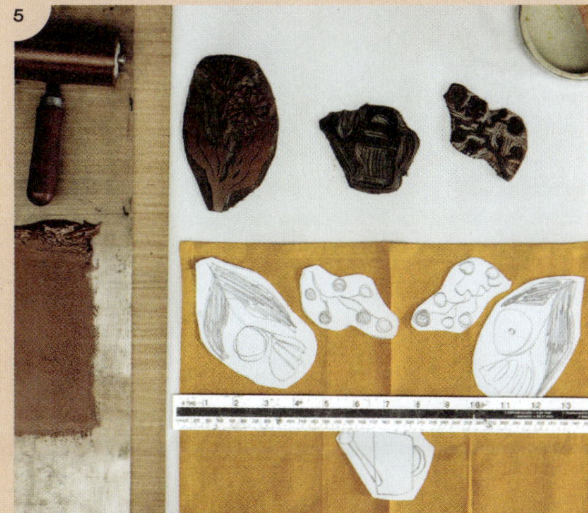

6. Work out from the central point and use scrap paper underneath the fabric to catch any overprint.

7. Once you've finished, hang up to dry on a washing line, taking care not to peg the inky areas as your design may smudge. When ready and dry to touch, iron to set the inks in place.

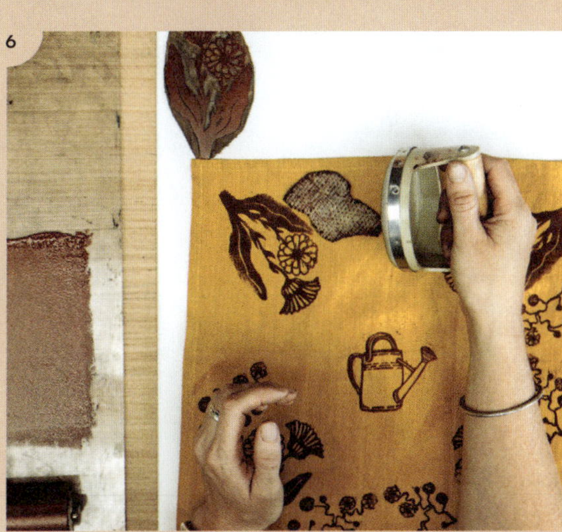

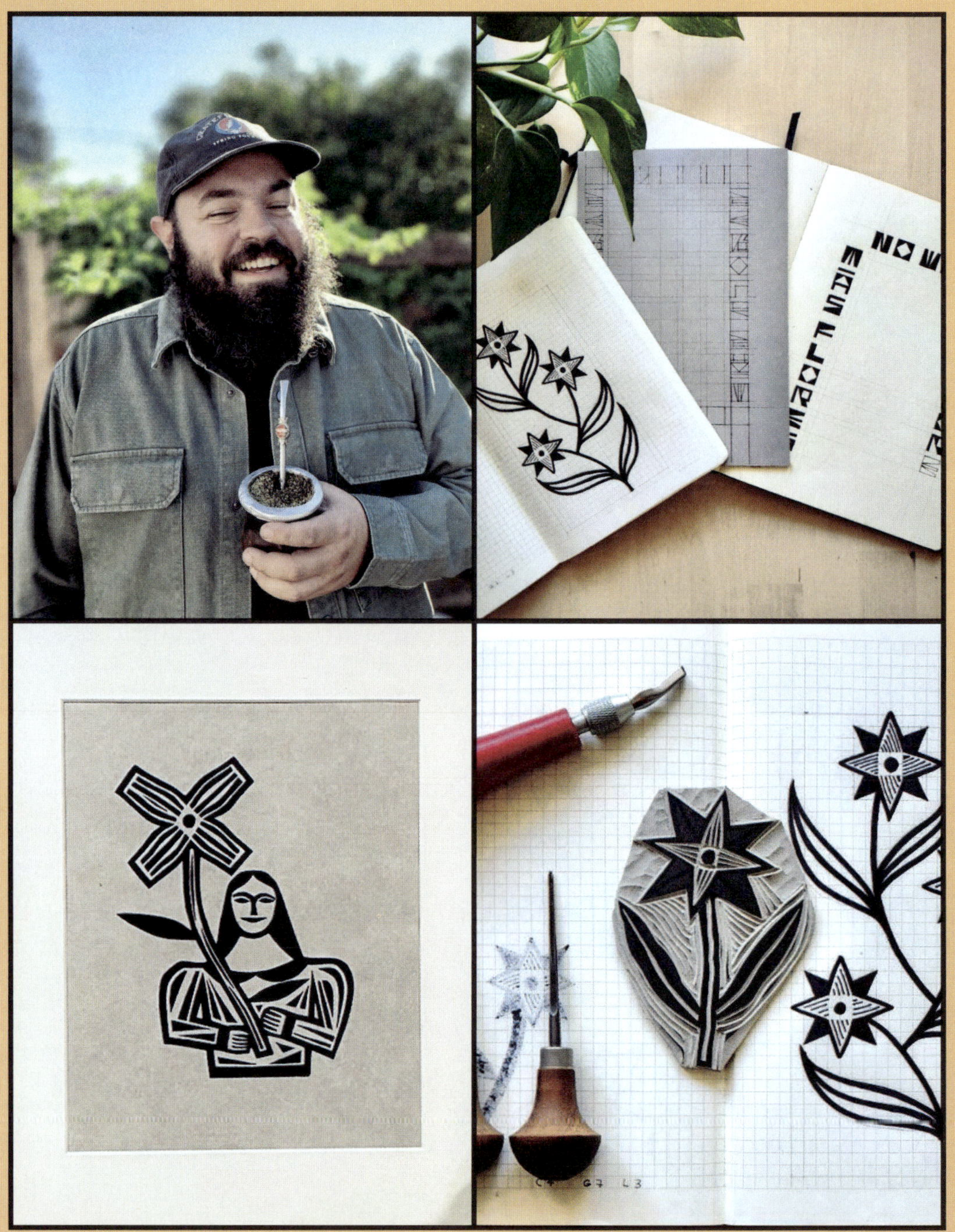
NOW

Ysidro

Where do you work and what materials do you work with?
I don't have a studio. The stress of adding another bill for a studio lease is unappealing to me. I do all my work from my one-bedroom apartment. Admittedly, it's a cramped working space, so maximizing room is key. I've got a small folding desk I bought from Ikea which is where I do most of my sketching and carving. I ink up and hand-pull my prints on the kitchen countertop.

How did you start making prints?
My path to becoming a printmaker was unconventional, to say the least. I didn't go to art school and started when I was in my late 30s, after being fired as a commercial pipefitter. While I was collecting unemployment, I decided I wanted to give printmaking a try. And, voila, here I am! I haven't stopped since.

Where do you go for inspiration for your work?
It's easy to slip into a rut. When I do, it's time to shake things up; I've got to get out of my head. That's when I pick up a rod and go fishing. I love angling in the evening. It's relaxing, and, usually, the bite picks up, which is always a plus.

What does a typical day in the studio look like for you?
I don't have the luxury of starting my printmaking session with a routine to get myself psyched. I'm a full-time commercial truck driver for a nationwide corporation, which means I work 12 to 13 hours 5 times a week simply to keep a roof over my head. On the weekends, I've got my two little girls. They are still young enough that they enjoy spending quality time with me. I don't do anything else on the weekends that isn't centred around them. So, how much time does that leave me for printmaking? Not much at all. I've got about one or two hours at night to sketch or carve. That's about all I can do for now; I still have to make ends meet, unfortunately. The life of a working stiff, no matter how romanticized it is by people who don't work blue-collar jobs, is a hard one. Being reminded, daily, that you don't matter, that the lives of your loved ones don't matter compared to the importance of the external, arbitrary, socioeconomic forces that shape our lives is soul-crushing. But pushing back for one or two hours a day to recapture my humanity is worth it; it's a direct act of joyful rebellion.

What's the best advice you'd give to a new printmaker?
As a child, I internalized all the negative labels that my teachers and the religious community members of my parent's faith had assigned me. Admittedly I was, like most boys, a handful. I was rambunctious, loud, confident, and uninterested in work. By the time I reached adulthood, I'd become hireable. For two decades, I picked up any job I could whose cheques wouldn't bounce when I'd cash them weekly. I had no interest in pursuing higher education, much less attending art school. The thought of institutional learning nauseated me. I couldn't imagine being anything other than a manual worker.

Where am I going with all this? Here's the hard-earned advice I'd share with anyone who'd listen: start small. I began my journey as a printmaker (albeit, I had no intention of becoming a printmaker) when I bought the cheapest spiral notebook at Walmart with the simple objective to sketch in it for 30 minutes a day. That seemingly inconsequential decision has snowballed into what you see me doing now. So, start small. Be consistent. Everything else, in due time, will fall into its proper place as your journey unfolds.

COLOUR PRINTING

Once you've got to grips with the basics of pulling a print, you may feel ready to start exploring colour. At first, this can feel intimidating, for there's so much more to consider in terms of labour, processes, and time. However, it doesn't have to be daunting. In this chapter, I introduce four simple techniques for printing in colour that'll hopefully dispel some of that trepidation and allow you to confidently develop your print practice.

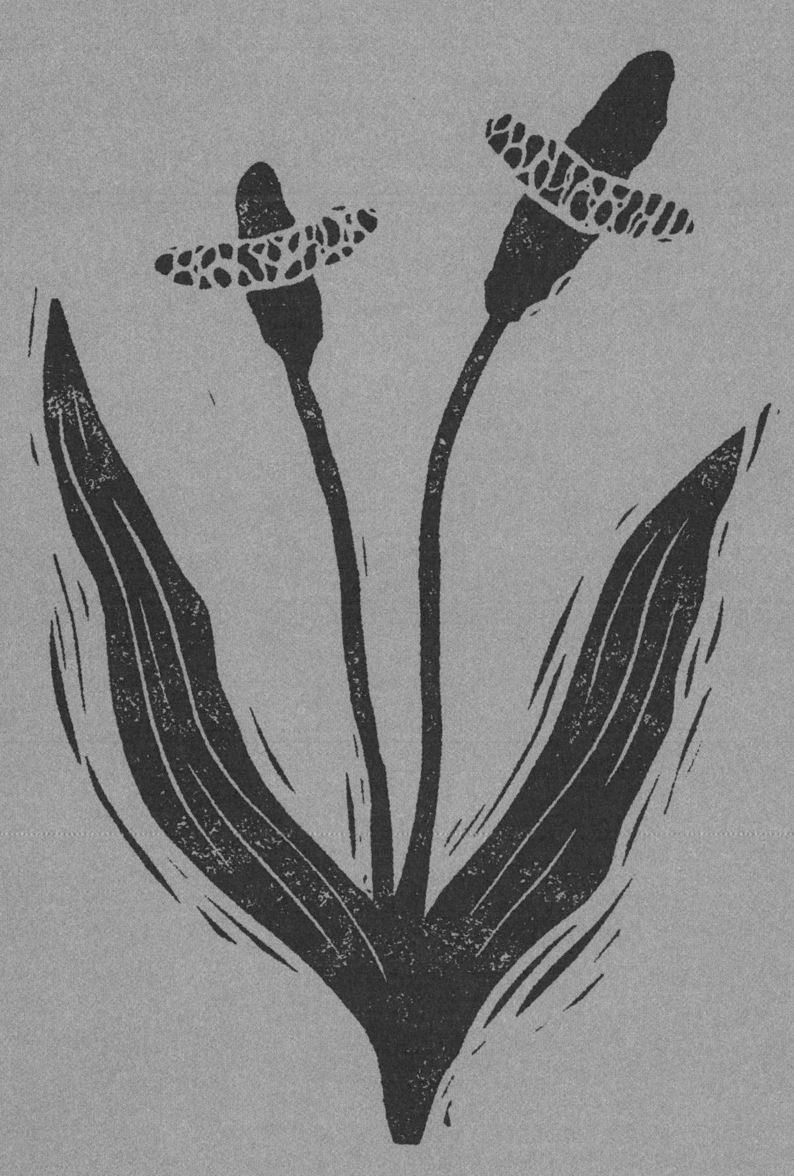

Colour Theory

Before you begin designing with colour, it is worth having at least a basic understanding of colour theory and how different colours interact with each other.

You will already have a subconscious understanding of colour from everyday life, from the clothes you choose to wear to the artwork you are drawn to. Learning how to understand those choices and how to pair colours together for harmony or contrast, is a vital step in making beautiful prints.

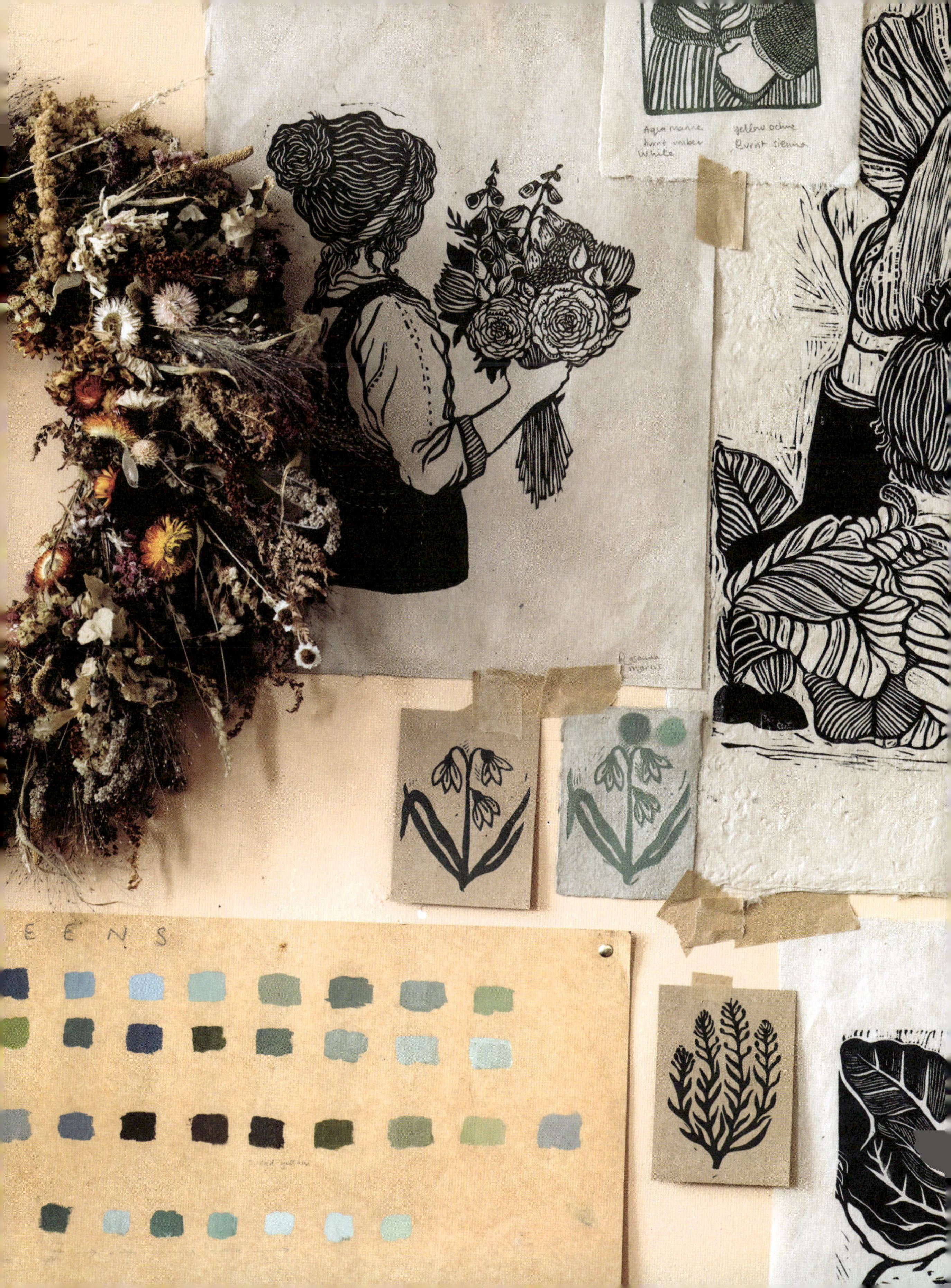
Aqua marine
burnt umber
White
yellow ochre
Burnt sienna
EENS

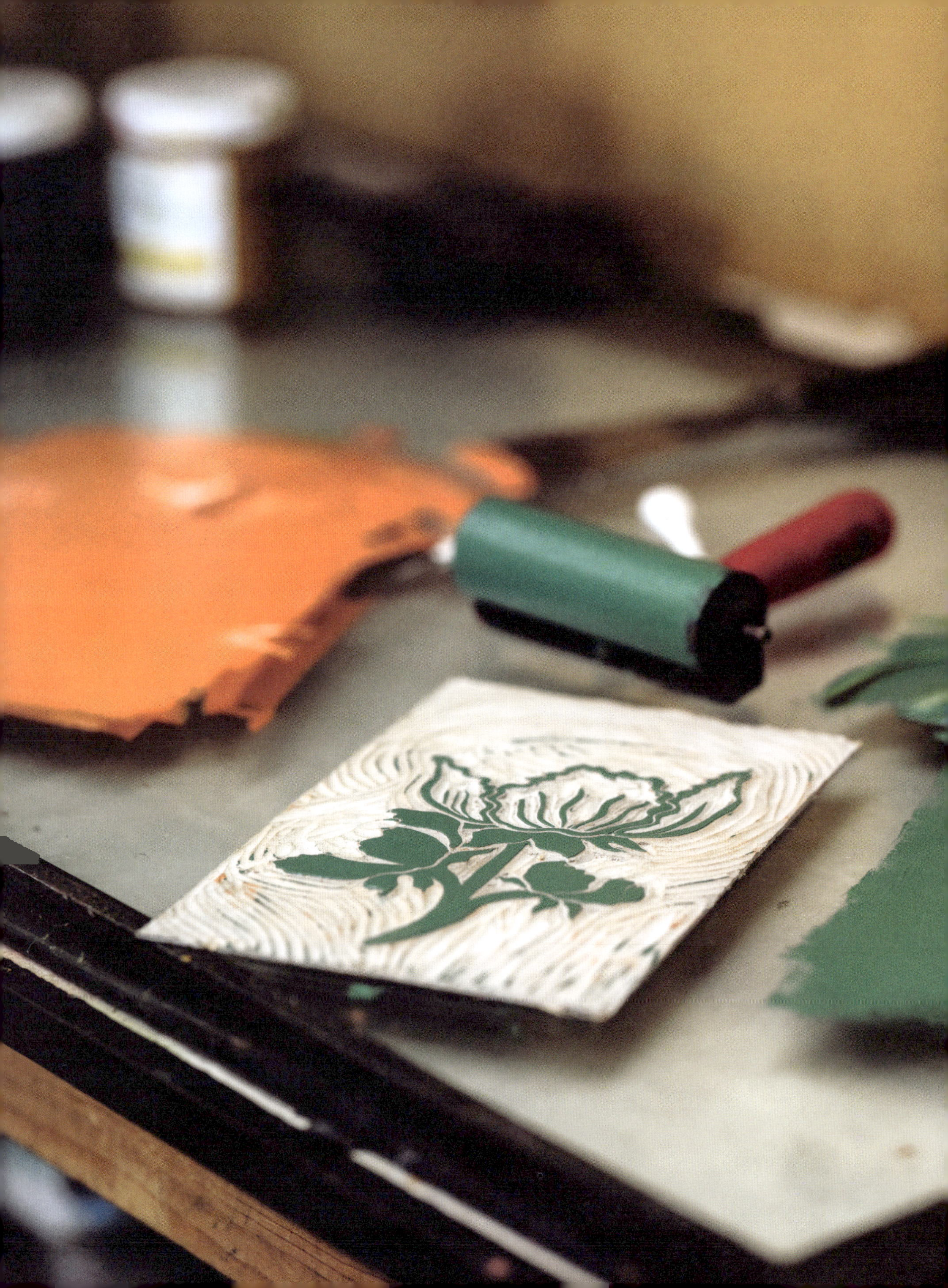

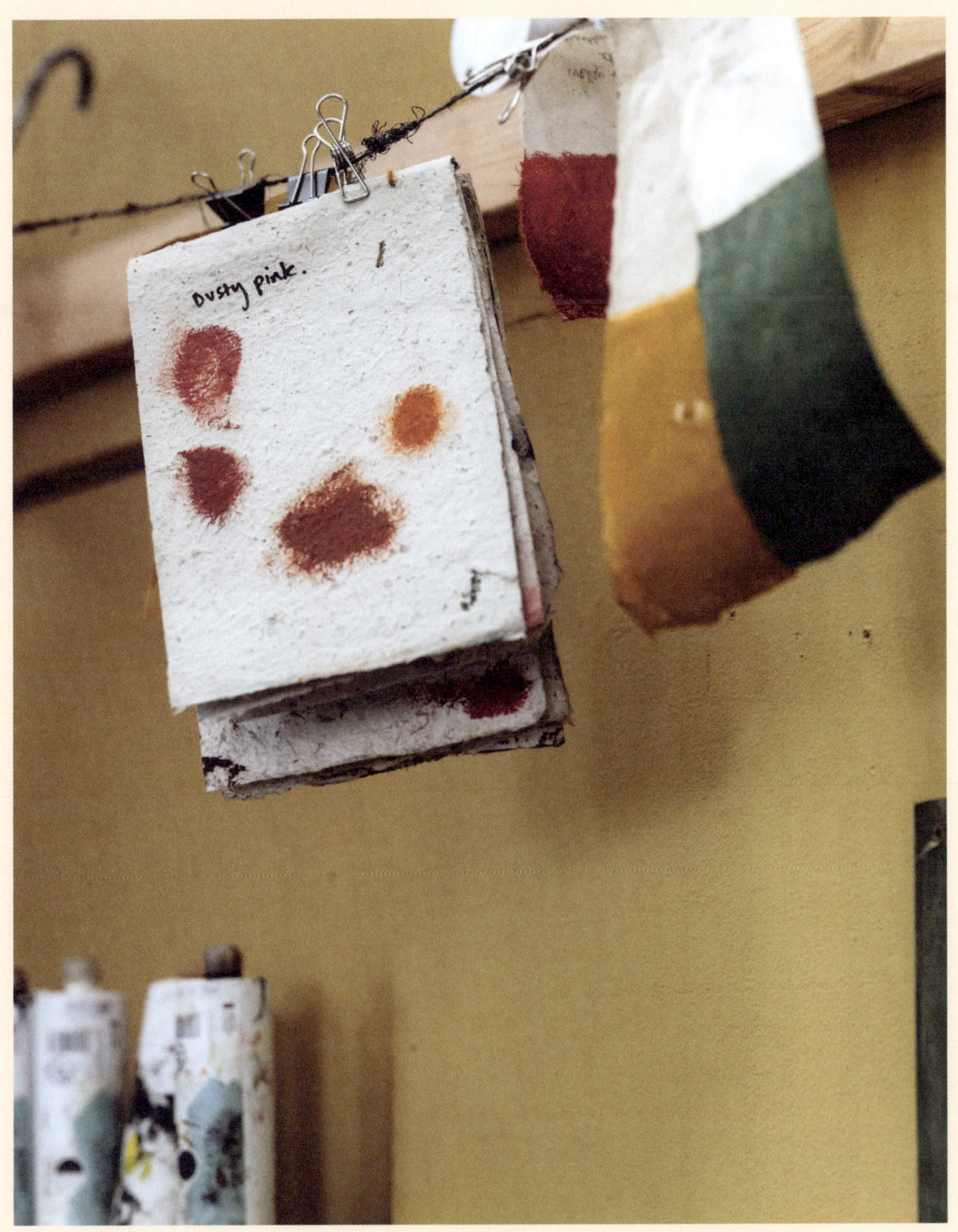
Dusty pink.

The Colour Wheel

A great place to start is with the good, old-fashioned colour wheel. First conceived and drawn out by Sir Isaac Newton in his work *Opticks* in 1704, it has been redrawn and referenced by artists, scientists, and poets throughout the ages.

The colour wheel shows the relationships between colours. It is a helpful tool for using colour placement in your work, for understanding the effects that colours have on each other, and of our perception of them when seen in different combinations.

HARMONIOUS COLOURS

To create harmony and a 'gentleness' on the eye in your prints, choose colours that sit next to each other on the tertiary colour wheel, with one dominant colour and then shades of this blended with the next colour on either side. As with many things in life, these combinations usually work best in combinations of three.

COMPLEMENTARY COLOURS

These colours are positioned directly opposite each other on the tertiary colour wheel – red and green, blue and orange, yellow and purple. When used next to each other in a design they can create dynamic contrast. They kind of clash but also complement each other, can be uplifting or dramatic to the eye, and make for punchier prints.

I love the effects that orange and blue create for bright and satisfying contrast, or the warm, sickly sweet combination of pinks and greens.

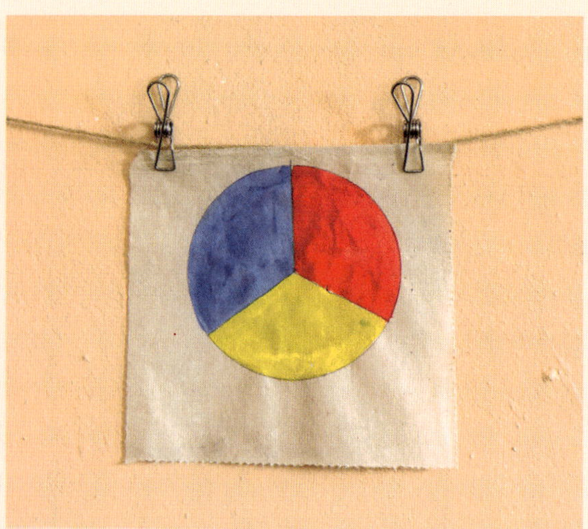

A primary colour wheel shows the three primary colours – red, blue, and yellow – from which all other colours are derived and that cannot be mixed by combining other colours together.

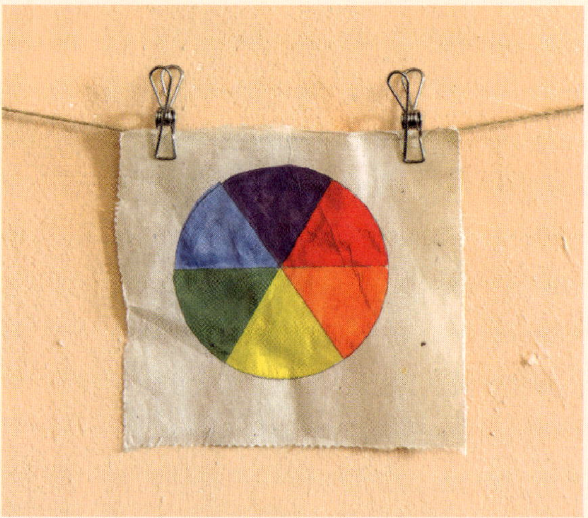

A secondary colour wheel is formed by mixing the primary colours with each other; red and yellow make orange, red and blue make purple, and blue and yellow make green.

COLOUR TEMPERATURE

You can use the 'temperature' of colours to influence the perception of depth (cool colours recede, warm colours advance), and also to have an emotional impact, where cooler colours are calmer and quieter, and warmer colours convey more drama and excitement.

ADDING WHITE

Treating white as a colour and adding it to your inks to create varying tints is another way of creating balance and harmony in your prints. A great exercise that explores this is to create a colour chart: take some scrap paper and see how many increments of your main colour can be achieved as you mix in differing amounts of white. Pin it up in your studio and use it as a reference the next time you are planning a print.

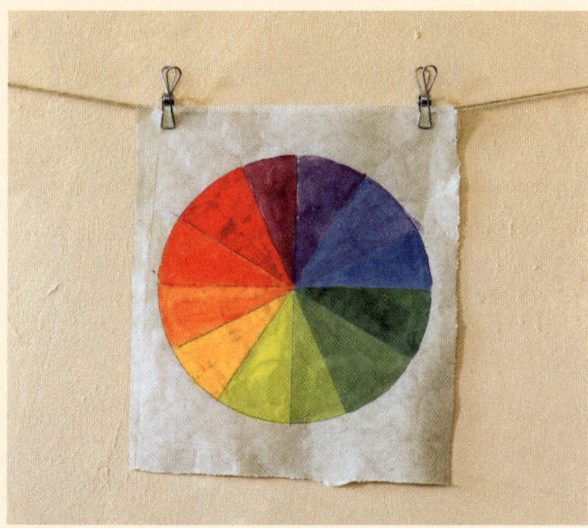

The tertiary colour wheel contains the colours that you get from mixing the secondary colours together: yellow-orange, red-orange, red-purple, blue-purple, blue-green, and yellow-green.

Choosing Colours

In my own work, I'm drawn to the natural tones found in earth pigments: raw and burnt siennas, raw and burnt umbers, and ochres. They have a warmth and weight to them that I love to combine with handmade papers. I also tend to go for the phthalo blues and phthalo greens, which can range from spring green tones through to deep warm blues.

I keep a sketchbook to record the blends I mix for specific prints so that I can come back to finish editions later. It's also a place for me to play and experiment with colour, although it's all very much by eye and I tend to record ratios rather than specific measurements.

KEEPING TRACK OF YOUR COLOURS

Once you start paying attention to the colours and combinations you are drawn to, it's a good idea to keep a note of them somewhere: a scrapbook of collected imagery, a pinboard in the studio, or an album of screenshots on your phone. Get into the habit of collecting this material and you will always have something to fall back on when you're stumped for choice.

To explore colour further, research how to combine colours and then take the time to make your own colour palettes. Mapping out the colours you love and their most effective combinations onto large sheets of paper is a time-consuming process but can form a brilliant resource when you're deep in the design stage in the future.

Printing from Nature

Making botanical prints directly from found materials is the most satisfying printmaking experience. Essentially, it's a foolproof technique for making beautiful imagery. You are printing directly from the natural world and utilizing its beautifully pre-formed flora to create bold designs.

I really love how accessible this method is for those who find image design difficult, or those who find carving and cutting tools tricky; this is the project for you. Ideally, you need a press with high and even pressure to get a clean print.

Colour Printing Leaves

Because of the fragile nature of the leaves, you're unlikely to be able to make large editions of these prints. If you're careful, then an edition of three to four is possible, but in general these are one-off pieces to be treasured.

However, for the second step where you run the plants through the press with only the paper, you need to remove the runners and set the pressure to the bed. Do a few blind prints, to make sure you've got the pressure just right.

YOU WILL NEED

Foraged plant material (see pages 86, 95)
Flower press or other drying method (see page 93)
Paper and pencil to plan composition
Three A5 lino blocks
Scrap paper
Thick printmaking paper
Ternes Burton pins
Oil-based inks in three colours
Press
Tweezers

PRESS PRESSURE

For these prints, the first step where you roll your plants through on top of the inked lino blocks allows for you to set the pressure with your runners (see page 118).

1. Begin by pressing your foraged flowers and leaves (see page 93). How you organize your natural materials in the press will affect your final print, so be mindful about this and think about your final design as you arrange them.

2. Make a composition on a piece of newsprint or scrap paper: draw around your printing paper, so you have a basic matrix, then arrange the leaves within this and draw an outline around each of them. You can use coloured pencils to help you plan where each leaf goes when inked. For this print we are using three colours.

3. Prepare three different-coloured ink blocks by thinly rolling out a layer of ink onto plain pieces of lino.

4. Lay your selection of leaves onto each inked-up block. Run each block through the press with a layer of newsprint or scrap paper on top, to transfer the ink to the leaves.

5. Once out the other side, use tweezers to gently remove the leaves from the ink blocks, and set aside carefully.

6. Prepare your jig and paper for printing, cutting the paper to size and taping in place using Ternes Burton pins or your preferred registration technique (see pages 110–113). Now lay your prepared template from step 2 onto the centre of the press. Add each of the inked leaves ink-side up onto their pre-drawn places.

7. Line up and lay your printmaking paper over the template and run through the press.

8. Repeat the process for each of the prints in your edition and, once dry, name, sign, number, and record your edition.

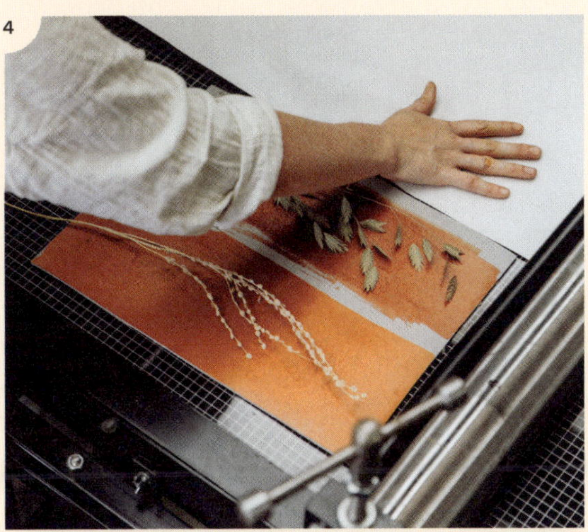
4

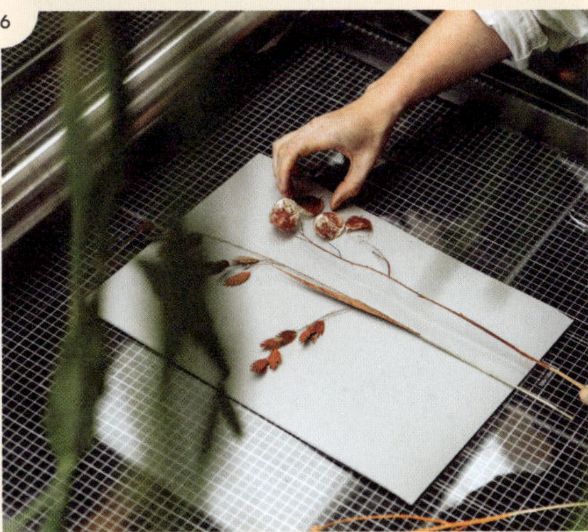
6

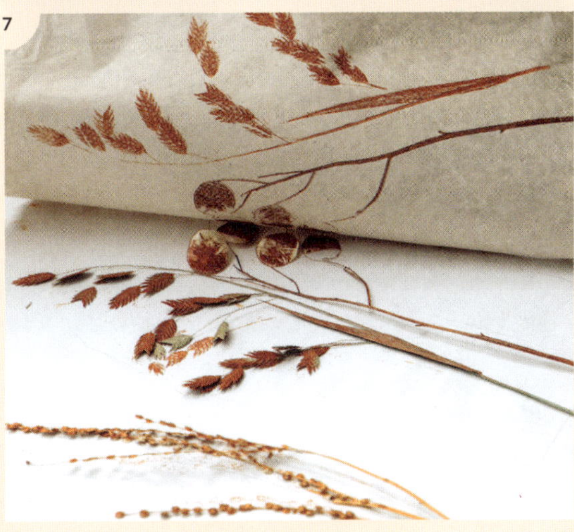
7

Multiblock Colour Printing

Making a multiblock print is a lot less tricky and daunting than it may seem at first. It's just a case of getting your registration right and some organized pre-planning. I like to plot my multiblock prints first in my sketchbook, then to size on loose sheets of paper with pencils or gouache paints, and then finally I go over them with tracing paper, so they are ready to transfer to the block.

For your first multiblock, start simply with three blocks, which means three layers of ink. Later, once you've mastered the technique, you can create as many layers as you like, there's no limit to how technical and complicated a print can become.

Marigold Multiblock Print

For this multiblock design, find a flower or a leaf with at least three different colours on show. We will then break down the design into three separate layers and mark them up on the block. If you are finding it hard to choose or create a design, try making your own version of the one shown here.

YOU WILL NEED

- Foraged botanicals with three areas of colour
- Three blocks of lino or wood, cut to the same size
- Sketchbook
- Coloured pencils or gouache
- Tracing paper
- Masking tape
- Permanent marker pen
- Carving tools
- Print paper ready for your edition
- Ternes Burton pins
- Hard cardboard
- Tape
- Ink rollers
- Three colours of ink
- Ink drier (optional)
- Press or baren

TIP *When printing a multiblock there are so many variables; it's natural and human to mess up at least a few in an edition, especially when you are first starting out. I always print more than I think I may want. If I'm aiming for an edition of ten, I would print fifteen to have some spare for the inevitable mistakes, misalignments, and dirty thumbprints that come from making so many prints.*

1. Begin by planning your design in your sketchbook and then to size by drawing around the outside of your lino block. Use three distinct colours as you separate out each layer on your page. I particularly love using gouache here because its flat and solid nature reminds me of printmaking inks. This helps me to block out an area and really see what I'm planning and how the colours will interact.

2. Take three sheets of tracing paper and trace each colour layer of the design out separately, including the outline of the block as a reference point for when you line them up in the next step.

3. Now you need to be meticulous as you line the edges up for each of the three lino blocks and transfer the images over to them (see pages 104–107). Cut the tracing paper down to size and use a tape hinge at the top. A small slip up in alignment here could ruin your final image, so take your time to make sure you are lined up perfectly.

4. Prep and carve all your blocks (see page 39). Prepare your jig and paper for printing, cutting the paper to size and taping in place using Ternes Burton pins or your preferred registration technique (see pages 110–113).

5. Prepare your rollers with ink and mix in driers, if using, to speed up your editioning time or factor in waiting at least 24 hours between printing each layer.

6. Ink up and slide your first block into the jig. Clip the paper into place and run through a press or burnish by hand with a baren.

7. Hang the print to dry and repeat until you've made your way through all the prepared papers in your edition.

8. Once the first print is touch-dry (allow 24 hours), repeat steps 5–7 with the next layers to print three colours in total. Once all three layers are dry, name, sign, number, and record your edition.

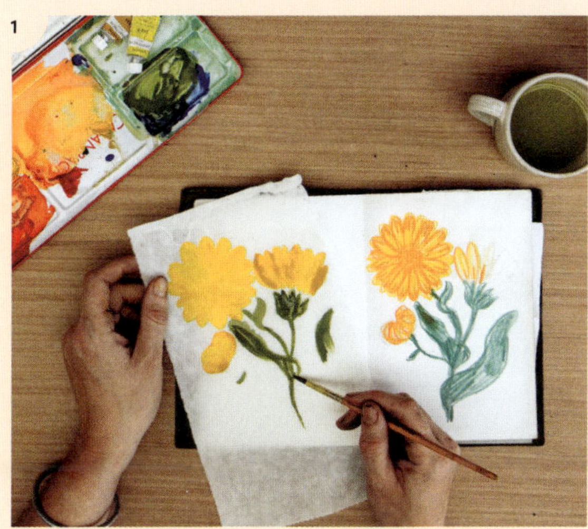

1

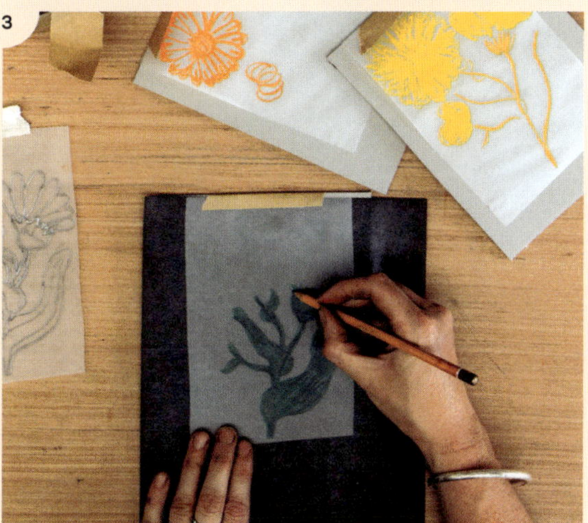

3

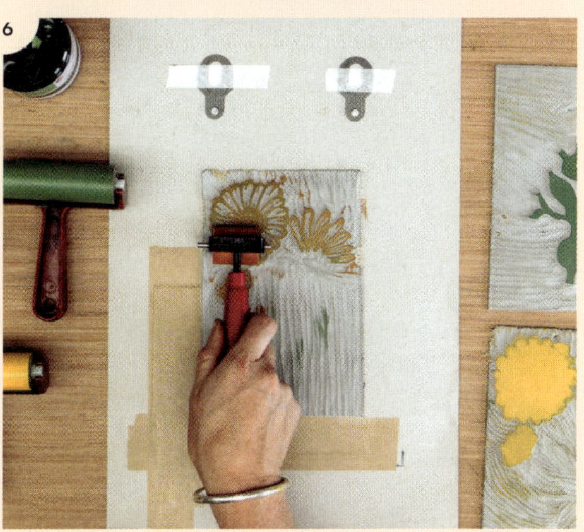

6

Reduction Colour Printing

The reduction print method requires a lot of planning ahead, patience, and attention to detail. To make a reduction print, you start with one block and with each new layer the previous layer is carved away – there is no going back. Your edition is final, and so are any mistakes made along the way. There's a magic in this finality, which, if you are to become a master of this technique, you must embrace.

Limiting your design to one block makes this colour print technique so much cheaper than other colour layer techniques, and it also helps make registration a breeze.

Layers of Colour

Colour application in the reductive approach usually works backwards, printing the lightest layer first and carving away stage by stage through the layers until the darkest and smallest details are printed. Whatever you carve away before you add the first layer of ink will be empty of ink, and the colour of your paper will shine through. For your first try at reduction printing, plan for two layers and a relatively simple subject matter while you get your head around the process.

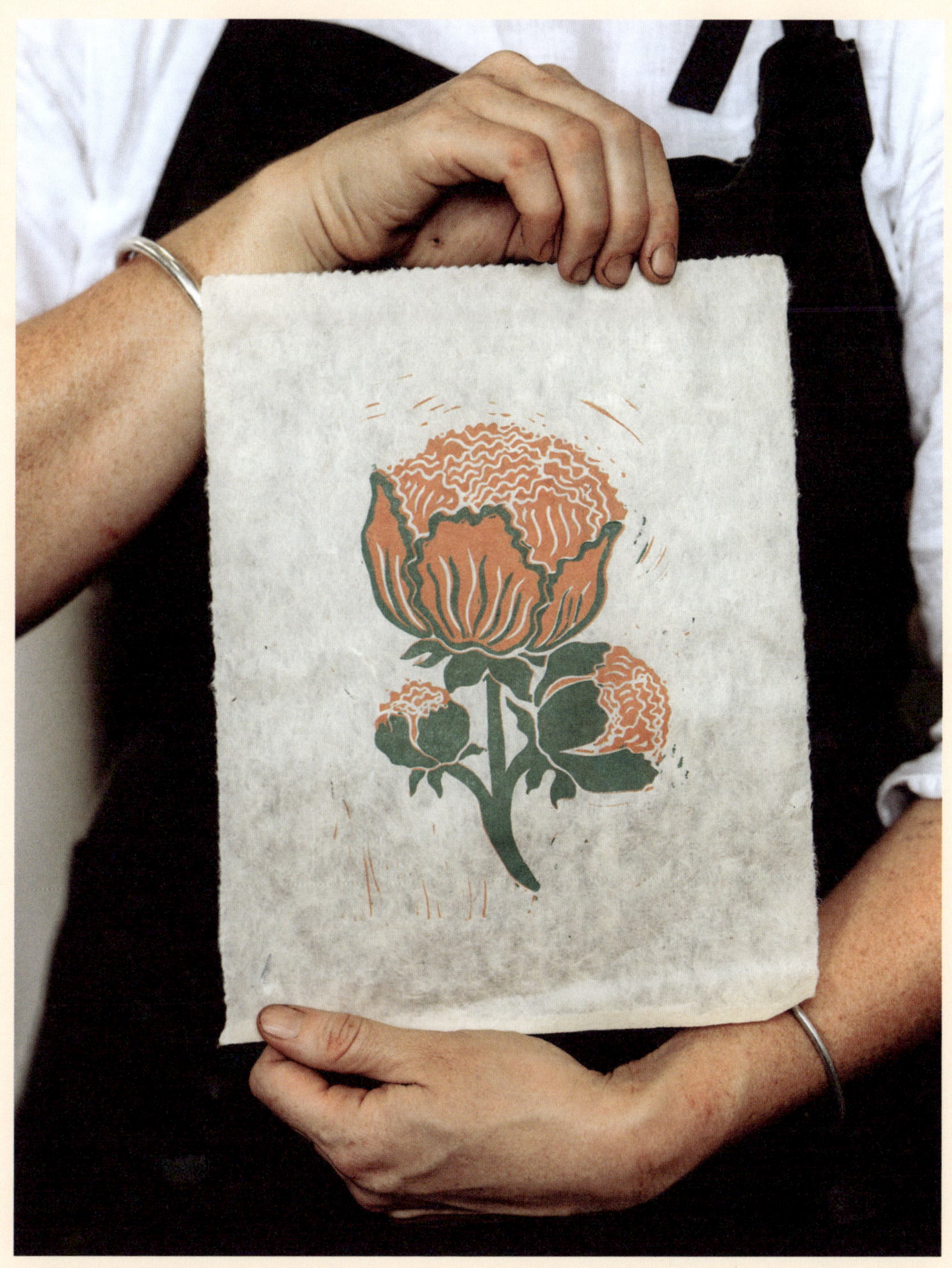

Peony Reduction Print

In this project we start with a simple two-colour reduction print. However, as with the other colour block print methods, once you get the hang of it the world is your oyster and there's nothing stopping you planning and executing your layers into the double digits.

YOU WILL NEED

Sketchbook
Tracing paper
Masking tape
Permanent marker pen
Prepared lino or wood block
Pencil
Ternes Burton pins
Hard cardboard
Printing paper
Carving tools
Newsprint or scrap paper for testing
Multiple rollers
Multiple colour inks
Press or baren

2

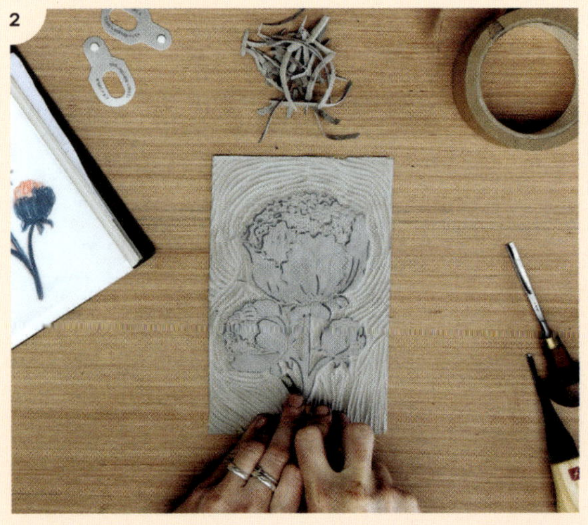

1. Begin by planning out your design to size. It's helpful to create a map at this stage so you can plan out each of your block's layers as you go along with shading or colour pencil for each layer. Transfer your design to your block (see page 104).

2. Following your plan, carve the largest and lightest layer first in your lino block – remember, anything you cut away here will be the colour of the paper it is printed on in the final design.

3. Prepare your jig and paper for printing, cutting the paper to size and taping in place using Ternes Burton pins or your preferred registration technique (see pages 110–113). Ink up, align, and print your first layer.

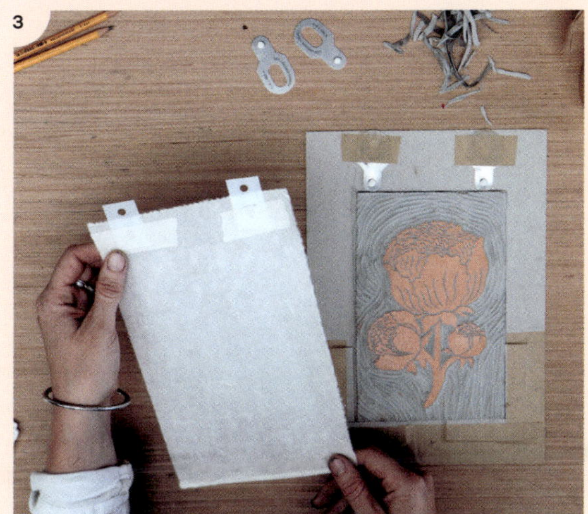

4. After printing, clean your block down thoroughly, dry it, and carve the next layer. At this point you are carving away anything you want to remain in the previous colour. It's a tricky one to get your head around at first, but with practice it will become second nature.

5. Before printing directly onto the previously printed layer in the edition I like to do a little test print on scrap paper to make sure I've carved everything away that I'd intended. Once you're happy, and the first layer is dry, print the second.

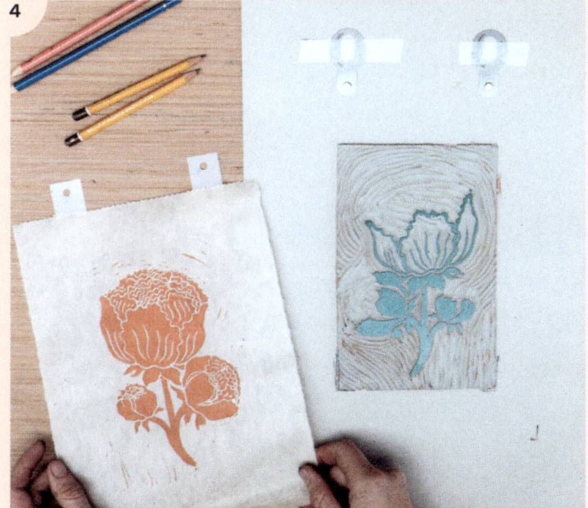

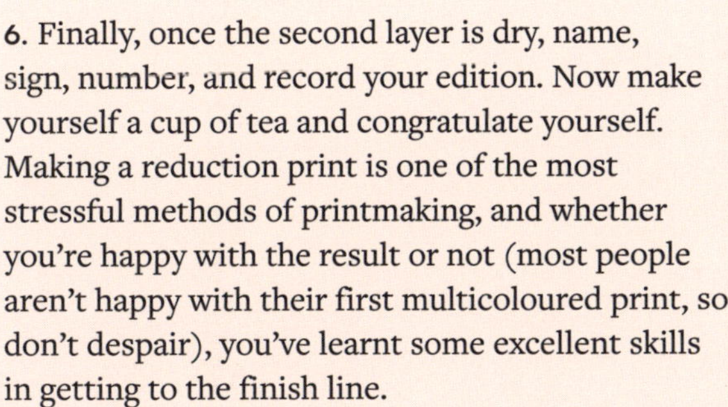

6. Finally, once the second layer is dry, name, sign, number, and record your edition. Now make yourself a cup of tea and congratulate yourself. Making a reduction print is one of the most stressful methods of printmaking, and whether you're happy with the result or not (most people aren't happy with their first multicoloured print, so don't despair), you've learnt some excellent skills in getting to the finish line.

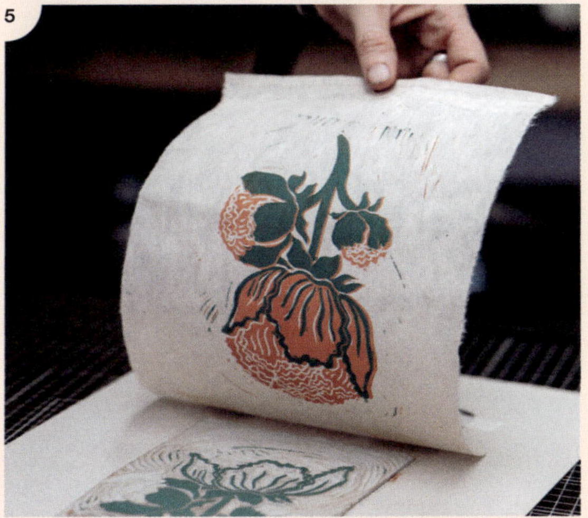

Jigsaw Colour Printing

Jigsaw prints are a brilliant way to bring immediate colour into your prints without having to invest in too many materials. Essentially, a jigsaw print is a one-block design that is cut up into pieces, these pieces are then inked with different colours and reassembled for the press. This removes the need for complex and finickity registration techniques, and massively speeds up the editioning process. With a little careful planning you can create striking, balanced, and bold images with so much less labour than with other colour techniques.

Lino or Wood?

You can make a jigsaw print with either lino or wood. For lino blocks, use a Stanley knife to cut along the hessian at the back. For ply blocks, it's best to use a jigsaw, or handheld mini saw and lots of clamps to hold it steady. For both types it's worth being mindful of how your pieces sit back together once inked; you may need to trim or sand the edges to allow them to slot into place before printing.

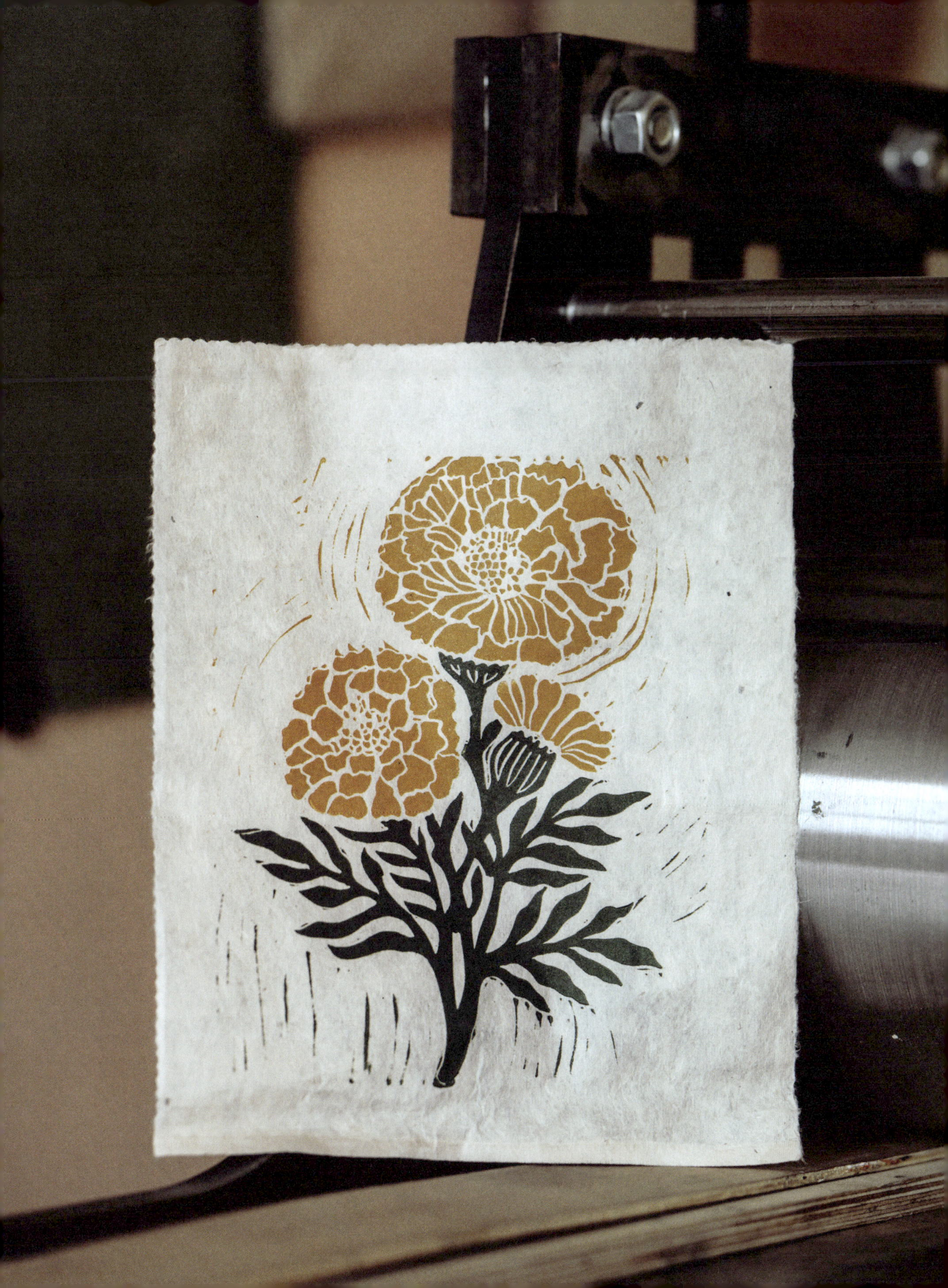

Making a Marigold Jigsaw Print

YOU WILL NEED

Sketchbook
Prepared lino or wood block
Pencil
Permanent marker pen
Carving tools
Scissors or craft knife for cutting lino
Jigsaw or mini handheld saw for cutting wood
Paper
Multiple rollers
Colour inks
Palette knife
Press or baren

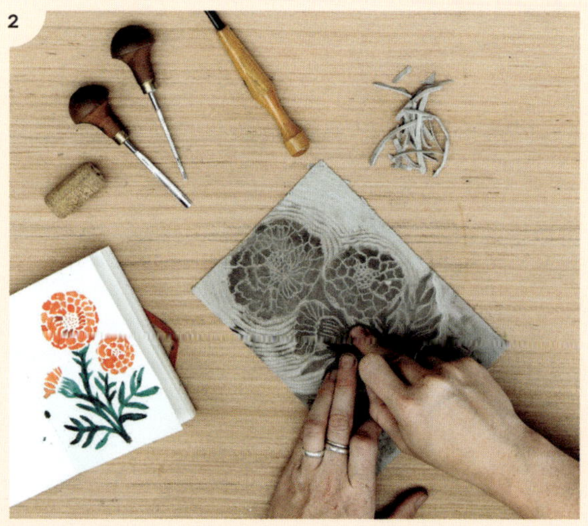
2

1. Begin by creating your design, planning areas that can easily be cut away from the block and inked up separately. Try to keep things simple: think big bold areas of colour, rather than lots of tiny separate pieces that will give you a headache when reassembling later.

2. Transfer your design to the block and carve (see page 39). Don't cut out the individual colour areas yet – it's much easier to carve a large block than lots of separate small pieces, so save that for the next step.

3. Once you've finished the carving process, it's time to create the jigsaw. For lino, you can either use strong scissors if there are big gaps between colours, or, if you need to be more precise, use a craft knife. For wood, use a mini handheld saw or jigsaw machine. Follow all manufacturer's safety instructions for workshop machinery.

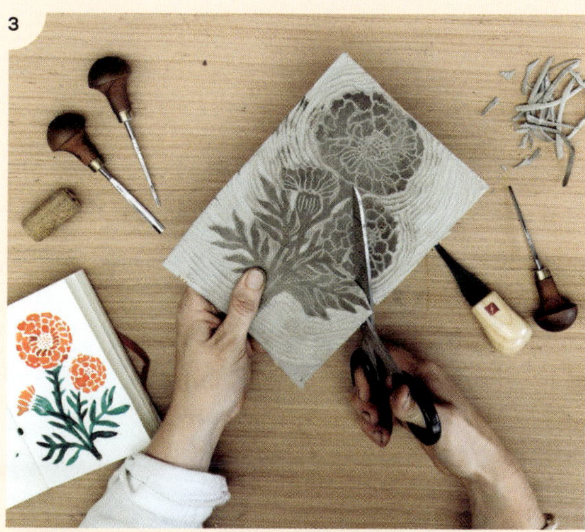

4. Once all your pieces are separated, take some time to tidy up the edges and thoroughly wipe down the blocks before you begin to ink. Watch out for frayed edges on lino and sharp edges on wood that might need a light sand.

5. Prepare each of your separate ink beds and ink up your blocks (see page 44). Once each part is inked up, be careful not to smudge the ink as you bring each piece back to the press. I use either a palette knife to carry them, or a piece of strong cardboard.

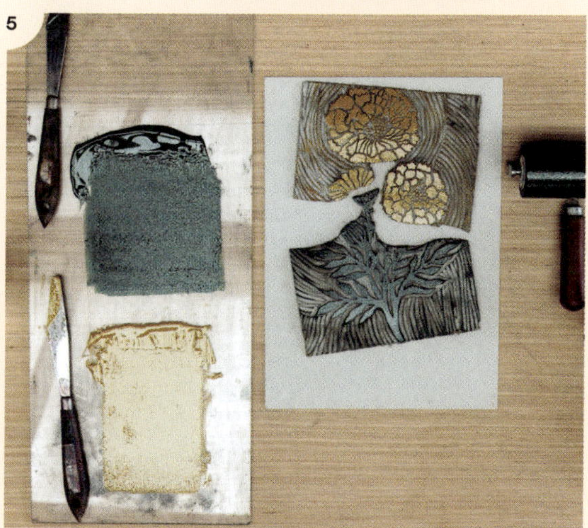

6. You may want to use a simple paper matrix here to make sure your print sits nicely in the middle of your paper. Reassemble all your pieces in the centre of the press and layer your paper on top.

7. Run through the press and when lifting your paper on the other side, go slowly; small pieces may get stuck to the paper as you lift, so use a palette knife to carefully remove them. Finally, once dry, name, sign, number, and record your edition.

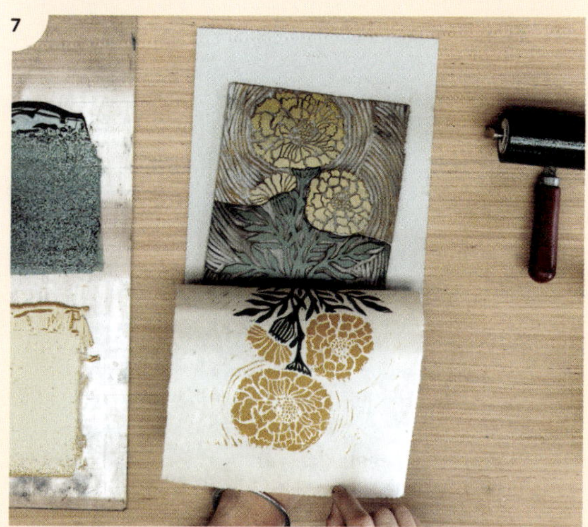

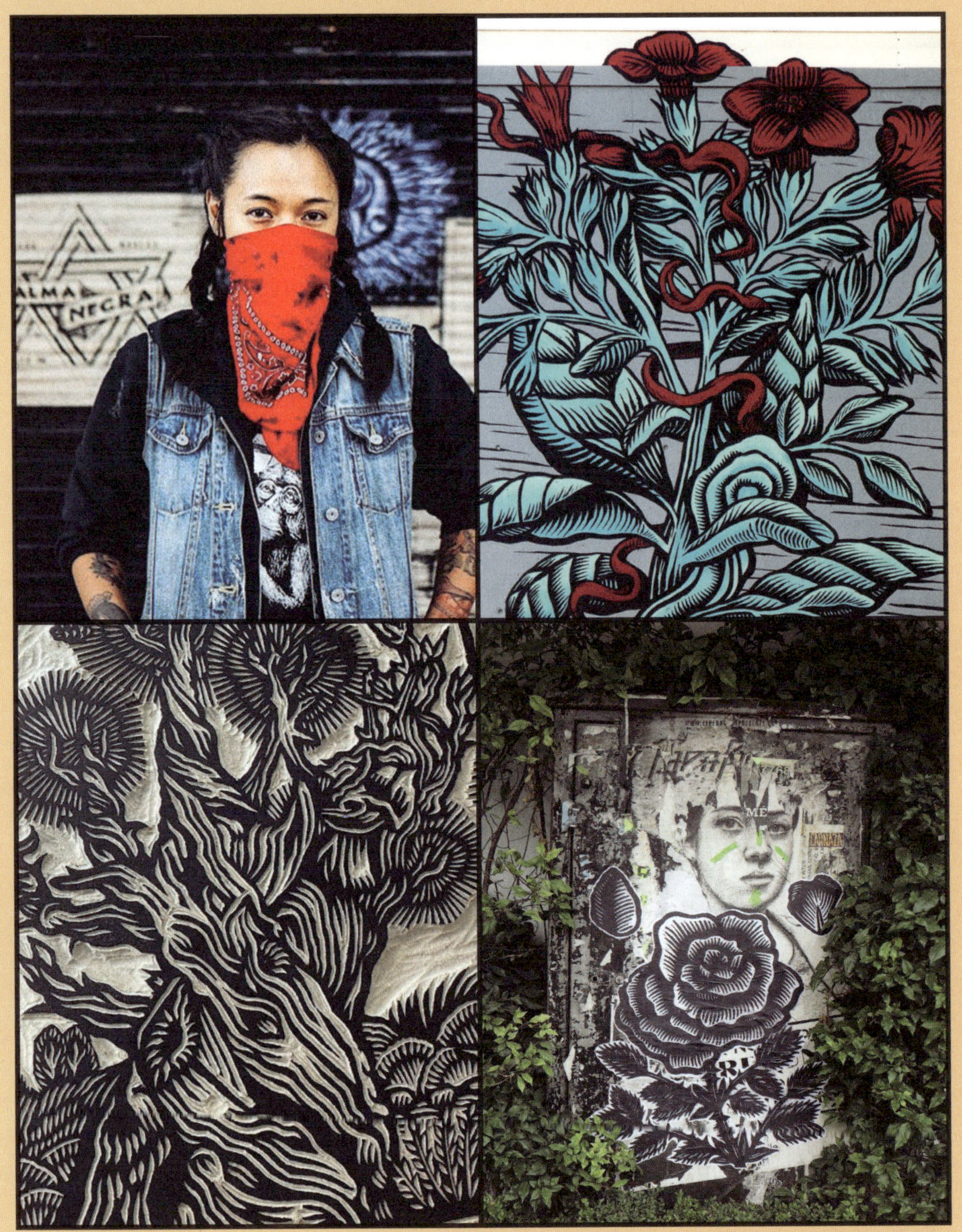
ALMA
NEGRA

Kill Joy

Where do you work and what do you work with?
My house was built in 1941 and the layout is unique in a way which means that, to get to my bedroom, I must pass through my shotgun-style studio. This means that there's never a day at home that I'm not thinking about my work. Embracing this set-up, my partner and I spent two years renovating the dilapidated, outdoor guest house into a relief, letterpress and serigraphy printshop. My style is usually centred around carving linoleum or wood blocks – but I like painting murals and making puppets, too.

How did you get started making prints?
My initial plan was to study painting, but it felt too pretentious. I contemplated taking up Communication Design, but that still felt too corporate. I landed on printmaking because it felt punk in its nature: you can express what you want, it's a democratic medium, and at the time, it took the least number of hours to finish an art degree. At that point in my life, I felt done with formal academic training. The printmaking students looked like they were having the most fun out of everyone, and that appealed! However, it wasn't until I lived in Mexico, three years after graduating, that I really dedicated myself to my carving practice. There, the cultural importance of printmaking and its bold graphic quality has left a lasting impression on me.

Where do you go for inspiration for your work?
I always refer to the TGP masters (Taller Grafica Popular 'People's Graphic Workshop'), a print collective founded in Mexico in 1937. I was able to visit a retrospective of Leopoldo Méndez's work in Mexico City and it revolutionized the way I viewed striking mark-making. I enjoy travelling to different places and learning what types of flora and fauna are native or important to the region. Talking to local people about what's important to them and translating their words into a visual language through plants feels like putting together pieces of a puzzle, which I really enjoy.

Your favourite botanical piece you've made?
Either a large wall mural featuring a tobacco plant, or the carvings of the bristlecone and fiddlehead pines. The rose was one of my first botanical prints, which is why it's special. I take the time when studying plants, as each has a unique character to portray. I spend a lot of time researching the significance and symbolism of each, so it's hard to choose which is my favourite.

What does a typical day look like for you?
I'm a night owl by nature, I typically go to sleep around 4am and wake up around 10am. I drink a mushroom tea, practise yoga, journal, and do some gardening on an ideal morning. By the time I'm done with all of that, it's lunch time. I get easily distracted so I'm finally ready to work usually around 7pm, with a break for a small dinner before working non-stop until about 4am. Sometimes I take a nap at 11pm and wake up at midnight to start making 'serious' work.

What's the best advice you'd give to a new printmaker?
Ignore the rules of formal training in print etiquette, but keep and refine the technique. Also, I think it best not to limit yourself working solely as a printmaker – keep your practice open to all mediums. It's a lot more fun that way.

MAKING EARTH PIGMENTS & INK

Connection to the land is at the root of most of my image-making, so it was natural progression when this interest extended to the inks I use. I had always been drawn to earthy colours, and my watercolour palette had telltale signs of wear on all the brown earth tones and yellow ochres. It was a huge eureka moment when I realized there was nothing stopping me from collecting earth and processing it into pigments, in turn rooting my practice in the very land it was depicting.

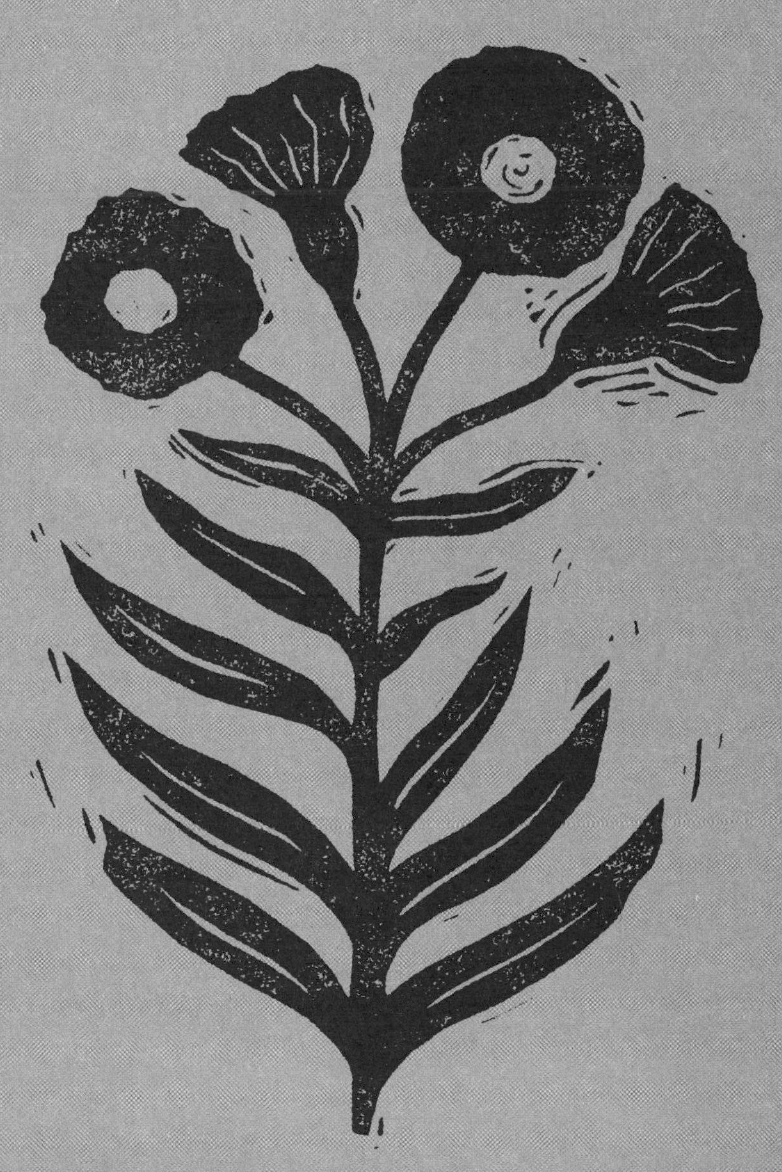

Earth Pigments

Earth pigments are naturally occurring compositions of minerals found in the soil. Once ground into a fine powder, they can be added to different binders to make watercolours, oils, gouache, and even printmaking inks. A huge range of pigments can be achieved from minerals, and their colour is determined by various levels of oxides, usually iron and manganese, which are present in a specific mineral's make-up.

Pigments have been collected and mined for human use from all over the world, from France to Cyprus, Spain to Italy, and the American Appalachian valleys to Pakistan. Our beautiful earth is abundant in rich pigment, and we've been utilizing it for centuries, since the first cave paintings of prehistoric man. As a species we have always been drawn to mark-making and expressing our existence, utilizing whatever colours and pigments we can get our hands on.

Will Earth Pigments Last?

Earth pigments are some of the strongest and most consistent pigments. They are extremely lightfast and permanent, making them ideal for artist colours, and tend not to be affected by their environment and generally do not degrade over time. This means they can be considered archival, which is a great plus for artists in the long-term. They are also non-toxic and some of the most inexpensive pigments you can get your hands on.

THE SCIENCE BEHIND EARTH COLOURS

Earth pigments are made up of three main components:

Main element *– iron oxide, found all over the earth, is usually the main component that affects the resulting colour of your pigment.*

Secondary element *– these are generally minerals such as calcium, manganese, rutile, silica, or limestone. The presence and quantities of these other minerals alter the main element and can create a whole range of hues.*

- *Where manganese is present you will find pigments are darker or brown.*
- *Where rutile is present rocks will be brighter, lighter, and more yellow.*
- *Where celadonite or glauconite is present, you can find beautiful greens. These are often from ancient ocean deposits and found along coastlines.*

Base element *– all earth pigments have a clay base; this holds the pigments and minerals together. This clay can also affect the main element, usually by lightning it.*

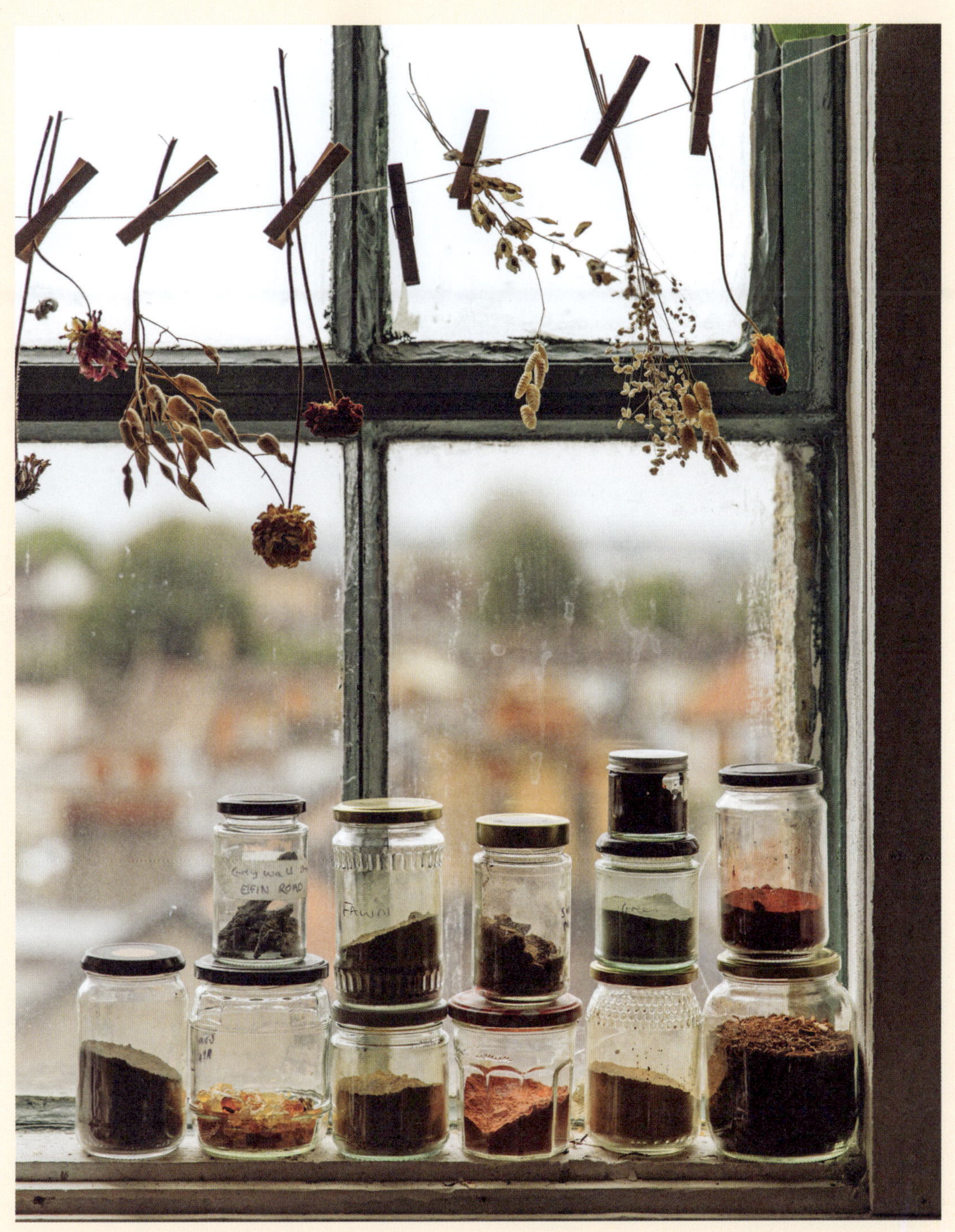

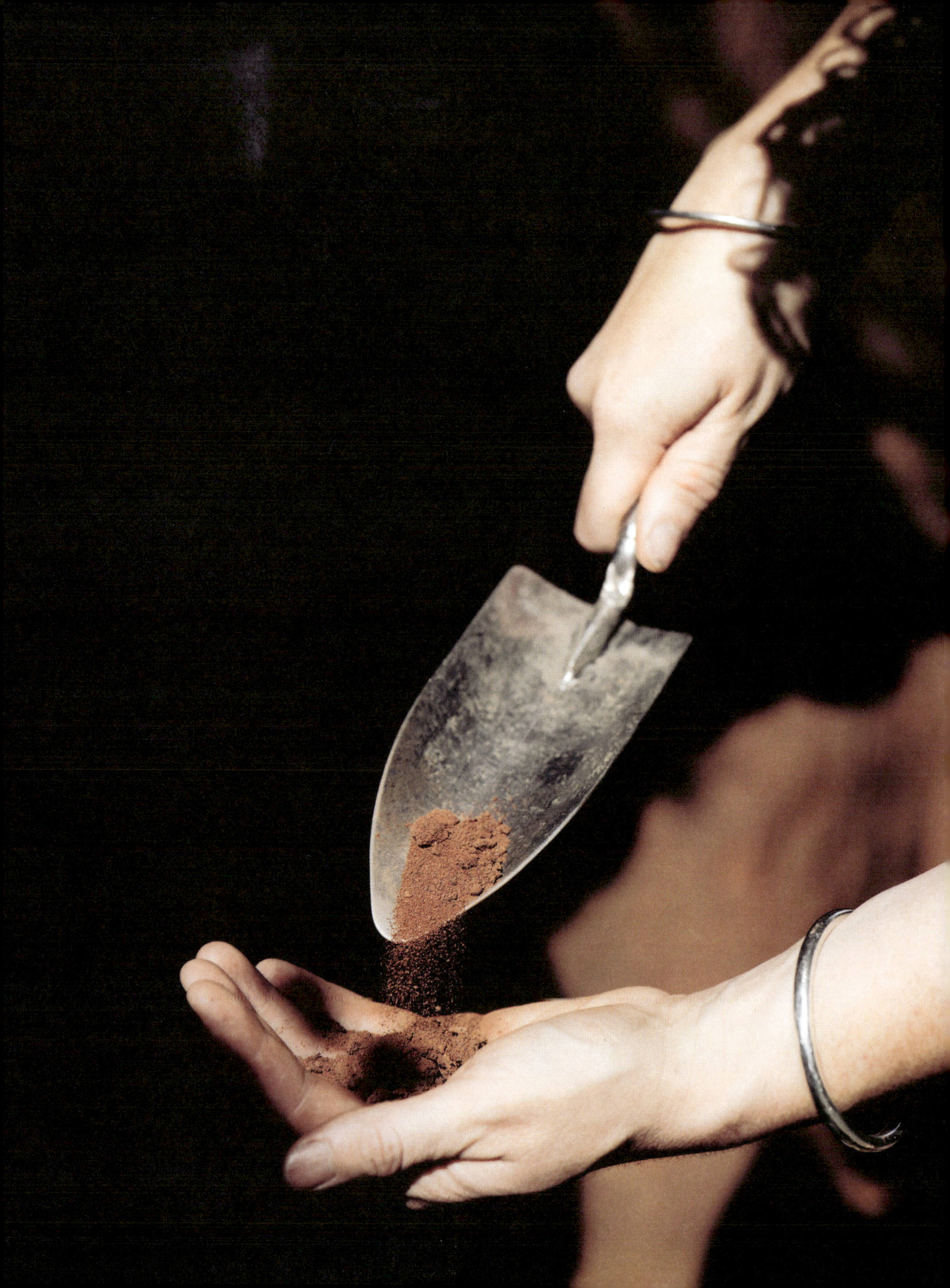

Collecting Earth Pigments

When you begin collecting, it can be tempting to travel further afield to find the purest pigments. However, I really recommend beginning with where you live. There is something special in collecting your pigment from within a couple of miles of your home, thus grounding your work in your own specific location and connecting to the land around you.

Heading out to find pigment feels a little like a treasure hunt, and you never know what you're going to find. Be curious and explore your local spaces – I recommend starting with a nearby park or river. As you get more experienced, you'll find it easier to know where to look.

Pigment is technically everywhere; you just need to dig a little below the surface to find it. I have found lots of beautiful pigments along riverbanks and riverbeds in summer, where the natural movement and flow of water brings up all sorts of riches from further upstream.

Do your research; ask local artists and people interested in pigment if they havc found any particularly good resources locally. You can also investigate geological maps of your area: Were there pigment mines nearby in the past? What can you discover about the local history of your land that might lead you to a new pigment source?

What to Look For

Earth pigments are purest the deeper down you go. Choosing locations where the top layer of earth has already been removed will make your job easier. Construction sites, newly built roads, and old abandoned quarries where people have already excavated the top soil, are a great place to start. Generally, I've found that the purest pigments come in patches and have an immediate vibrancy to them. You're looking for exposed land, rather than the rich black humus of the woodland floor.

USING ROCKS & STONES

You may not have easy access to a loose earth pigment source. Crushed stones and rocks are also considered earth pigments and the colour is derived from the minerals within. Using rocks as your pigment source is not for the faint-hearted and requires some serious muscle and patience as you sit with your pestle and mortar to grind them to a powder. However, if you are committed, you can get a beautiful array of pigments from rocks.

When looking for rocks to create pigment, you're hunting for the softer rocks, which when rubbed against another easily leave a mark. This is called a scratch test and will give you a good indication of the final colour you'll render after processing. The easiest rocks to process with the highest pigment content will leave a mark on your hand as you test them and may even crumble under pressure. Hard and brittle rocks will take an age to grind down, and are best avoided.

URBAN PIGMENTS

You can also make pigments from found materials in urban environments, such as brick or cement. It goes without saying that being sensible and taking care of yourself by wearing suitable protective equipment is important when experimenting with found resources.

BEST PRACTICE FOR SOURCING PIGMENTS

Gloves – Wear gloves when collecting and processing your pigments. Although earth pigments are mainly non-toxic, unless you have the means to test the specific scientific make-up of each collection you make, it's worth wearing gloves just in case.

Mask – It's not a good idea to inhale a lot of dust, especially if you don't know the specific contents of the earth you're working with. When out collecting very dry earth and pigment, wear a good face mask and again when processing your earth to turn it into pigment.

Mindful sourcing – In the beginning, it can be easy to get excited and bring back bags full of collected earth and pigment that you will never get around to processing. Making earth pigment is a long and laborious process and you need very little to make a good-quality ink. If you are collecting locally, you can always go back for more if necessary.

Check with the landowner – I believe everyone has a right to nature, to roam the natural land and to access its minerals. However, most people might prefer to be asked before you start digging in their flower beds.

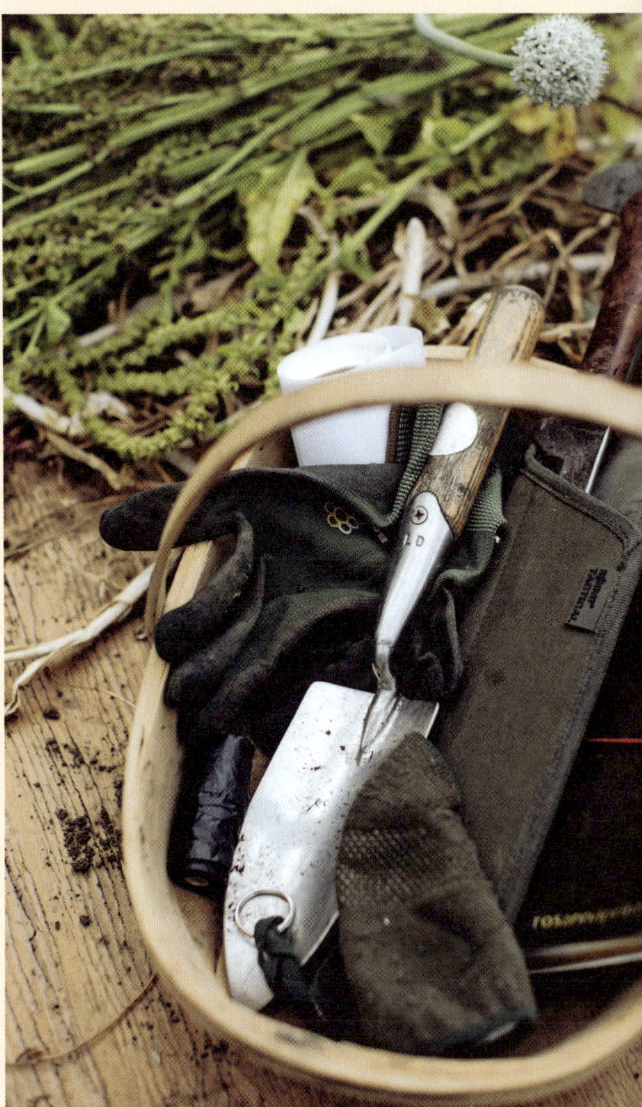

COLLECTING KIT

- *Hard-wearing gloves*
- *Trowel*
- *Multiple plastic bags (to collect and transport earth or rocks)*
- *Permanent markers and stickers to label your bounty*
- *A notebook to record your collection locations, so that you can go back later for more*
- *A mask, if it's particularly dry and dusty*

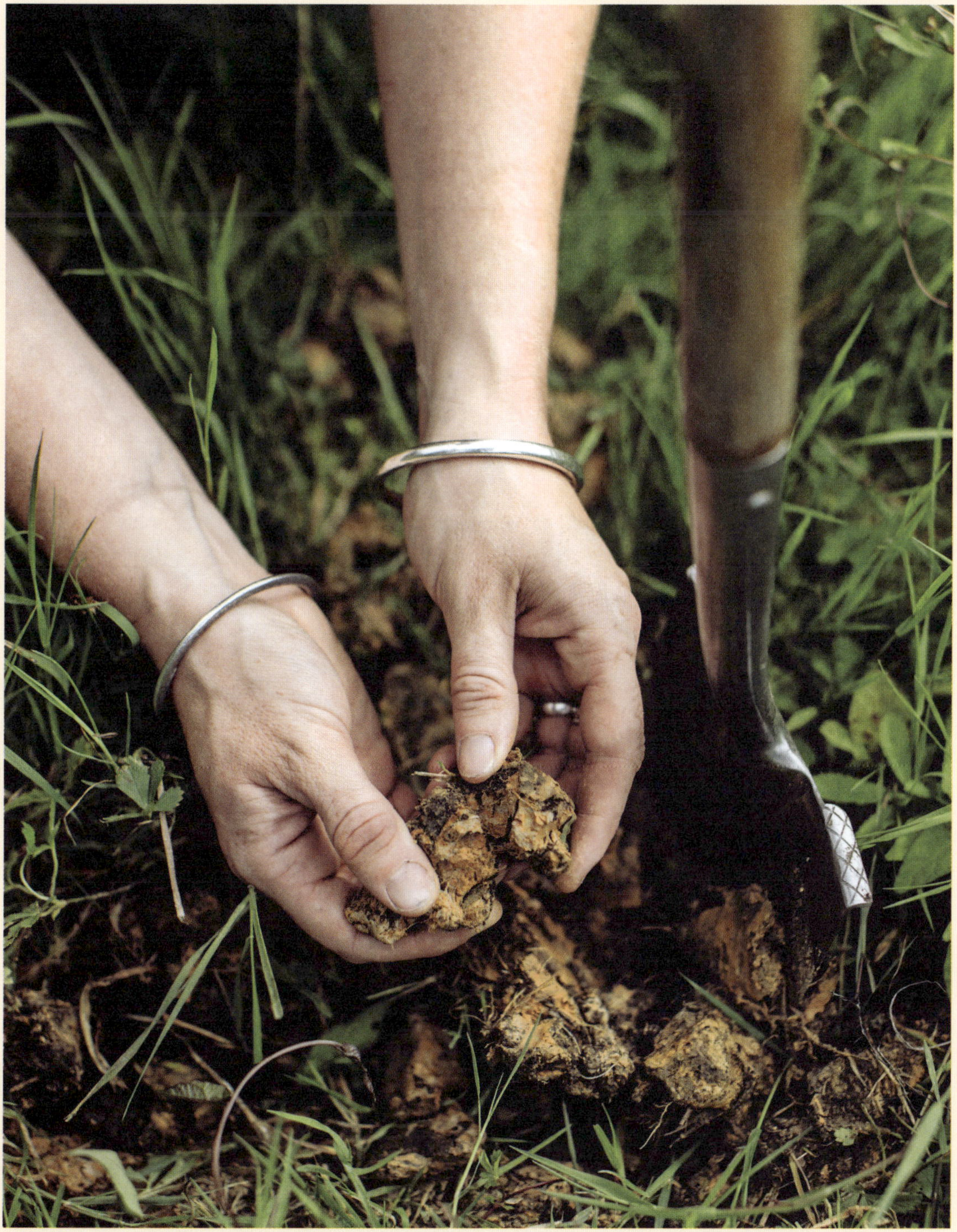

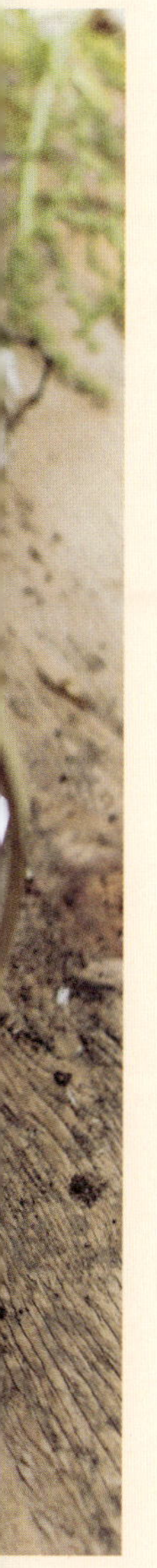

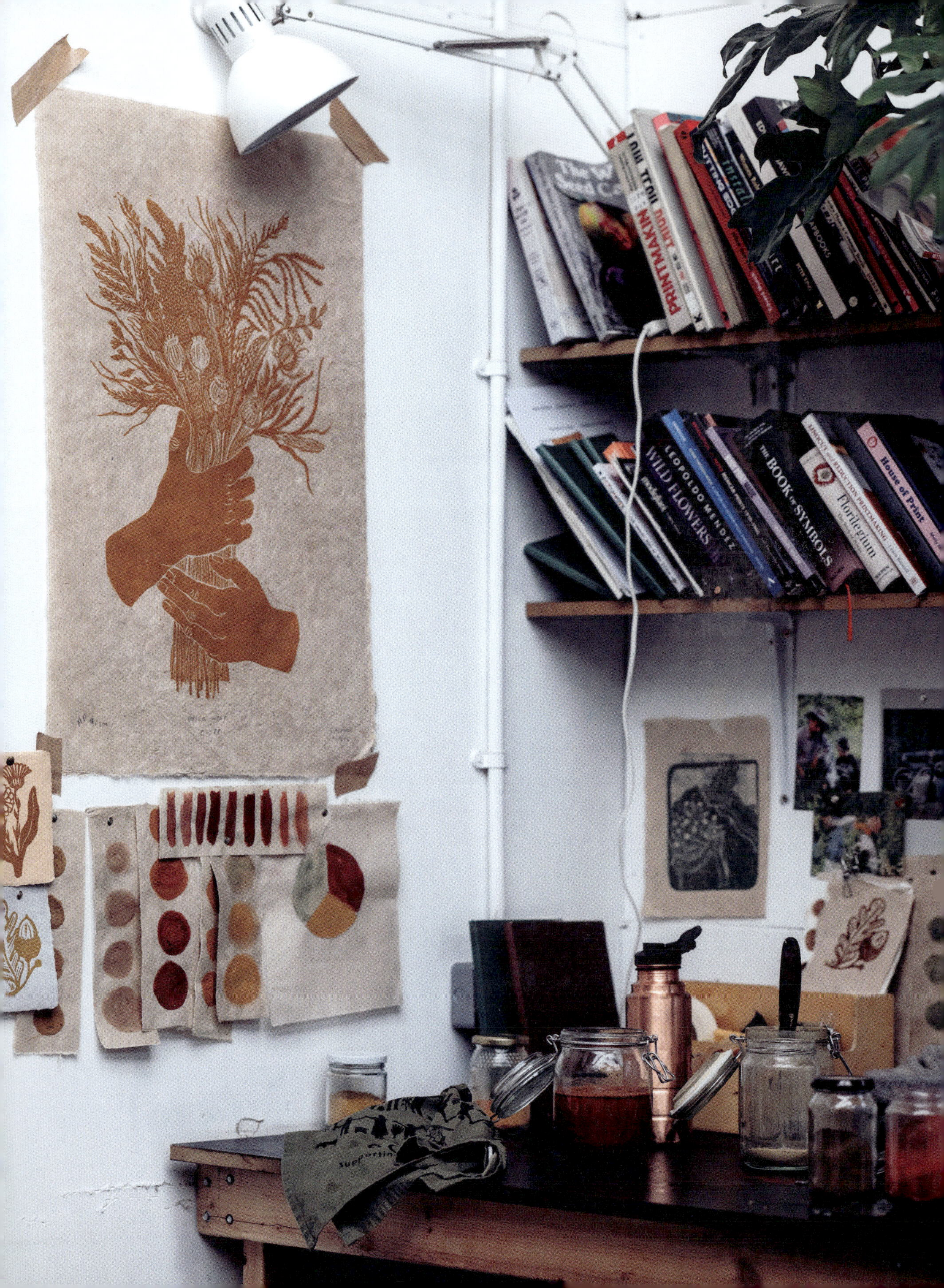
PRINTMAKIN
LEOPOLDO MENDEZ
WILD FLOWERS
THE BOOK OF SYMBOLS
LINOCUT and REDUCTION PRINTMAKING
Florilegium
House of Print

Processing Your Pigment

Once you've done the hard work of collecting your soils and heaving them back to your workspace, you'll be ready to begin the labour-intensive process of turning them into pigment, ready to create beautiful printmaking ink. There are two main methods for cleaning and processing your earth, which I've outlined on the following pages.

If you plan on processing stones and making mineral pigments, you can use either of these methods to clean your pigment once you have crushed your stones into a fine powder using a pestle and mortar.

Tools and Materials

These tools are very specific and are part of advanced practice for processing pigments for use in printmaking. Keep them separate from your general printing tools and materials.

LABORATORY SIEVES

Available from specialist laboratory suppliers with varying levels of mesh count. You need at least three if not more different mesh counts – starting with around 40 mesh and working your way up in increments to a mesh count of around 180 – to be effective.

LARGE JARS

For the water levigation method I use large Kilner jars, but if you get really into the process, some artists use buckets to enable them to process large quantities of pigment at a time. You'll also need lots of general sterilized jars for storing your pigments once processed.

PESTLE & MORTAR

Many of us already own a pestle and mortar for grinding up herbs and spices. When processing earth pigments, it's important to have a separate set that you use only for this purpose. Choose a stone set as large as you can handle comfortably; avoid wood or ceramic as they will get damaged under the immense pressure that is needed to process pigments.

MULLERS

These are usually glass with a flat, textured base that works to distribute your pigment through the binder. You can buy them in a variety of sizes from specialist art supply shops. They are an investment and essential for processing your own pigments. If you aren't completely set on the process, I'd recommend trying to borrow one first.

MULLING SLAB

In order to grind your pigments down, you need a strong surface on which to mull. I use reinforced glass; sandblasted glass is good as the texture helps to break down the particles. You can also use marble or granite, as long as the surface is strong and won't shatter under continued and sustained pressure.

COPPER-PLATE OIL

Used traditionally by printmakers the world over before the invention of traditional pre-mixed printmaking inks, copper-plate oil works really well as a printmaking ink binder. It is, however, oil-based and requires the same clean-up process as other oil-based printmaking inks (see page 54).

PRINTMAKING EXTENDER

An accessible printmaking material (see page 23), this works well when combined with enough pigment. If you use the safe-wash extender, it also has the benefit of an easy clean-up.

Dry-sifting Method

This is a fast and efficient method for purifying your collected earth, but it does create a lot of dust and so requires a mask. Processing outside is possible, but a strong wind could interfere with how much pigment you lose, so it's best done in a studio that you don't mind getting a bit dusty, with some good ventilation.

TIP *Using a large sock (that you don't mind getting dusty) to cover your mortar really helps reduce how much dust spreads when grinding and crushing your soil.*

YOU WILL NEED

Collected earth
Gloves and a dust mask
Large sheets of white paper
Large sock that fits over your pestle and mortar (see Tip)
Large pestle and mortar
Two sieves, one with a fine 40μ mesh and another with a finer 100μ mesh
Palette knife

1

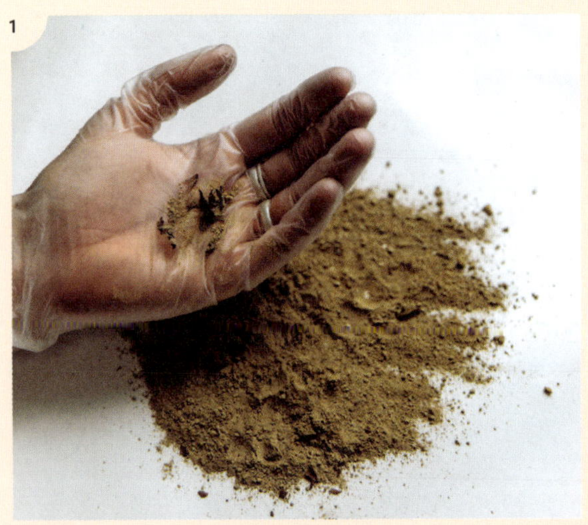

1. Wearing a dust mask and gloves, lay your collected earth out on large sheets of paper to dry. At this stage you can also finely comb the earth to remove any organic matter such as leaves or grass.

2. Once dry, wearing a mask and gloves, put a small handful of dry earth into the mortar. Place the sock over your mortar and begin to crush the earth and grind it down to an even and powdery consistency. Once ground, place on a fresh sheet of paper and repeat until all your earth is processed.

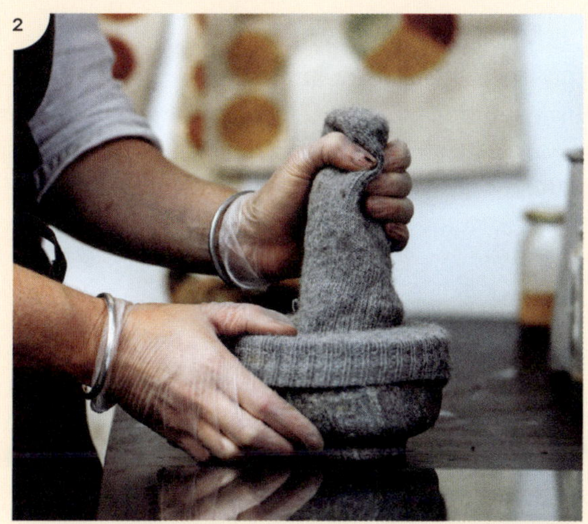

2

3. Next, you can begin to sieve the earth, starting with the larger mesh and working down to the finer-meshed sieves. Shake your sieve gently back and forth over a clean sheet of paper to remove any fine organic matter. If the earth gets stuck as it moves through the sieves, use a small palette knife to break it up.

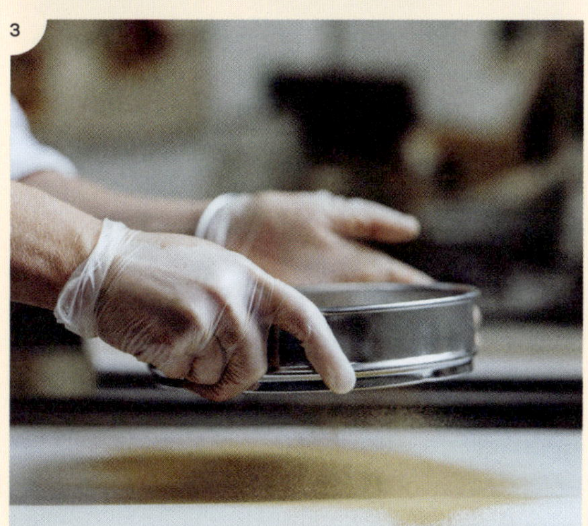

3

4. Once you have passed all your earth through the sieves and removed any leftover organic matter, it will now be ready for the mulling process (see pages 182–183).

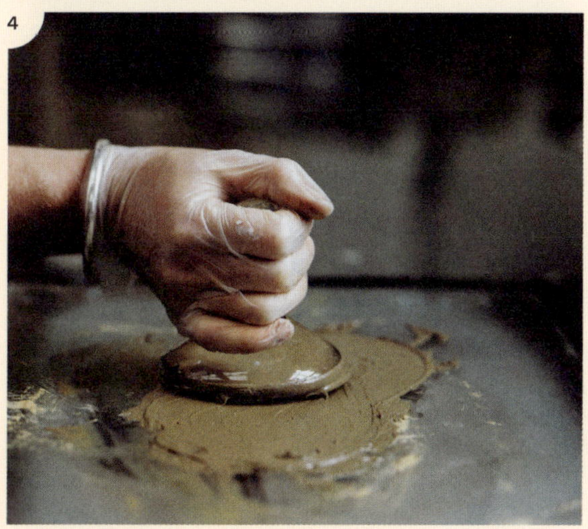

4

Water or Levigation Method

This method for separating out pigment relies on gravity. It takes a little longer than sifting, as you must wait in between processing for your pigments to settle and to dry, but generally in my experience this results in a smoother, cleaner pigment.

YOU WILL NEED

Collected earth
Gloves and a dust mask
Two or three large jars
Distilled water
Large pestle and mortar
Glass muller
Mulling slab – sheet of tempered glass
Palette knife
Scraper
Sterilized jar for storage

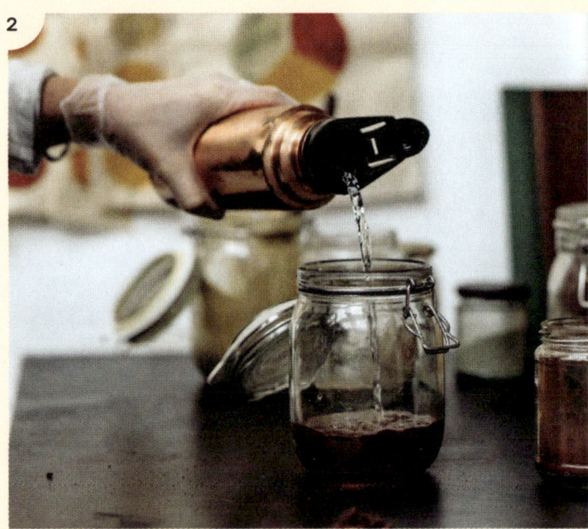

2

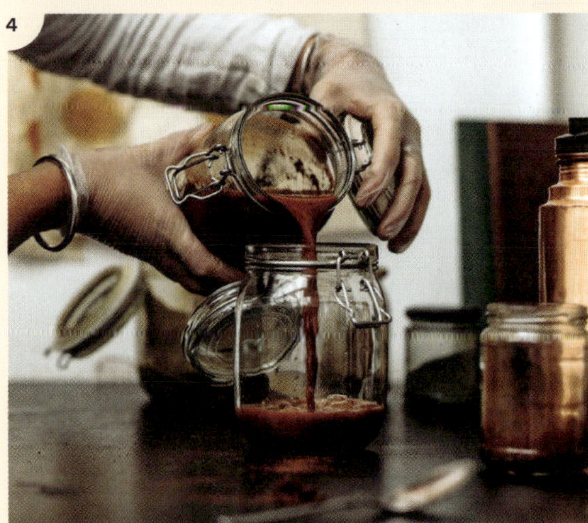

4

1. Wearing gloves, quickly comb through your earth and remove any extra organic matter, such as grass or leaves.

2. Put a couple of handfuls of your collected earth into a jar, about a quarter full. Fill the rest of the jar with some water, about three-quarters full, swish it around a little and then count to 15 before pouring off any organic matter that has floated to the surface.

3. Repeat again if your collected earth still has a lot of organic matter mixed in. Then repeat the process a third time, filling the jar with water again, and stir. Allow to settle again for around 30 seconds.

4. Pour this clouded liquid off into a second jar and discard anything that has settled on the bottom. This is likely to be soil, sand, and grit and not useful for pigment making.

5. Next, allow the cloudy liquid to settle in the second jar. Depending on the specific make-up of your collected earth, this will take varying amounts of time. Some are ready in a few hours; others take 24 hours or even days to settle. You will know when it's ready when the water is completely clear, and your earth pigment has settled in a thick layer on the bottom.

6. Slowly pour off the clear water, using the lip of your jar to hold the settled pigment paste back when pouring.

7. Depending on the quality of the earth paste you have left, you can either decide to repeat the levigating process again, by stirring and pouring off the coloured liquid (the pigment is heavier), then waiting for it to clear, or you can begin to process the resulting paste with a pestle and mortar.

8. Put a small handful at a time into the pestle and mortar, and grind the paste into an even and consistent quality. The more time you spend on this the better, as you want to get the pigment particles down to the smallest possible size. As a guide, try and aim for five solid minutes per handful.

9. Once processed, transfer your paste to the middle of your glass slab. Place your muller into the centre of the paste and move in circular motions, around and around, spreading the paste across your glass. Every now and then use a palette knife to gather up your paste to the centre and begin again. Repeat for around 15 minutes.

10. Once you are happy with the consistency of your paste, spread it out as thinly as you can across your glass and leave to dry overnight. The water will evaporate and when you come back to it, your glass should be caked in a hard layer of pigment. Wearing a mask, scrape all your pigment into a jar ready for processing into inks.

5

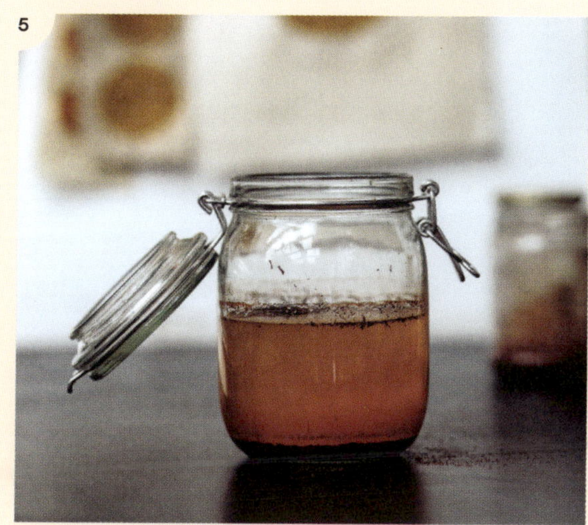

9

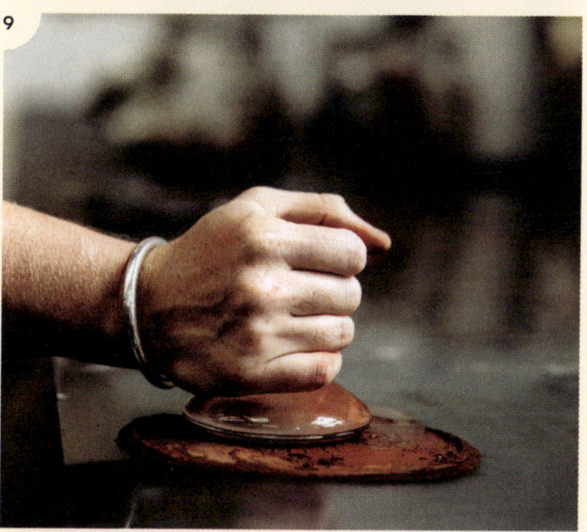

10

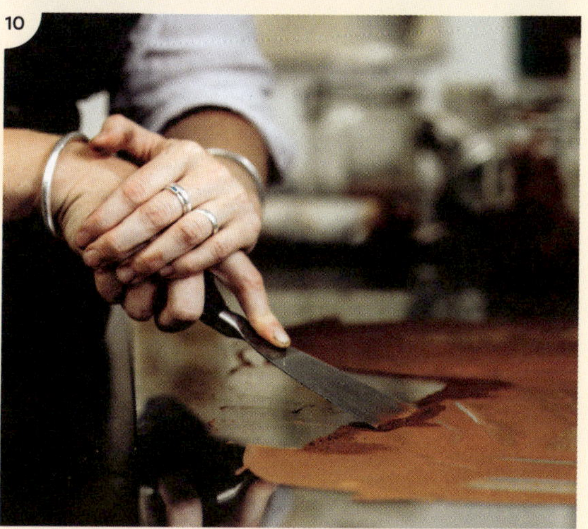

Making Your Own Ink

Once you have processed your earth pigments, you now need to turn them into printmaking inks by mixing with a binder, such as copper-plate oil. This process also involves mulling, to disperse the pigment evenly throughout your chosen binder. You need every small particle of pigment to be suspended in the binder and well-coated in oil to make a consistent colour and to allow the pigment to really shine brightly in your prints.

Blending Pigment with Oil

If you are using glass as your slab surface it helps to lay some newsprint below the glass to make it easier to see your progress. Pay attention as you mull and take time to test your blend as you go on scrap paper, adding more oil or pigment intuitively to get the perfect consistency.

YOU WILL NEED

Processed earth pigment
Mulling slab - sheet of tempered glass
Copper-plate oil or extender
Palette knife
Muller

1. Begin with a small pile of pigment in the centre of your glass. Create a well in the middle of your pigment and add your chosen oil at a 50:50 ratio; go steady, less oil is better at this stage. Bear in mind that different pigments need differing amounts of oil to make a good ink.

2. Using a palette knife, begin mixing the pigment and oil together into a soft paste. Then move this paste with your palette knife to the side of your glass.

3. Start with about a third of the mixed paste, move it to the centre of the glass, and begin mulling. Lay your muller into the centre of the paste and move it in circular motions, backwards and forwards in different directions, spreading the ink as thinly as you can across the glass. Moving the muller through the ink takes a lot of elbow grease and pressure to blend it really well.

4. Use your palette knife to gather it all up again into the centre and repeat. You should start to see your ink and pigment mixture becoming silkier and smoother as you process it. The amount of time you need to work on this varies from pigment to pigment but as a rough guide I usually aim for around 15 minutes for each small handful of ink.

5. Once you have processed one part of your paste, move it to the side with your palette knife and process the rest, repeating the same process until all your ink is silky and well mixed.

6. You can either use the ink straight away or store in airtight jars. Be sure to label them for further use and make a note of the final oil ratio, and the time spent mulling, so that if you really love it, you can replicate it in the future.

1

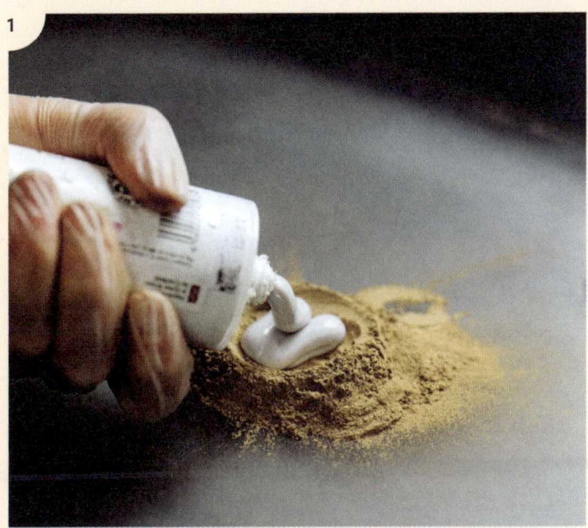

2

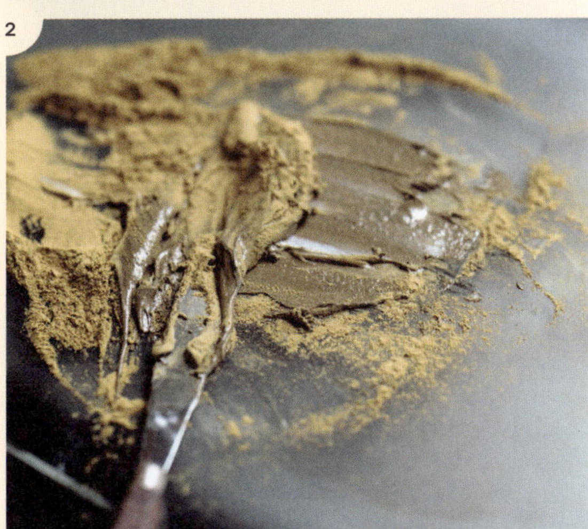

5

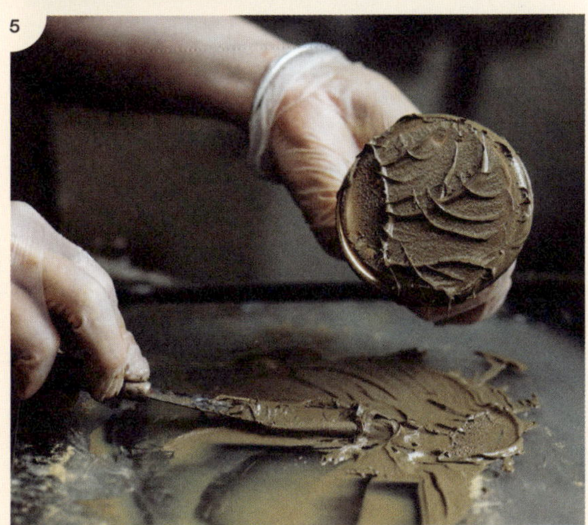

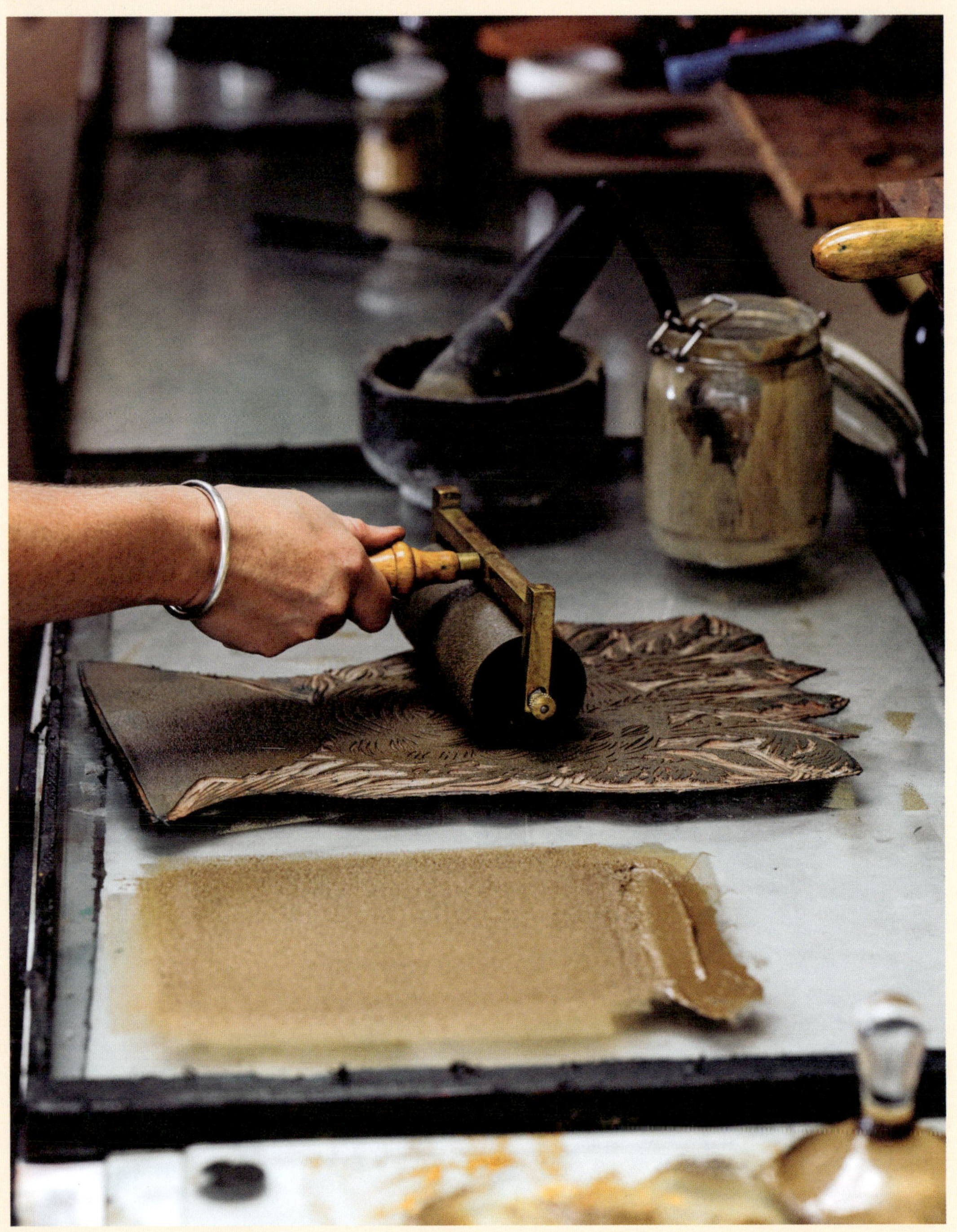

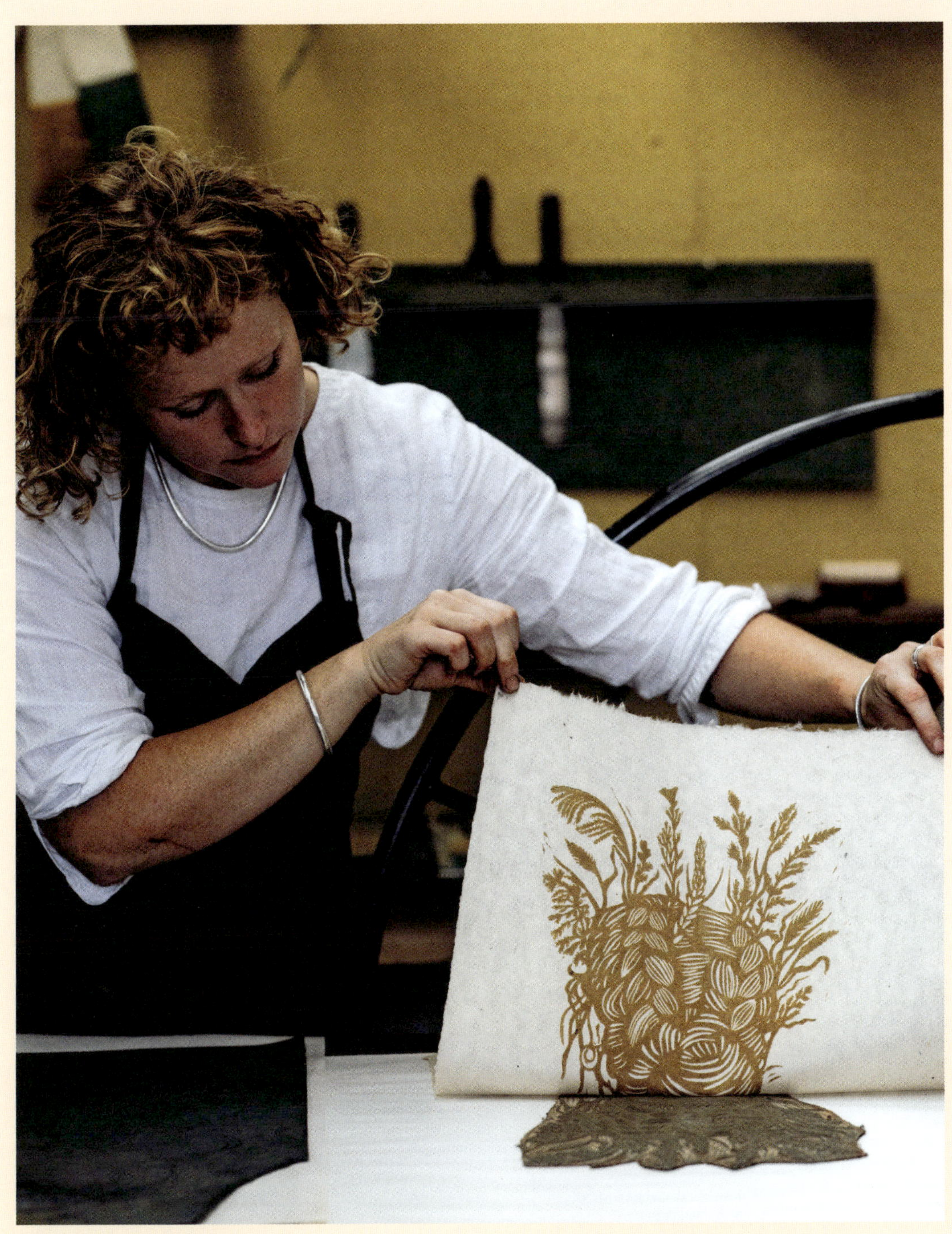

Suppliers

Suppliers in the UK:

HANDPRINTED
For printmaking inks, tools, lino and paper:
www.handprinted.co.uk

T N LAWRENCE
For printmaking inks, tools, and papers:
www.lawrence.co.uk

INTAGLIO PRINTMAKERS
For specialist printmaking equipment, tools, and papers:
www.intaglioprintmaker.com

JACKSON'S ART SUPPLIES
For all sorts of art materials, printmaking inks, tools, and papers:
www.jacksonsart.com

HAWTHORN PRINTMAKERS
For beautiful inhouse inks and presses:
www.hawthornprintmaker.com

IRONBRIDGE
For expertly made printmaking presses:
www.ironbridgeframing.co.uk

BRISTOL BALL RACKS
For brilliant, beautiful handmade drying racks:
@Bristol_ball_racks on Instagram

International suppliers:

SPEEDBALL ART + PRINT SUPPLIES
www.speedballart.com

McCLAIN'S PRINTMAKING SUPPLIES
www.imcclains.com

WOODCRAFT CARVING TOOLS
www.woodcraft.com

ARTIST CRAFTS MAN
www.artistcraftsman.com/printmaking

Acknowledgements

Creating this book was a huge feat for me – being diagnosed as severely dyslexic at school, I never in my wildest dreams believed I would be able to achieve anything like this. I'm so grateful to my brilliant husband, Konstantinos, who supported me through it all. When insecurity and anxiety kicked in, you picked me up and believed in me – even when I really didn't believe in myself. Also, my wonderful children, Robin, Daphni and Yani, who brought me cups of tea while I worked and gave me a reason to keep pushing when it felt so hard to keep up.

Thank you to everyone at Pavilion that supported me and patiently advised me throughout building this book. Thank you for giving me the opportunity! Thank you also to the wonderful Eva Nemeth for being the most incredible photographer I could have asked for and helping to make this book as beautiful as it could be.

Thank you also to my supportive peer group of brilliant printmakers who were my listening ears and sounding boards as I worked my way through each of the chapters in this book. Thank you especially to the wonderful Rachael Hibbs, who pushed me to believe I could write a book in the first place. Thank you also to Lou Tonkin, Ysidro Pergamino, Lili Arnold, Kill Joy and Tenjin Ikeda for contributing your beautiful work to these pages and giving us an insight into your diverse practices.

I also want to give a special thanks to my friend and brilliant printmaker Nichola Goff, from whom I learnt all I know about earth pigments and processing them into printmaking inks. And to Luke Wade, for your beautiful print racks that made it just in time for the photoshoot. Thanks also to Amy Gillespie, for your extra help when it came to the final edit of the book and for making sure I made sense!

Without all the support and encouragement of my friends, family, and peers, this book wouldn't have been possible. I am so grateful – thank you, all of you, for helping make this dream come true!

Index